TRACKING DOWN OREGON

Other books by Ralph Friedman
OREGON FOR THE CURIOUS
TALES OUT OF OREGON
NORTHWEST PASSAGES
A TOUCH OF OREGON
IN SEARCH OF WESTERN OREGON
THE OTHER SIDE OF OREGON

TRACKING DOWN OREGON

by

Ralph Friedman

Photographs by Phoebe L. Friedman
(except as individually noted)

The CAXTON PRINTERS, Ltd.
Caldwell, Idaho
1997

First printing September, 1978
Second printing October, 1979
Third printing September, 1984
Fourth printing March, 1990
Fifth printing March, 1997

© 1978 by Ralph Friedman and Phoebe L. Friedman
All rights reserved

Library of Congress Cataloging in Publication Data

Friedman, Ralph
Tracking down Oregon.

Includes index.
1. Oregon — History — Miscellanea. 2. Oregon — Description and travel — 1951- — Guide-books.
I. Title.
F876.F74 979.5 76-6647
ISBN 0-87004-257-2

Lithographed and Bound in the United States of America
162712

Table of Contents

	Page
List of Illustrations	vii
Invitation to a Journey	xi
Oregon, this Oregon	1
The Untypical Smiths	6
A Closeness to Hug Point	11
A Rising of Spirit at Munson Falls	13
The Seasons of Randolph	15
Tichenor and Associates Present Port Orford	19
Ghost Towns of the Lower Columbia	30
The Small Drama of Hamlet	35
Baptism at Bacona	43
The Not So Meek Joe	51
A Peacefulness at Pike	55
High Tide for Sam Simpson	58
Saga of a Gunslinger	71
Kinton Has Some Little Lambs	71
The Pittsburgh Dream of Lake Oswego	79
A Corner of History at Oregon City	82
Great Day at New Era	88
Battle Hymn of Abigail	95
Long Road to the Cook House	104
The Search for Jennyopolis	111
Irish Bend Nightmare	115
The Romance Back of Latourell	118
"Mighty Peak of Tremendious Hight"	125
That Wonderful Ingleside Farm	131
The Saga of Silverton Bobbie	135
A Requiem for Homer	146
A Name for Opal Creek Falls	150
No More Elephants in the Bohemia	155
Pioneers! O Pioneers!	160
Sunny Valley Scene	165
Bridge over Evans Creek	169
A Grave Marker to Ponder On	171
The Log Town Rose	173
Portrait of Van Gilder	178
A Tolling Bell at Boyd	181
A Dreaming at Dufur	184
A Friend in Time	189

Page

A Varied Song in Sherman County 193
Come Along to Hay Creek 203
The Wonderful Baldwin Hotel 206
Two Apart: Winema and Captain Jack 211
Phantom Legend on the Crooked River 221
Fording on the Oregon Trail 225
Ghostly Sequel to the John Day Fording 229
The Sage of Pilot Rock 233
A Long Way from Old Long Creek 242
Mattie's Monument 245
Wings in an Odd Fortress 248
Sawdust at Seneca 251
The Gray Ghost of Hines 254
A Stately Meeting at Wagontire 256
Great Basin Blues 259
Great Register on Crooked Creek 261
The (Maybe) Fantastic Walls of Rome 264
The Divided Hill House of Jordan Valley 267
In Search of Monahan 270
Leslie Gulch: A Fantasy for Real 277
From Rob to Riches at Joseph 280
The Wrong Kind of Monument 283
That Troublesome Oregon Trail 288
Oregon Names 294
Index 297

List of Illustrations

	Page
Roberta Symons of Ashwood	vii
Lake Owyhee	3
Plaque on boulder	7
Solomon Howard and Helen Celiast Smith	8
Hug Point	12
Munson Falls	14
"Beach Gold Diggins"	15
Whiskey Run	17
Third site of Randolph	18
William Tichenor	20
Battle Rock	21
Joaquin Miller	25
Minnie Myrtle Miller	26
Grave of William Tichenor	29
Bradwood RR Station	31
Clifton	32
Old Brownsmead School	33
Mayger	34
Marie Pottsmith at Hamlet	37
Bacona marker	43
Bacona Schoolhouse	47
Arlena Jeppesen as young woman	47
Arlena Jeppesen at eighty	49
Joe Meek as Mountain Man	52
Joe Meek as farmer	53
Meek grave	53
Hines gravestone	56
Sam Simpson	60
Simpson grave in Lone Fir Cemetery	69
Grave of Virgil Earp	72
Oregonian photos (Xeroxed)	73
George Law	75
School at Kinton	77
Lake Oswego Smelter	80
Oregon City in 1845	83
Plaques on wall	83
Old buildings	85
Ben Holladay	91
Spiritual Camp Hotel	94

Page

Abigail Duniway House 97
Abigail Scott Duniway at voting booth (tent) 101
Grave of Abigail Scott Duniway and her daughter 103
Amos Cook House 110
Site of Jennyopolis 113
Irish Bend Covered Bridge 116
Drawing of Ft. Vancouver 119
John McLoughlin 120
Latourell street scene 123
Mt. Hood 129
Monte Rumgay and friends 132
Monte Rumgay on a wagon ride 133
Grave of Silverton Bobbie 136
Silverton Bobbie's "family" 139
Silverton Bobbie on car 143
Homer Davenport 146
Homer Davenport panel in Geer House 147
Riding Whip Tree 148
Exploring party 151
Opal Lake 152
Upper falls 153
Lundberg Stage House 157
Grave of Jesse Applegate 161
Radio Park Store 165
Grave Creek Covered Bridge 167
Evans Creek Covered Bridge 169
Grave of Bill Bradley 172
Log Town Cemetery 174
Log Town Rose 175
Van Gilder diary 179
Louis Hanna of Boyd 182
Old Dufur 185
Balch Hotel 185
The Friendly Store 191
DeMoss Cemetery 195
John M. DeMoss 197
Old Hay Creek Ranch 204
Round barn at Hay Creek Ranch 205
Baldwin Hotel 207
A Room at the Baldwin 209
Lava Beds 213
Captain Jack 214
Winema 215
Grave of Winema 219
South Fork of the Crooked River 222
Stephen Meek 223
John Day River at fording point 226
Oregon Trail marker near John Day River 227

Page

Warrant for arrest of Mary Leonard ... 231
Jim Hoskin ... 234
Theron Keeney ... 243
Mattie Stubblefield and great-grandchildren ... 246
Stone barn near Mount Vernon ... 249
Sawdust on floor in Bear Valley Tavern ... 251
Hulk of Ponderosa Hotel ... 255
Oswald West ... 257
Buggies at Wagontire ... 257
Great Basin marker ... 260
Cliffs above site of Camp Henderson ... 262
A name on the cliffs above Camp Henderson ... 263
The Walls of Rome ... 265
Stateline Ranch house, Jordan Valley ... 269
Jo Monahan dressed as a man ... 273
Leslie Gulch marker ... 277
The road through Leslie Gulch ... 278
Leslie Gulch formations ... 279
Joseph bank ... 280
Homer Hayes ... 281
Old Joseph Monument ... 284
Chief Joseph ... 285
Weatherford marker, on Oregon 19 ... 288
Scotts Bluff ... 289
Old Oregon Trail rut in Umatilla County ... 291
Horsetail Falls ... 295

Invitation to a Journey

Allons! whoever you are come travel with me!
Traveling with me you find what never tires.

Walt Whitman, *Song of the Open Road*

Oregon is more than places. It is people, past and present, history, legend, folklore, breath and stillness in every form within its boundaries.

For the storyteller, should the broken-down old cowpoke nursing a lone bottle be less important than the millionaire with a cellar full of good wine? Is Portland more fitting for the printed page than an abandoned village rotting away on the naked plain? Must a thin Cascade foothill stream, which has its own nostalgia to tell, be inferior to the broad Willamette? Would you tell me that an arthritic sheepherder living out his last days in a sagging shack is not as rich in story material as the governor? Or that a rimrock-raised woman who runs a sagebrush country store is not as representative of Oregon as any senator?

You know better — and that is why I invite your company on this journey.

For some years now I have been asked — at least a thousand times — how I came to find this place or that, or how I discovered the women and men I put into my books. Eventually, as it had to be, I began to tinker with the idea of writing a book on how I tracked down people and places and legends and folktales. But then I realized that, when it came down to it, readers would be as interested in who and what I found as in how I did my detective work. So I covered all, and the where is given, too, so that you can get there.

Not all places or people or folklore will be new to all of you. But I have tried to avoid what has been said to the point of monotony and to present new perspectives. Frankly, I am not so much interested in the specific date something happened as in why it happened, and I am less concerned with an individual's achievements than in what motivated that person to act. We know the achievements; we have been less enlightened about the motivations.

So come with me to find an Abigail Scott Duniway who is human to the core, to locate a waterfall seen only by a few, to hunt out a burial ground soaked with the juices of history, to discover the amazing Jim Hoskin of Pilot Rock, the tragic Captain Jack, the remains of Log Town, the cavalry names etched on a desert cliff, the legend of a gunslinger.

Hold to my arm as we stride through forests and over plains and up mountains and sink our feet into the Pacific foreshore.

Come with me, woman, man, girl, boy, and take your dogs along — for there is a dog story here that broke my heart to write — and let us greet the morning, noon, and eventide in every corner of this state.

Shall we share our thoughts and food and water as we dance to the wind and sing to the rivers and find in north, east, south, and west an Oregon that cries to be heard — or clasps silence so tight to its bosom that we must gently unlock it?

Come, Camerado, here is the open road. I bid you join me.

Ralph Friedman photo

Roberta Symons, who runs the store, post office, rock shop and first aid station at Ashwood.

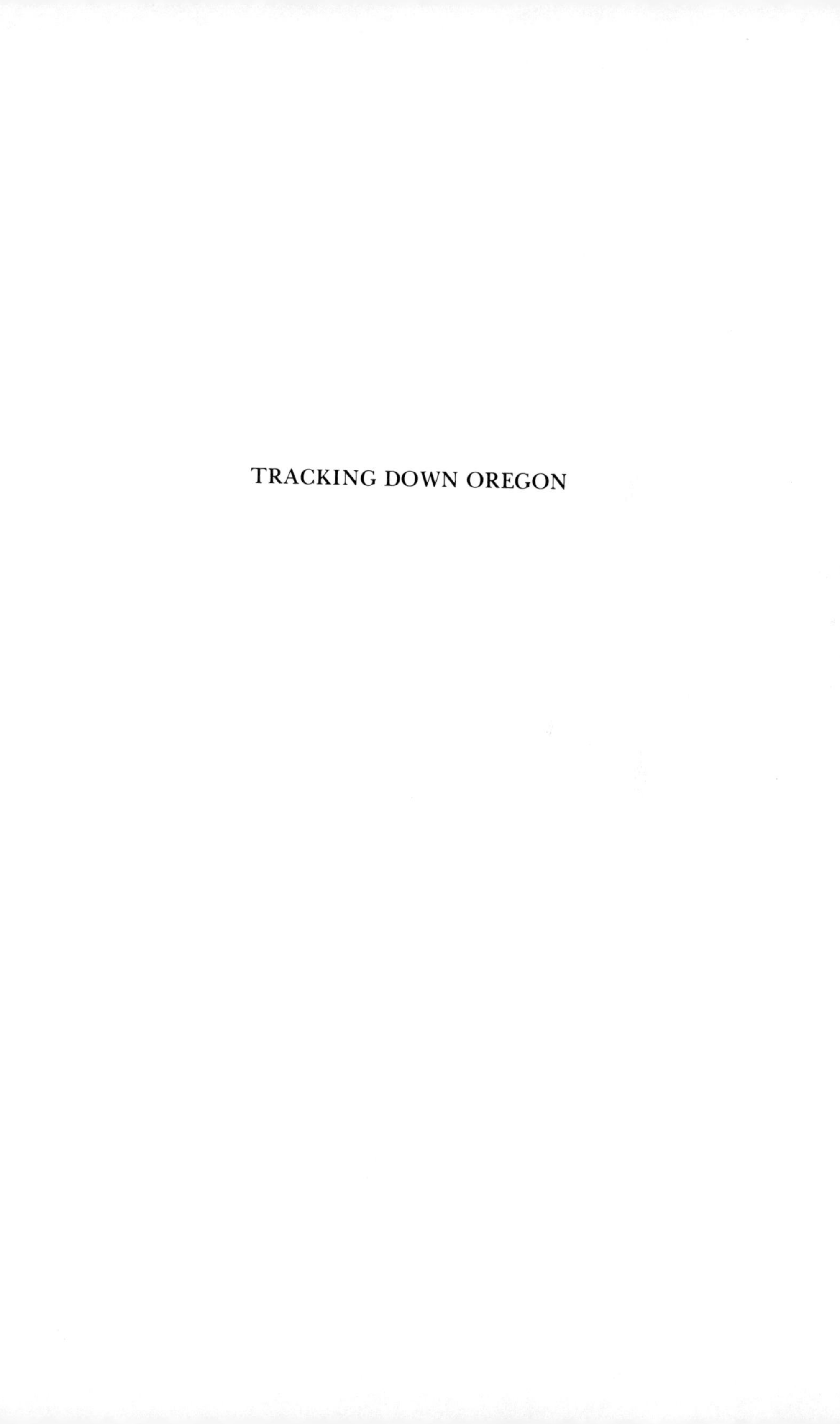

TRACKING DOWN OREGON

Oregon, This Oregon

Fair is the white star of twilight
And the sky clearer
At the day's end;
But she is fairer, and she is dearer
She, my heart's friend!

Fair is the white star of twilight
And the moon is roving
To the sky's end;
But she is fairer, better worth loving,
She, my heart's friend.

From *Path of the Rainbow*, a book of Pacific Northwest Indian poems edited by George W. Cronyn

The sun first touches Oregon on a flocculent hill of silvery Engelmann spruce high above the maw of Hells Canyon, deepest gorge on the continent.

Turning to his dog, the sheepherder reckons, "It'll be another nice day, huh?" The dancing tail agrees. "It oughta be," growls the herder. "It's May."

On the half-moon Wallowa Mountains, the "Alps of Oregon," the sun has rippled the pure-snow slopes with golden fire and painted a faint blush on the cheek of 10,000-foot-high Sacajawea.

"Someday," swears the sheepherder, facing the peaks, "I'm going to climb them. I wonder if Joseph ever did."

Joseph is the great Chief Joseph, whose Nez Perce people were driven from their bountiful Valley-of-the-Winding Waters, the Wallowa, meeting now with moist green lips the morning kiss of the sun.

Southward the sun has laid its warming breath upon the torrefied hills of Burnt River and violet-flecked the broad belly of the Snake River at Farewell Bend. A trailerite at the state park explains to his wife: "Covered wagons camped here, right on the Oregon Trail. They called it Farewell Bend because that's as far as they could follow the Snake."

"It's a nice place to relax," she answers. "Let's stay another day."

Still south, the shafts of the rising sun furrow the sugar beet and potato fields of eastern Malheur County, which is on Mountain Time. "We really belong in Idaho," a dairyman argues. "But we'll never change."

Near Westfall, the only Oregon post office in a totally unpopulated town, wild flowers pop out of the ground like prairie dogs, bobbing their heads and sniffing at the feet of sun-painted rocks. Across this choppy sea of sage — now only forty miles from the swimming pools of Ontario, on the Idaho border — the battered prairie schooners of Meek's Cutoff Party groaned. Somewhere — here, there, or anywhere — gold was said to be found, and never again seen. And the lost Blue Bucket Mine remains the state's foremost legend.

Below the Grand Canyonesque formations above Owyhee Lake, morning comes unheralded to the desolate Owyhee Hills, the Jordan Craters and the desert of southeastern Oregon. The land lies so still it seems under the sea, and yonder so deep in tones of yellows and purples, like coral on the ocean bed. Stealthily the recluse Owyhee River creeps from cached canyons to breathe free upon the grotesque playa before plunging in dithyrambic cry down into another gorge.

At McDermitt, a guest at the White Horse Inn steps out of his Oregon room and walks across the lobby to play a slot machine in Nevada.

Westward the sun advances, tinging the edges of a sailboat cloud over a pioneer ranch. "Another day, another dollar," an old vaquero mutters, then climbs into the saddle to gallop off after an errant heifer.

An antelope turns toward Catlow Valley from a shelf on Hart Mountain, an 8,000-foot-high massif jutting out of the desert, and rolls its pronged head in the virgin hours of the sunny morning. No one will do it harm here; the mountain is a national antelope refuge.

Northward, beyond the steep and seldom-explored Steens Mountain, the sun has reached Pete French country, a hushed world of rock-rimmed juniper buttes and haunted canyons soaked in the history of a man who audaciously built the largest cattle empire in Oregon. He has been dead eight decades, gunned down by a feuding homesteader, but in Harney County he is still alive. Fire and wind, however, have taken almost a complete toll of his once-fabled ranch headquarters, a small piece down a dirt road from Frenchglen, whose twenty or so inhabitants make it the most populated settlement in an area of 6,000 square miles. Outside the Frenchglen Hotel, an old stagecoach inn, the bird watchers take pictures of the branding irons hanging below the enclosed porch before departing for the nearby marshes of Malheur National Wildlife Refuge.

Still north, the sun soothes the high plateau where stood sixty and seventy years ago more homesteader hamlets than anyone can recall. Lured by slick promoters, tens of thousands of hungry innocents poured onto the bunchgrass plains, denuded the earth to plant crops that couldn't grow, turned the earth against them, and fled for their lives. Some of the towns remain, withering on the vine. Drewsey, for instance. In its youth it was so wild folks called it Gouge Eye. Its population is down to forty, the general store is still in the nineteenth century, and the only violence now is on television.

Cattlemen took over the homesteader lands. In the beef-rich John Day Valley the flow of sunlight which has squirmed through the passes of the darkling Blue Mountains sees the cattle being moved on hoof from winter feedlots to highland pastures. Right through John Day town the cattle are driven, one of the several cattle drives left in Oregon.

Lake Owyhee

Several of the herds are pushed north to hills that more than a hundred years ago were roaring gold camps. Like Roman candles, they peaked quickly and sputtered out. Nobody now knows where most of them stood. A few ghost towns live on — one with a population of three.

Other cattle are moved to the whispering hills above the polychrome fossil beds on the clear John Day River, and still others to the grazing forests of ponderosa pine looking down on leathery cow towns.

The northern rim of the Oregon sun sweeps the lavender shadows from the streets of Pendleton, already preparing for its great September Round-Up, and scrawls lemon waves upon the Columbia River. McNary Dam is a block of gold.

Westward, the sun follows the Columbia and the covered-wagon trace drawn inland over a glut of naked ridges to The Dalles, "End of the Old Oregon Trail."

South in this span of land, morning glow washes the undulating wheatlands of Sherman, Gilliam and Morrow counties, now so emerald green; lustres the Painted Hills of sparsely settled Wheeler County; awakens the Warm Springs Indian Reservation spa of Kah-nee-ta; thaws the Moorish redoubt of Fort Rock, alone and aloof on the High Desert; unfolds the stirring rivers, cold deep lakes and ponderosa-scented parks of central Oregon; releases from fetal dawn the high peaks of the Cascades, coned clouds frozen in the blue-burnished sky. At Klamath Falls, a Canadian who has just driven the 137 miles of pine-fringed highway from Bend in the tang-of-cider morning, pulls in at a gas station, his last Oregon stop before crossing into California, and tells the attendant: "You've got some mighty wonderful country out here." The reply is typical: "That's why we moved here. We've got everything except the rat race — and who needs that?"

The probing fingers of the westering sun inch up the Cascade Mountains, from the California line to the Columbia River. South to north the solar alchemy transforms the cordillera, unveiling the Skyline Trail and the faerie-blue volcanic pit of Crater Lake; the blue-green west slope forest of Douglas fir; the hundred-fold lakes and infant rivers; the great peaks erupting from the ponderosa plateau; the volcanic fields where astronauts destined for the moon walked on lava; the east-slope apple orchards of the Hood River Valley; and the state's loftiest peak, 11,245-foot Mt. Hood. Down over silvery stands of Noble fir a jet plane follows the glide path into Portland. A skier darts a glance at the metal bird and continues downslope to Timberline Lodge.

"Somehow I thought of Oregon as all green," the visitor from New York tells his waiting friend at Portland's International Airport. "I didn't realize so much of it is arid. In some places I didn't see a tree for miles."

"That's right," she agrees. "Two-thirds of the state is east of the rain belt. That's where our Old West is."

The May sun which has spilled Portland's green-thumb city dwellers and suburbanites onto their flowery lawns is flooding all the heartland valleys of Western Oregon. Between Portland and Salem, the cradle of Oregon, the pioneer houses, churches and hamlets seem reborn in the prelude to summer. But at Champoeg, on French Prairie, a retired farmer from Molalla cusses to himself. He has brought his grandchildren to see the meeting ground where the fate of Oregon was settled, and he had to pass five California cars before he could find a place to park. "This state's gettin' too crowded," he gruffs. "I wish they'd a-closed the borders long ago."

"When long ago?" his grandson asks.

The old man shakes his head. "I dunno. The day after my grandfolks arrived." And he laughs. "Ain't that what they all say — keep everybody out of Oregon the day after they come? I guess you can't stop progress. Damn it!"

The longest, most populated, most industrialized valley of all — the Willamette — has started another day. An engineer in Albany asks his wife: "What's the weather prediction?" "Your guess is just as good," she shrugs. So he looks out the window, sees the sprinkle of sunshower on the sidewalk, and leaves his umbrella at home. The weather could change — but he won't drown.

In the big cities the movers and shakers are plotting to attract new businesses; in the grassy towns of Scotts Mills and Scio the people hold fast to the rustic life.

So, too, the day opens in the vale of the Umpqua and on the fruited plains of the Rogue River Valley. At Ashland, facing the Siskiyou Mountains which drop into California, a young Hollywood actor points to the replica of the Globe Theater in idyllic Lithia Park and tells his honeymoon bride, "Here's where I got started, at the Shakespearean Festival."

Now the sun curves over the Coast Range, turning the boils of fog on the wooded hills into shimmering bonfires. The rivers that charge to the sea are naked now, free of the shrouds of night and fog. The Chetco, Pistol, Coquille, Rogue, Siuslaw, Umpqua, Alsea, Yaquina, Nehalem, Klaskanine, and more.

And on the slopes of the Coast Range, the sun filters into the logging operations of Douglas fir — so mechanized compared to the burly era of the axe-swinging Paul Bunyans. A forester stands in a patchwork quilt of a harvested area, roams his eye over two-year-old seedlings and remarks to a young faller: "Tree farming is our salvation, son. Never forget that."

Beyond a stately grove of redwoods, the sun reaches the Pacific in the southwest corner of Oregon. At that moment, or near it, all of the littoral has been focused in the eye of the infinite fire globe. The multitude of state parks, already filling with trailers and boats; the lighthouses and the long sandy beaches strewn with driftwood; the fishing towns whose fleets are already at sea; the charter boats starting out ("Maybe I can get a few salmon today," a Portland business executive says with a grin to his wind-scoured pilot); the spray-dimpled forests of Sitka spruce and Western hemlocks; sand buggies specking the ever-mutable dunes ("Our Sahara by the Sea," a driver laughs as he starts his buggy down a steep yellow hill that chills an Alaska tourist); the bays and headlands — and above all, the long vistas. "Beautiful, just beautiful," gasps a Nebraska woman, entranced by the serrated cliffs twisting into and away from the restless sea, so piercingly magnificent on a translucent day.

Near Astoria, where the Columbia discharges the thousand tributaries it has gathered in its 1,200-mile voyage since birth, a school bus halts by the replica of Fort Clatsop. On this site the Lewis and Clark party — the first white Americans to cross the continent — spent the winter of 1805-1806.

Among them was the Shoshone girl-mother who had shared their agony and their triumph and for whom a snow-painted mountain is named. And across the state, where the sun first touched Oregon an hour earlier, the Wallowa sheepherder keeps vigil on a hill of golden fleece and vows that someday he'll climb the peak called Sacajawea.

The Untypical Smiths

Nothing in the world is single,
All things by a law divine
In one spirit meet and mingle.

Samuel Butler, *Love's Philosophy*

Do you stop with the plaque on the boulder in Clatsop Pioneer Cemetery that states, simply and unequivocally, that Solomon Howard Smith and Helen Celiast Smith were the first schoolteachers in Oregon?

No, start from there, and in the building up of fact and unraveling of legend you will mold a story that is alive with pioneer drama, rich with frontier pageantry, and tender with a love that transcended race and culture.

Solomon Smith was twenty-three when he arrived at Fort Vancouver with Nathaniel Wyeth in 1832. A native of New Hampshire, he had studied medicine at Norwich Academy, in Vermont, but gave up what might have been a promising career for adventure and wealth in the West. When the empty-handed Wyeth returned East, Smith stayed on in the new land.

John Ball, another Hampshireman, had also been with Wyeth, but parted from the expedition at Fort Vancouver. Dr. John McLoughlin, the Chief Factor of the post and the head of Hudson's Bay Company's Western operations, considered himself a man of culture and had been pleased to have the Dartmouth graduate and a seasoned lawyer as his guest. But Ball was reluctant to stay on for free and was ready to depart the stockade when McLoughlin came up with an attractive suggestion. "You're an educated man," he said. "I'll employ you to instruct the children of the fort." Ball accepted and became the first schoolteacher in the Oregon Country.

Since none of the children had any grasp of English — being the product of mixed marriages and raised by their mothers — and since Ball knew none of the Indian tongues spoken by the children, his success was far from complete. At any rate, he wanted to try his hand at farming, and with McLoughlin's blessing he did, moving down to French Prairie in the spring of 1833 and putting some acres into wheat. But the crude frontier life was too much for him; he was more firmly inclined to a different kind of culture, he said, and in mid-October of 1833 he boarded a vessel bound for his New York.

Finding himself with nothing to do, Smith volunteered to replace Ball as tutor. With no other applicant in sight, McLoughlin hired him. By then

Grave of Solomon Howard Smith and Helen Celiast Smith

the children had learned some English, and Smith, out in the wilderness, had acquired the basics of Chinook, the common jargon of the Northwest Indians and the language bridge between Indians and whites.

In later years Smith would recall teaching at the fort only because it was the rationale for his presence there. Had he not been employed at the fort he would not have met the woman who would become his mate for the rest of his life.

She was Celiast, princess daughter of Coboway, supreme chief of the Clatsops. That much is for sure. She was slender and lithe, with flowing black hair, features finely chiseled, a voice compared to a songbird, eyes that were soft as a doe's, and a smile that had the warmth of summer morning. That, too, is known. But the early part of her life with Smith is imprecise.

It seems almost certain that she had been married, without benefit of clergy or civil authority (simply because there was none around) to a French baker at Fort Vancouver named Porier and had three children by him. The Clatsop and the Yankee took a quick and strong liking to each other, and soon nothing could turn them away from the path their hearts marked. He saw her as fairer than any woman he had ever met; to her he was tall, broad-shouldered, courteous, hard-working, and with burning eyes that would not let her go.

Was she living at the fort when they first looked upon each other, as some scholars believe? Or had she deserted her husband and taken up residence with her sister, Margaret, who was living in common-law marriage at French Prairie with the old trapper, Joe Gervais? There is a story that McLoughlin, upon discovering that Porier had another wife in Canada, urged Celiast to flee the baker and take with her only the youngest of her children.

Those researchers who hold that Celiast was with her sister add that she frequently visited the fort, where she was initially seen by Smith. Almost immediately he was hot on her trail, imploring her to marry him.

She could not live at the fort with Smith and he could not remain at the post without her, so the two ran off together, taking her three children.

They traveled only as far as French Prairie, which was far enough from problems then, and there for two years Solomon and Celiast, now Helen Smith, taught school, thus becoming the first schoolteachers inside the boundaries of what later became the state of Oregon.

One of the eight entries in the marriage page of the Oregon Mission record book bears the following terse declaration: "Saturday, 11th Feb. 1837 — Mr. Solomon H. Smith was married to Miss Ellen of the Clatsop tribe at the house of Mr. Smith Willamette settlement by Jason Lee."

Solomon Howard Smith and Helen Celiast Smith *Courtesy Oregon Historical Society*

Lee, who had come to the Oregon Country as the Methodist agent on the straight-and-narrow railroad to God, had lived long enough on the edge of the wilds to have gained some tolerance. He had learned that no angels resided in Oregon — if they did anywhere — and that if complete morality could not be obtained, a step below it was better than none. Without reproach and with straight face he tied the knot, thus legitimizing a marriage that had started four years earlier. To her dying day Helen insisted that she and Solomon had been wed in 1833.

There is another story about Celiast that cannot be verified but adds interest to the account of her life with Smith. By 1840 she had "experienced a change of heart" and hungered to return to her own people as a missionary. She was so staunch in her desire that Smith sold the French Prairie farm and the family started west, holding religious services with Indians encountered en route to the coast.

For whatever reason he left French Prairie, Smith took up a land claim on Clatsop Plains, the first or second homemaking farmer to settle west of the Coast Range. Upon his claim, "extending from the Skipanon creek to the ocean beach" he built a one-story structure 20 by 30 feet, and in it the family settled. By then Helen had the first of her seven children by Solomon. Together with the three earlier, the seven gave her a total of ten.

Now Helen became a frontier wife, working the farm and holding the family together while Solomon was away, as he often was in the early period on the Pacific littoral. The year their first house was built he went inland and came back with the first cattle brought to the Oregon Coast. Turning around, he journeyed again to the Willamette Valley, purchased some horses, and drove them to St. Helens, on the Columbia, from where the horses were boated to Clatsop Plains. Then, as if he had not done enough for one year, Smith started the first Columbia River ferry, lashing boats together.

For a while, until succeeded by one of Jason Lee's recent arrivals from the East, Helen and Solomon operated a missionary station, but it was abandoned. The conversion rate was too low and the remoteness intolerable. After that the Smiths proselytized no more.

An early partisan for the Americanization of the Oregon Country, Solomon Smith was a participant at Champoeg on that eventful day of May 2, 1843. Having studied medicine in Vermont, he practiced it in Oregon. In the versatile style of the pioneers he was also a sawmill owner, dairyman, storekeeper, riverman, and, at the age of sixty-three, a state senator. The last survivor of the first American settlers in Oregon, he had done much, but to the last day of his life he was proudest of his Helen. To him she was always the princess daughter of a great chief, an unflinching co-worker, and the best friend he ever had.

He died in the summer of 1876, at the age of sixty-seven, ending a marriage of thirty-nine years by doctrine and forty-three years by love. She survived him by about fifteen years, majestic to the close. A third of a century before, a journalist describing the middle-aged Celiast wrote of "the come-hither look of Solomon Smith's magnetic squaw." And in 1889, when she was eighty-eight and still living on the Clatsop Plains, she was, in the eyes of all who saw her, a beautiful old woman.

So you look at the plaque on the boulder in Clatsop Pioneer Cemetery and if you stop there you know only that Solomon Howard Smith and Helen Smith were the first schoolteachers in Oregon. (Not in the Oregon Country — that honor is due only John Ball — but in what became the state of Oregon.)

But beyond the plaque, beyond the stone, beyond the cemetery itself, is a tale worth seeking out, and this we tried to do in our tracking down Oregon.

Directions: From Astoria, 8.3 miles south on U.S. 101 to Clatsop Plains Pioneer Church. Clatsop Pioneer Cemetery is back of church.

A Closeness to Hug Point

She'll be comin' 'round the mountain when she comes,
She'll be comin' 'round the mountain when she comes,
She'll be comin' 'round the mountain,
She'll be comin' 'round the mountain,
She'll be comin' 'round the mountain when she comes.

American Folk Song

When the stagecoach came 'round the mountain four miles south of Cannon Beach, the driver kept the reins tight, for a slip could plunge horses, people and carriage into the cold, frothing, quickly-deep ocean.

Hug Point was a literal description: the road hugged the point where the hill met the sea. Today the rough, crude, brine-worn bend seems archaic, almost primitive beyond belief, but when the well-cemented sandstone was cut and blasted out of the hill, it marked a great advance of progress in coastal travel.

At long stretches between Astoria and Tillamook, early settlers used the beach for a highway. There are tales of pioneer mailmen riding their horses belly-deep in the sea to make their rounds. When the wagons came to Hug Point at high tide, their travel was halted. Elsewhere they could navigate on the upper end of the sands, but not here. There was no beach.

The average elevation of the Coast Range is about 1,500 feet. But behind Hug Point, Sugarloaf Mountain and Onion Peak rise to 3,000 feet. The slopes were too steep for the wagons to swing eastward. If there was to be passage at high tide, a road had to be hacked out of the sea cliff. Late in the last century this was done.

This oddest of all Oregon roads continued to be used after the automobile replaced the horse. It must have been murder on tires and springs and hell on nerves. When two cars met at the bend, one of them had to back up, or down, and that surely was a chore.

By coincidence I met there a man who had driven a horse-drawn stage as late as midway into the second decade of the 1900s. His wife was with him. They had become acquainted when she was a passenger on one of his runs. Now they lived in Texas, but they had come back to the Coast to see how much had changed since they had departed many years ago. It was their first return to Hug Point. "Everything around here seems different," he said, "but this road looks very familiar to me. See those grooves? I remember them well."

As he spoke a picture came to me. The bright-eyed but white-haired

Hug Point at low tide. Author on edge of road.

man, lank but bent, is a young stagecoach driver again. He is on his way to Nehalem, with mail, light freight, and passengers. The wind is rising and the rain is thick. Through slits in the thin fog he can see the ocean, lunging and lashing, lathery in its wild dance of frenzy, each wave rising ominously from the deep, like a sea monster. At the far border of the foreshore the horses strain across the sodden sand until they are almost to the hill. Then the driver bends them right, toward the high-tide Pacific. And now he turns them evenly onto the sandstone trace and holds hard to the reins. The horses have been here before, but he can feel the jitteriness spark out of them. He knows his passengers are tense. Not one of them is saying a word. He calls out to the horses, "Easy, boys. Easy there. Easy now. We're doin' fine." The horses shake their manes, to throw off the rain or in understanding, and walk cautiously, pausing at each step to hoof firmly down on the slippery rock. Then a pull to the left and they are rounding the point. This is the hardest part. The ocean is throwing itself at the coach. Disaster is only a falter away. But the horses stay steady. Down the grooved slope they come and when they touch sand they throw up their heads in relief. The driver grins and someone inside the stage applauds. It will be Nehalem for sure.

Directions: Stagecoach road is about 400 yards north of parking lot at Hug Point State Park. Park is 2.3 miles south of south end of Cannon Beach-Tolovana Park Loop and 1.5 miles north of Arch Cape, on U.S. 101.

A Rising of Spirit at Munson Falls

I never found the companion that was so companionable as solitude.

Henry Thoreau, *Walden*

Few people seem to come here. The solitude is one of puzzlement and reverence. The words of Emerson in *Nature* sift through the trees as an ethereal mist: "In the woods, too, a man casts off his years, as the snake his slough, and at what period soever of life, is always a child. . . . In the woods, we return to reason and to faith. . . . Standing on the bare ground — my head bathed by the blithe air, and uplifted into infinite space — all mean egotism vanishes. I become a transparent eye-ball; I am nothing; I see all; the currents of the Universal Being circulate through me: I am part or parcel of God . . . ."

Thus is constant my mood at Munson Creek County Park, south of Tillamook. Five times I have been here and only once, besides my wife, was another human present. That was a young graduate botany student from Oregon State University. She replied to our soft greeting even more softly, as though the ears of the rain forest would be wounded by anything above mild tone. Then, pack on back, she took off slowly up the trail to Munson Falls, pausing every few feet to acquaint herself with a flower or shrub. If she had wanted to make an in-depth study of each species she would have been on that relatively short trail all year.

The park is a darkling mass of moss-hung firs, maples, cedars, spruce and hemlock. Sunlight filters in as though it were holy water meted out to the anointed. A shadow sleeps on until new lightness or dark dissolves it. The next shadow rests on the same bed of cones or couch of ferns.

Look up and down and all around you. Here is the forest primeval, as it was a century ago, as much of the northern Coast was a hundred years back. Here are mighty firs that are the watchtowers of the woods, looking out with the vigilance of mother giraffes, while huddled around them spruce and hemlock shiver in the wind that makes its unscheduled count. Above the fallen trees, their bones still hard, and the long-dead logs turning to pulp by rain and time, the standing aged maples and cedars nod pensively, knowing their hour will come, and glance at the brash youngsters swelling so arrogantly. The ancients, too, had felt youth, and when the sun is overhead and unclouded they can still remember another season.

We took the trail through the mossy, dank, magnificently sombre forest, hiking half a mile, as I counted our steps, to the pool of Munson Falls. A white knife cutting through a tangle of hoary trees, the falls, at a

Munson Falls

319-foot drop, are the highest in the Coast Range and the second highest in the state. But statistics do not somersault my heart.

In the lowland forest I had felt tranquility and had put myself in perspective. Infinitesimal I saw myself to be, a tiny, flitting creature, no more durable than a summer fly. Yet, because I was alive, I was in league with the trees and the flowers and the shrubs and the ferns and the creek that strayed from the pool. We were linked together simply because we were, we existed, we had to share, to be of sustenance to each other, our survival as living beings dependent upon each other, and having voiced this sense of personal responsibility, I cannot be more profound.

So up the narrow, winding, branch-strewn, twigged dirt path I started with this peace of mind, the calendar of petty chores and festering bickerings put aside. Up and down the trail, the flowers shy and the ferns smiling along the path and the interior woods opening to receive me in their maw. And then we saw Munson Falls, the sheer power of the cataract an electric, life-giving, throbbing, awakening, pulsating surge, pouring down with the exaltation of the "Hallelujah Chorus" from Handel's seismic oratorio.

It was then, as I looked upon the white, sunlit stream, every drop of it a voltage cell of life, hurling itself with abandon into the outthrust forest, that my spirit soared, and on top of no mountain have I ever felt so tall.

Directions: From Tillamook (U.S. 101), south 7.1 miles to turnoff for Munson Creek County Park. 1.1 miles, turn into park. 0.5 mile, parking.

The Seasons of Randolph

Such was the golden summer of Roaring Camp. They were "flush times," and the luck was with them. The claims had yielded enormously.

Bret Harte, *The Luck of Roaring Camp*

You won't find Randolph at its first location, on Whiskey Run. It hasn't been there for more than a century.

During the Coos County Gold Rush of 1853-1855, a creek dribbling into the ocean was named Whiskey Run, either because of the heavy drinking or because the creek suggested firewater to some thirsty prospector. There is a legend that the amount of booze consumed outweighed the gold panned, but legend is as intrinsic to gold-camp history as the metal itself, and when you fall in with the tales of Argonauts, make sure that a shovel is handy. You may not have to use it, but be prepared.

For instance, consider this story of buried treasure at the first Randolph, on Whiskey Run. Two miners who had made a rich strike buried a

Illustration in Harper's Magazine, October, 1856

five-gallon can of gold dust beneath a tree in the woods back of the beach and went off for supplies. During their absence a forest fire swept the mining district, leaving thousands of black-charred snags and stumps and obliterating any mark to identify the site of the cache. The two miners searched for weeks before giving up — and there is no record of the gold ever having been found.

You can use the shovel for the disposing of this yarn, or for digging up dirt as other fortune hunters have done.

In the spring of 1852, some Indians prospecting on the beach north of the mouth of the Coquille River made the first discovery of gold on the Oregon Coast when they stumbled upon an abundance of the yellow metal in the black sand near where Whiskey Run enters the Pacific. The gold was finely particled, they soon learned, and unevenly distributed in the thick sand. Sometimes there was scarcely a trace of color; at other times a panful of sand yielded eight to ten dollars.

The following summer the Indians sold their claim to two brothers, who worked out a small fortune there; as much as $100,000 in gold may have been taken from the claim.

One of the first white men on the scene, a dour, secretive fellow named Joe Crowley, toiled hard, kept his mouth shut, and departed in the middle of the night with a mule load of gold. He made it safe to a bank all right, but from then on life was downhill. As happened with so many other miners who catapulted from beans to bonanza, Crowley squandered away his wealth or was fleeced of it, and he died a pauper, without even a mule.

The summer of 1853 brought the gold rush, with men hustling in from as far as San Francisco. The ocean beach was staked off with claims for miles north and south. More than a thousand men gathered here. A couple of the early comers named the settlement Randolph, for John Randolph, an earlier congressman from Roanoke, Virginia, whom history remembers best for his having fluttered Philadelphia in 1803 with the happy announcement that he had fathered a child out of wedlock. He also duelled with Henry Clay and popularized the term "doughface," applied to Northern congressmen who voted with Southern slave-holding interests.

The town, thrown together on a bluff overlooking the beach at Whiskey Run, mushroomed almost overnight. Within a few weeks of the first shack Randolph had saloons, restaurants, stores, lodging houses, cabins and tents. A trail was built to Coos Bay, connecting the camp with ocean-going vessels. At the height of the rush, Randolph rivaled Jacksonville, the most famous gold town in the history of Western Oregon, in importance, if not exactly in population.

But, as happens to all placer camps, the gold petered out and the Argonauts made tracks to other rumored rainbows. Two years after the Whiskey Run stampede started, Randolph was practically deserted. A bleak picture of the settlement, as it looked in the autumn of 1855, appeared in the October 1856 issue of *Harper's New Monthly Magazine*. Authored by William V. Wells, the article was titled, "Wild Life in Oregon." Here is Randolph as seen by Wells:

"We found two or three disconsolate families collected in the public

Whiskey Run entering the Pacific. Near here stood first town of Randolph.

pond, or corral, making an 'arbitration,' as a very talkative lady informed us, of the cattle of a couple who, having been married a year, had found the hymenial chains to hang heavily, and were about separating for life. Leaving nearly the entire population, consisting of nine men and women and a number of children, to this occupation, we drew up at the door of the least ruined house, and dismounted, to the satisfaction of a flock of flaxen-haired urchins, to whom our arrival was evidently a matter of great moment. A very pretty and interesting woman welcomed us, and was soon busily engaged preparing our supper. Meanwhile we strolled out to see the lions of Randolph. Several vacant lots in a 'streak' of deserted pine dwellings attracted my curiosity enough to inquire what had become of the houses; when our hostess responded that they had fallen a sacrifice to the fuel-gathering hands of the remaining population — in a word, they had been used up as fire-wood. What a picture! A town springing from nothing — growing — culminating in its career of prosperity, and burned as fuel in its decadence!

"In another year not a clapboard will remain to tell the whereabouts of Randolph. Our hostess — whom we thought far too pretty to be wasting the bloom of her beauty in this bleak corner of Oregon — soon spread before us an excellent supper, to which we did such extreme justice that even she, not unused to the voracity of her Oregon visitors, stared up from her sewing at the rapid disappearance of the edibles. The master of the house announcing that our beds were ready, we tumbled into our blankets and slept soundly until daybreak, when the adjacent

Third site of Randolph

frizzling of some elk-steaks operating upon the olfactories of H ——, he opened his eyes, sprang out of bed, and hastened to array himself. Breakfast dispatched and the bills paid, we remounted, and leaving the silent town to its requiem of the eternal surf, we struck off from the coast, and plunged directly into the woods."

Some of the miners at Randolph took the town with them — at least they took the name — to the mouth of the Coquille River, near where the lighthouse in Bullards Beach State Park now stands. Then Randolph was "moved" again, inland on the Coquille, and in the 1860s established as a "true town."

The prophecy of Wells was fulfilled a few years after he left the first Randolph. There is no trace today of where the gold camp stood, though we know its location. There is even less knowledge of the exact site of the second Randolph. And all that tells us of the place of the third Randolph, the "true town," now in the winter of its seasons, is a marker, denoting not a village but a rural area.

For romance and imagery, I like the setting of the first Randolph best. The beach at Whiskey Run contains not only agates, agatized myrtlewood and jaspers, but unfolds a superb Pacific vista. And some days prospectors, having left their television sets behind, work the sands for the grains of gold the Argonauts of a century and a quarter earlier left behind.

You can't find enough gold at Whiskey Run to pay for your gas (if you're that lucky!) but if you know your history, and let your mind roam, it isn't hard to come up with a panful of fanciful lore. And that, having tracked down the story of Whiskey Run, is why I return to it.

Directions: For Whiskey Run Beach, go north 3 miles from Bandon on U.S. 101 to Seven Devils–Whiskey Run Jct. Turn left, or west. 1.5 miles, Whiskey Run Beach.

For Bullards Beach State Park, go north 1 mile from Bandon on U.S. 101 and turn west. 2.8 miles, lighthouse at mouth of Coquille River.

Third site of Randolph is 1 mile north of Seven Devils Jct. and 1 mile east of U.S. 101.

Tichenor and Associates Present Port Orford

If this were played upon a stage now, I would condemn it as improbable fiction.

Shakespeare, *Twelfth Night*

Without William Tichenor there would not have been Battle Rock State Park. Nor, perhaps, Port Orford, whose downtown is half a mile north. Tichenor was to this area what Hamlet is to Hamlet, Macbeth to Macbeth, and King Lear to King Lear. But though he headed the cast in the drama of Port Orford, he had some important supporting players, whom in due time we will meet.

Like all the illustrious pioneers, Tichenor was a many-talented soul who stepped upon the stage of history at the right time. That he faded from the limelight tells less about him — and others like him — than it does about the growing-up of the state. Past deeds are forgotten in a crowd of strangers falling over each other to climb their own peaks. Many of the elders became known to the newcomers as "characters," good only for an anecdote.

Still, Tichenor fared better than most of his early contemporaries. Even in the late autumn of his life he was a familiar figure on the streets of this small Curry County coast town, more often than not formally dressed, his slightly bent frame still bearing the stamp of authority. His lean face, with deep-set eyes, and a long, narrow beard that sometimes gave him the appearance of a hayseed farmer come to the carnival and at other times that of a stern nineteenth century banker, attracted even the attention of schoolchildren, who had their own heros and legends. They had heard he had been a sea captain and an important man, but what had he done? Then they shrugged off the momentary puzzle and returned to their own times. At that, they knew more of Tichenor than do most of the adults in today's Port Orford.

Tichenor had already lived a full life when, at the age of thirty-eight, he brought his small propellor-driven steamer, the *Sea Gull*, here on June 9, 1851, and landed nine men and supplies on the large rock at a map point soon after, for sound reason, to be called Battle Rock.

At twelve Tichenor had left his New Jersey home to go to sea, as cabin boy on the brig *Martha* bound for Europe. Returning, he studied navigation. When he was sixteen he shipped as mate on the steamer *George Washington*, which ran the Mississippi River in the New Orleans trade. Tichenor was not yet twenty-one when he married Elizabeth Brinkerhoff, who was full well to know the woes of a mariner's wife and the ordeals of a frontier woman. But at least the first eight years of their marriage, on a farm in Knox County, Indiana, were without crisis and anguish.

By the time he bought a vessel, in San Francisco, in late 1849, Tichenor had been an Illinois state senator, a trader, and a California Gold Rush miner (for decades afterward the site of his discovery on the middle fork of the American River was called Tichenor's Gulch.)

He sailed the ship he purchased in San Francisco to the Gulf of California, where he spent the winter trading between Lower California and Mexico. He returned to San Francisco on March 12, 1850, with the first green turtle cargo to hit the city.

The landing of the nine men on the huge seaward shoulder that has been known as Battle Rock for a century and a quarter was no accident. Tichenor was precise in his location. Two factors influenced him. First, he was keenly aware of the new gold diggings in southern Oregon and he aimed to make his own pot of gold from the gold miners before his com-

Courtesy Oregon Historical Society

William Tichenor

Battle Rock, Port Orford

petition got to them. He would establish a supply point on the coast so that freight could be hauled from San Francisco, unloaded at the nearest feasible coastal point, and then packtrained overland to the mines. He had sailed up and down the Oregon Coast and — this was the second influencing factor — had determined exactly where to establish his base of operations. The nine men he recruited at Portland were to be the first contingent of a settlement to be founded for supplying the miners. Little did he realize that, after failing to reach them, miners would come to him.

It was George Vancouver, the famed British explorer, who bestowed the name Tichenor would take for his colony, honoring Vancouver's good friend, the Earl of Orford. Actually, Vancouver was then looking at Cape Blanco, but eventually the name crept south a few miles and Cape Orford became Port Orford. Vancouver had passed by in 1792, almost six decades before Captain Tichenor, plying the coast, picked out a place to start his settlement.

No sooner had the *Sea Gull* departed from the rock, on June 9, 1851, than Tichenor's nine, one of them named Cyrus Hedden, were attacked by the resident Indians, the Coquilles, who resented white intrusion. Fortunately for the palefaces, Tichenor had had the foresight to equip them with a four-pound cannon. Without it, the state park might now be called Massacre Rock. You know how it is: when the whites won, it was a victory; when the Indians won, it was a massacre.

As soon as the Coquilles relaxed their vigilance the nine fled northward, to settlements near the mouth of the Umpqua River. But the days of Indian sovereignty in their own land were numbered. Tichenor returned on July 14 — Bastille Day, by coincidence — with sixty-seven men under the command of James S. Gamble and proceeded to build two blockhouses "inside of heavy logs," which he called Fort Point after a landmark just northwest of Battle Rock. The men were recruited from the streets of San Francisco, which "were thronged with idlers who were destitute and willing to go anywhere as long as their wants were supplied." Before the month was out, "it was found necessary," complained Tichenor, "to send fourteen of the most desperate and insubordinate of the crew back to the city."

All was going well until a party of ten men, led by William Green T'Vault, the peppery first editor of Oregon's first newspaper and the first Oregon postmaster general, was ambushed by Indians.

An expedition of twenty-three swashbucklers had started from Port Orford to blaze a trade route to the mines and settlements in the interior. After a week of floundering to nowhere, thirteen of the men returned to Port Orford. The others carried on under the bumbling leadership of T'Vault, who did not seem to be able to turn around twice without becoming disoriented. Their wayward course brought them to the Coquille River, where their horses were helpless in the river-bottom jungles. Instead of retreating — T'Vault seemed to have an innate penchant for choosing dubious valor over discretion — the men hired Indian canoes. Probably seeking vengeance for the warriors felled at Battle Rock, the Indian guides maneuvered T'Vault's weary, luckless, and totally incompetent explorers to a Coquille village. There other Indians were waiting, armed to the teeth with bows and arrows, war clubs, and long, sharp knives wrought of band iron from a vessel wrecked in the Rogue River.

Only five of the whites escaped, including T'Vault and Cyrus Hedden, who had returned from an Umpqua settlement to Port Orford. T'Vault and another man, saved by an Indian lad, abandoned their sodden clothing and traveled all night along the beach until they found refuge among the friendly Indians at Cape Blanco, who canoed them to Port Orford. There is no record, alas, as to whether the hospitable Blancos regarded the unclothed strangers as immodest or quaint.

Hedden and two others stole through the woods until they felt safe; then they trudged to the same settlement on the Umpqua to which Hedden and his beleaguered friends had fled from Battle Rock three months earlier. Another old friend was a sailor of the pilot boat *Hagstaff*, the vessel that had been wrecked in the Rogue. Like Hedden, he was a two-time loser. After the *Hagstaff* had smashed up he and the rest of the crew had scurried to the woods for hiding and had wandered furtively for three weeks until rescued by the Umpqua settlers. With three scarred and famished parties arriving inside of one summer, the Umpqua settlers, who nursed and fed and clothed all refugees, must have wondered who would show up next.

T'Vault had made it into history before his pathetic and agonizing expedition; Hedden achieved some regional prominence later. He was a pioneer of Scottsburg, opening an early mercantile establishment. About

125 years later, Hedden's Store, in the third building to carry his name, still stood in Scottsburg and was still operated by a Hedden.

When word reached Port Orford about the fate of T'Vault's party, the news was swiftly relayed to California. Up sailed ninety U.S. dragoons, embarked on a punitive mission. It took the soldiers three weeks to find and corner the Coquilles and twenty minutes to smash their force. Fifteen Indians were killed, many wounded, and the Coquille village and stores destroyed.

Then the troopers marched back to Tichenor's village and built Fort Orford, where the old junior high school was later put up. It was, by the standards then, a rather large post: officers' quarters, barracks, blockhouse, guardhouse, kitchen, ordnance storehouse, stables — fifteen buildings in all. None of the troops, including the reinforcements who arrived soon after, was again called into combat, and in the early autumn of 1856 the garrison marched away.

Tichenor had other problems than finding his men bushwhacked. He seemed to have a proclivity for giving assignments to the wrong people. An exploring party he sent out made a 180-degree mistake in direction. The irreverent settlers, quick to advantage themselves in pricking Tichenor's dogmatic pride, derisively called the wrong peak Tichenor's Humbug, today known simply as Humbug Mountain.

But now, assured of protection, Tichenor laid out and named the town. He had an iron in just about every fire, but his best laid plans — to develop a stable community that would prosper from inland trade, the sea, the earth, and the woods — went up in smoke when gold was discovered.

We may be getting ahead of oursleves. Blame it on the rush of events. Tichenor slips in and out of the action so swiftly that it is difficult to hold fast to him. He keeps returning to the sea — he is a mariner first — and like all skippers he has his problems. On January 22, 1852, he loses the *Sea Gull* in a fearsome storm at Humboldt Bay but by quick thinking and bold strokes of seamanship saves the lives of all on board. For his heroism he is given a gold watch by a grateful passenger. Tichenor is touched and calls it the greatest honor he has ever received.

Five months later the captain brings Elizabeth Brinkerhoff Tichenor and their three children, Jake, Anna, and Ellen to Port Orford. Ellen, not quite four, is to become celebrated as the "Belle of Curry County." Her contemporaries remembered her as a bright, energetic lass who rode horseback up and down the beaches, sympathized with the Indians and walked amongst them fraternally, taught school, and then up and married a weathly San Francisco attorney, by whom she had eleven children.

The years 1854 and 1855 were the greatest boom in Port Orford's history. Tichenor could have done without the sprawl of prosperity but, since he had no way to stop it, he joined it, selling lots and supplying the miners with most of their wants.

Discovery of gold swamped the fledgling village. Five hotels were hastily erected; in addition, the town had five stores, twice as many saloons, two butcher shops, a bowling alley, and a sprinkle of individual dwellings. Soon, though, because there wasn't room in the hotels to accommodate all the gold seekers, a twisty string of tents arose on the beach. By then the town was so full of strangers that, despite Tichenor's activities, he meant nothing to the floaters.

For two years the town sprinted on the high voltage of gold fever. Every hour brought rumors of new finds. It did not occur to the miners that the gold would ever run out. And this may have been a big factor in the way they separated the gold from the sand, losing much gold. After a day of digging and panning, the miners put the sand in pans into the oven to dry and then blew away the black sand, leaving the gold dust. It was a careless and costly operation.

With the typical arrogance of the get-rich-quick invaders, the miners regarded all Indians as nothing better than attractive targets for sport shooting. Onslaughts upon the Indians were numerous and grisly and went unpunished by the authorities. If a white was arrested on the charge of murdering an Indian, the jury would acquit him in glee. In 1854, following a cowardly attack on an Indian village at the mouth of the Chetco River, Joel Palmer, superintendent of Indian Affairs in Oregon, reported to Washington in frustration: "Arrests are evidently useless as no act of a white man against an Indian, however atrocious, can be followed by conviction."

"Though the red man was savage and cruel," wrote regional historian Orvil Dodge, no great admirer of the Indian, "he learned much of it from the white man."

Chief John lamented that the land had belonged to his people ever since the tall Port Orford cedars were small. White men, in the same spirit of clearing the land, cut down both trees and Indians.

And where were the troopers of Fort Orford? Drilling and drilling so as to be ready when the Indians attacked. But when the Indians did rise up, in 1855, and lay waste the land between Pistol River and Port Orford, the troopers did not move. In explanation of a civilian force and in exasperation, William H. Packwood, a captain of the volunteer militia, griped to Territorial Governor George L. Curry of the garrison's inactivity.

"We had just cause; and should it be urged that there was the military at Port Orford, and consequently no necessity for organizing a company," wrote Packwood, "I would only refer to the fact that they remained there after knowing our situation, and would, I believe, have remained there all the same had all the Indians of southern Oregon been concentrating on us."

But there was another reason for the dragoons remaining put. The Port Orford people were deathly afraid that if the soldiers left to search for Indians, the Indians would fall upon Port Orford. The citizens were quite willing to help other settlements best they could, but they would not give up their protection and they insisted that the troopers remain.

Tichenor sent his schooner *Nelly* to take off the people besieged on a beach but strong offshore winds prevented the rescue. Finally, though, the combined strength of the military (not from Port Orford) and the heavily-armed civilians triumphed — and the "Indian troubles" were over.

End of hostilities brought only a short respite for Port Orford. In 1856, when the Indians laid down their weapons, many mines failed and

Port Orford declined. (Only a year before, a post office had been opened and Curry County established.) A few years later only three families remained, including that of Captain Tichenor. Orvil Dodge described the bleak scene: "Weird, silent, ghost-like stood the five hotels, the saloons and stores; homes for the birds, store houses for the wood rats, sport for the north wind that played at hide and seek through the broken windows and open doorways, broken fences, deserted farm yards, roofless dwellings . . ." The historian Bancroft dismissed the settlement in one curt sentence: "Port Orford is a little hamlet on the wrong side of the mountain with no reason on earth for being there."

But the town came back, revived by a resurgence of mining, however modest. In 1858 two men were awarded a contract for $800 to build a jail. At least Port Orford had that much money in its treasury and that much need for civic protection.

When Dr. Henry Hermann arrived by sea in late May of 1859 with his Baltimore Colony, to settle on the Coquille River, Port Orford received its strongest intake of solid hope since the arrival of the dragoons eight years earlier. Among those who gave their all to the town was George Dart, who married Tichenor's oldest daughter, Ann.

Then came 1862, and down the bustling main street rode Cincinnatus Hiner Miller, who was to gain renown as Joaquin Miller, "Poet of

Joaquin Miller *Courtesy Oregon Historical Society*

the Sierra." He was a literary man then and had come to meet Minnie Myrtle Dyer, "Poetess of the Coquille," whose poetry and bright prose he had read in Oregon newspapers. So much had Miller admired her writings that, always the romantic, he had to seek her out. He found her "tall, dark, and striking in every respect" and was confounded and overwhelmed, to listen to him, by this "first Saxon woman I had ever addressed." When he was sixteen, he claimed, he had married a Modoc princess in northern California and fathered the lovely Calli Shasta. (It is all told in a chapter of his *Squaw Wives and Squaw Men.)*

Minnie Myrtle "had it all her own way at once," Miller asserted. "I arrived on Thursday. On Sunday next we married! Oh, to what else but ruin and regret could such romantic folly lead?"

A somewhat more prosaic version is that Miller came to the Dyer homestead on Elk River, near Port Orford, to see the young poet, whose family called her by her given name, Theresa, and that, though they were wed within the week, it was Joaquin who pitched as much woo as Minnie Myrtle.

Eight years and three children later Miller left her, his poetry more important than his family. Divorce followed — and for a long while she

Courtesy Oregon Historical Society

Minnie Myrtle Dyer Miller

was so destitute that she had to farm out her children to family and friends. Joaquin, lionized in England, where he had gone to seek his laurels, tried to forget Minnie Myrtle. But she was in no mood for dropping the subject of their marriage. Until her death in 1883, thirty years before he died, Mrs. Minnie Myrtle Miller spent much of her time lecturing on "Joaquin Miller, the Poet and the Man." She was anxious to "let the public know what kind of a person he really was" and reveled in talking about their private life. A great poet he might be, she conceded — although she thought she was as good and, all things considered, certainly had as much talent — but as a human being he was, in today's lexicon, a male chauvinist pig.

All of the Oregon feminists, including Abigail Scott Duniway and Frances Fuller Victor, sided with Minnie Miller as she aired all but the most delicate details of her shattered marriage.

In a biting commentary that addressed itself more to the role of women in society than to a broken marriage, Mrs. Victor wrote: "Miller married a woman who as a lyrical poet was fully his equal; but while he went forth from their brief wedded life to challenge the plaudits of the world, she sank beneath the blight of poverty, and the weight of woman's inability to grapple with the human throng which surges over and treads down those that faint by the way; therefore, Minnie Myrtle Miller, still in the prime of her powers, passed to the silent land."

But Mrs. Miller's lecture routine began to wear on some of her champions, who didn't think woman's place was wallowing in pity, especially when listeners were charged money to the wallow.

Miller had first come to her and in the end she came to him, but not for romance. Sick, impoverished and alone, she traveled to New York City, where he was living, to appeal to him for aid. He could be compassionate, and he was. He provided shelter and summoned a physician. But it was too late. She died soon thereafter and was buried in Evergreen Cemetery, so far, far away from her Port Orford cedar and Pacific surf. He passed away much closer to the heartland of his poetry, in San Francisco. And so even in their graves she came away the worst of their relationship.

In a way, Tichenor, who knew Joaquin and Minnie Myrtle, touched both their deaths. She died only four years before Tichenor, and the sea captain breathed his last in San Francisco. But before he came to the final crossing of the bar he was to know other interesting people, such as Grandma Knapp's devoted son.

Louie Knapp was the kind of man to warm the cockles of the old mariner's heart. It wasn't so much that Knapp put up a plain, modest-sized hotel at the south end of Port Orford, which he named the Knapp Hotel, but that the inn served as a lighthouse and a sanctuary for sailors. Each night a lamp was placed in the window facing the sea to warn mariners off the rocky coast. Those who were shipwrecked anyway, or were left stranded, were welcomed into the open-armed hospitality of Knapp and his wife. Many a hair-raising sea adventure was told around the stone fireplace with its myrtle-wood mantel that brightened the men's parlor.

Later, as the famous who trooped through Port Orford stayed at

Louie Knapp's hotel, rooms were named for them. A Seward Room, for the secretary of state who had stopped over on his way to visit Alaska, whose purchase had become known as "Seward's Folly." A Sherman Room for Gen. William Tecumseh Sherman of Civil War fame, who was commander in chief of the United States Army when he came to Port Orford. A Joe Meek Room, for the Rocky Mountain trapper who became the first U.S. marshal of Oregon. A Jack London Room for the adored writer. Local legend has it that London wrote part of *Valley of the Moon* while staying at the Knapp Hotel. (Other hostelries have made the same claim; London would have had to have written more chapters than he did to meet the assertions of all the legends.) And an Ellen Tichenor Room, for the San Francisco resident daughter of the sea captain.

The Knapp Hotel survived the devastating forest fire of 1868, which burned or badly damaged most of the cedar near Port Orford and almost leveled the village. (It did burn to the ground the civilian fort Tichenor had built in 1851.) Once again the community looked out the window, saw the spectre of a ghost town, and turned to starting a new life.

The fire coincided with the end of sea life for William Tichenor. He settled down to be a landlubber but he could not keep away from boats. In 1869 he launched the little schooner *Alaska*, said to be the only schooner ever built in Port Orford, at least the only one built in the first century of the settlement.

Between sea voyages Tichenor had been active in all phases of the town and area. After his retirement he took on even more chores. He was sated with responsibilities, some of which he sought, but as he grew older he shunned some tasks and others were handed to younger men. He had long been out of the mainstream of politics, administration and commerce when at the age of seventy-four he took a trip to San Francisco. He died there that same year, 1887, on July 27. His body was returned to Port Orford and buried in the family cemetery.

But where was the cemetery? Atop a hill, we were told. But finding it was something else.

No one in the vicinity of the hill had heard of Tichenor, but all of whom we inquired knew that on this hill, near a TV tower, there were some graves. And so we continued.

No road — unless you severely abuse that word — goes to the knoll. The trace, difficult to locate unless you have precise directions, is rough, rocky, and high-centered. We halted our car where we saw trouble ahead and walked the last hundred yards.

Tichenor is there, beneath a simple marker. Around him are other early pioneers. Not many; not a new grave for ages.

The captain would have appreciated his last resting place. The knoll affords a magnificent overlook of freshwater Garrison Lake and, just beyond, the wild and boundless Pacific.

You look toward the ocean and think you can perceive the *Sea Gull* nosing in to shore. Nine men, their provisions, their personal weapons, and a four-pound cannon are put off, on the high rock that slopes to the beach. There is handshaking, a few slaps on the back, and the boat steams into the briny deep.

Is that what the spirit of the captain would see if it arose from the

Grave of William Tichenor, Port Orford

grave? And would it ask itself: If not for me, who would lie on this hill and who would walk below it? Oh yes, the miners came, they were bound to come, Tichenor or no Tichenor, but when they departed, what remained were the seeds I had planted. They carried on into the next act. And that leads me to a question which I ask all of you, you who are gone and you who are waiting to go: Would there have been this drama of Port Orford without me, the main actor? Tell me, would there?

Directions to Tichenor's grave: In Port Orford, turn west off U.S. 101 on 9th St. Go 0.2 mile. Turn left at fork. Go 0.3 mile. Take right fork of rough trace to cemetery atop hill.

Ghost Towns of the Lower Columbia

At Bradley Wayside on Clatsop Crest we looked down upon the flat, foot-shaped island in the Columbia named more than 180 years ago for Peter Puget, a lieutenant in the British navy, and our eyes swept the river, upstream and downstream, to the very limits of curve and smog.

When I first saw Puget Island in the 1930s, its grain fields and fallow lands were patterns of green and grey, and sluggish streams formed silvery canals. There is more green than gray now, and the canals are screened by trees. The houses seem more affluent these days and the road in much better shape, but there is one constant: Though Puget Island is close to the Oregon shore it lies wholly within the state of Washington.

To our left, westward a clue to its outline barely discernable from where we stood, is a smaller island, Tenasillahe, a compound of two Chinook words, *tenas* and *illahe*, meaning, in total, "little land." Lt. William Robert Broughton, who named almost everything in sight on his voyage of discovery up the Columbia in 1792 — he was the first white man to see the Willamette and got as far as where Troutdale, twenty miles east of Portland, now stands — described Tenasillahe Island as a "long, sandy, shallow spit." Other explorers called it marshy, and those who camped on it complained of dampness. Today it is part of Clatsop County agriculture.

I remember the Columbia when, from Astoria to St. Helens, the river was dotted with small, picturesque fishing and lumbering towns, ferries, and earthy main streets that pressed against the shore. Even before I arrived some settlements of yore had all but disappeared: Blind Slough, Quinn, Pyramid, Rinearson, Reuben, Hunters and Marshland. And others had moved uphill from the stream, leaving nothing behind but memories quickly forgotten.

Some of the villages I saw are virtually dead now. It doesn't seem logical, and it's hard to believe, but the Lower Columbia is a river of ghost towns, especially if you count those settlements that are reduced to Grange hall communities. There are virile cities, of course, and everyone traveling U.S. 30 sees these, but few know of the ghosts away from the highway.

A mile west of Clatsop Crest we turned north off U.S. 30 at a sign marked Bradwood-Clifton. For two and a half miles we wound through second-growth woods, tangled in their own confusion, with long downward roller-coaster stretches. Then at an obscure junction we swung right and in half a mile wheeled into Bradwood.

Ralph Friedman

Bradwood RR station

The town was incorporated by the Bradley-Woodward Lumber Co. in 1930, taking the hybrid name of Bradwood. It was a company town at the start and it was that way at the finish, when the mill folded about three decades later. Then Bradwood was auctioned off. Evidently there wasn't any big buyer, for shortly after that the village started to fall apart.

Except for a few occupied houses, the town stood empty. A cow grazed stolidly at the end of the street with the sureness that no car would go that far. The board sidewalk showed little wear lately, and the store-filling station was long ago shut. Somebody some years past had fixed a basketball net to the outside of the store, but in five years of going to Bradwood I never saw anyone playing.

All the machinery and equipment had been sold and moved following the auctioning off of Bradwood. The mill building was first a hollow shell, a dark and musty cavern. Bit by bit, over the years, it lost its hold on life and, gouged and torn at by intruders, slowly collapsed into a dank heap of debris. The little waiting station, no bigger than a double outhouse, that had stood alongside the railroad track, was removed. Someone has a faded board sign with BRADWOOD on it. Well, it was never of consequence. The hogheads and the town folks always knew where they were at.

Odd it was then, I thought, for Bradwood to have street lamps — the modern being an anachronism. I could have learned, with a little effort, whether the lights were still turned on at night, but the question was more intriguing than the answer. There is a time to seek facts and a time to fancy.

We returned the half-mile to the deep-shadowed junction, turned right, and practically dropped for one long mile to the end of the road, at Clifton.

In the 1870s a hamlet was established here. Then a cannery was built. It must have been quite successful, because a spur line was pushed into Clifton. The community was settled by Italians, Greeks and Yugoslavs, who traded old country fishing villages for new. Nationalistic feuding dissolved into a rich mixture of cultures, though for decades there were three colonies in that small strip along the Columbia.

About 1915 Clifton had a population of 200, a store, a school, a small fleet of fishing boats, and houses lining the river or set slightly back of it, along a wooden walk that looked like a pier. All the houses we saw seemed to be built on stilts. Most were unoccupied and a few had tilted or collapsed into the river. The wharf was still there, serving as a spread for gillnets, but no one was on the dock. This day the silence was so heavy we could feel its weight. By and by a middle-aged man, fishing for something or other, came down the river in a small outboard motorboat, a spaniel

Clifton *Ralph Friedman*

Ralph Friedman

Old Brownsmead School, now a barn

patiently a-set in the bow of the skiff. Both dog and man gazed curiously at us, each with the same manner, and quietly disappeared.

I have been up and down the Columbia and I tell you that nowhere on the Oregon side is there — or was there, the last time I saw it — a more eerie-looking village, in all its bizarre fascination, than Clifton.

That day we came also to Brownsmead, a child of diking and reclamation. You couldn't call it a ghost town as late as 1974 because a country store was open, right across the pavement from the Grange hall. Of course, the village had run down some — that was evident because a quarter of a mile up a rural arterial you could still make out Brownsmead School District on what had been turned into a barn — but the store was full of goodly items, including wheels of cheese whose odors dripped right through the door. "Folks come clear from Portland for this cheese," crowed the patriarchal proprietor, a lean, crisp man who brisked about on heels of pride, so we had some wedges cut for us. "You tell your friends," he repeated to each customer, and made a production of every sale.

He pointed to the section of mail boxes. "That was the post office of Blind Slough," he said, with a knowing nod. "A hundred years old; that's when Blind Slough started, a hundred years ago." It had started much later, in 1910 as a matter of fact, but we replied, "Is that so?" and bought some postal cards, which we addressed and had hand-cancelled. The post office, no bigger than a broom closet, was off a hallway leading to the rest room, and the most modern piece of equipment was the hand-cancelling stamp.

Still in good mood, the elderly storekeeper chirped, "The corn grows high around here. Must be the soil. Come back when we have the corn festival and you'll eat the best corn you ever tasted."

"Promise, " we replied. "We'll be back next year." And we kept our word, but when we returned the store was closed. Locked. Shut tight. One of the friendliest, homiest places on the Lower Columbia had gone out of business. And with the closing of the store Brownsmead became a ghost town, and for us a sad ghost whom nostalgia could not replace.

We went to Mayger, too, another skeleton of the past, with the dock looking like it was ready to cave into the river. Don't search for the post office, which opened in 1889. Or the stores. Or the livery stable. Or the 350 population that called the village home half a century ago. (Some of them sleep in the pastoral burial ground of the Mayger Downing Community Church, a mile away.) For all practical purpose, Mayger is just a place to take a picture of a creaky wharf whose pilings the river is slowly stripping away.

Directions: From Clatskanie (U.S. 30), west 13.1 miles to Bradley Wayside on Clatsop Crest. 1 mile, Bradwood-Clifton Jct. Turn right. 2.6 miles, forks. Turn right. 0.6 mile, Bradwood. Return to forks. Turn right. 1.2 miles, Clifton. Return to U.S. 30. Turn right. 3.7 miles, Brownsmead Jct. Turn right. 4.8 miles, Brownsmead. Return to U.S. 30. Turn left. Drive east to Clatskanie. Turn left on Nehalem St. (main intersection). Drive through downtown Clatskanie to W. 5th. Turn left toward Mayger. 7.6 miles, forks. Take left fork. 0.2 mile, Mayger wharf. Return to forks. Take left fork. 1 mile, Mayger Downing Community Church and Cemetery. 5.7 miles, U.S. 30. Turn left for Rainier and Portland.

Ralph Friedman

Mayger

The Small Drama of Hamlet

Part I

Is this not something more than fantasy?

Shakespeare, *Hamlet*

There is a community near the Oregon Coast called Hamlet and for years I wondered whether it had been named for that moody Danish prince.

If it had, then who was the literary soul who did the naming?

Intrigued, I journeyed to Hamlet and found that you can drive right through it without knowing you have been there. About the only evidence that there is, or was, such a place is an old building a bit off the road and a cemetery out of view from the narrow pike.

But there really was a community of Hamlet, though it was never incorporated, and for about thirty-five years it had a post office.

The post office was established in the home of Albert Hill, who built the house in 1891, the same year he and his two brothers founded the settlement.

I heard all this from Albert's son, Vernon, who was a mechanical engineer at Richland, Washington, but came home often as he could. "I like the peace and quiet and all the space to look at and knock around in, and so do my wife and children," he said.

Vernon Hill told us the story of Hamlet: "My father and his two brothers, Henry and Andrew, were Finnish fishermen out of Astoria. Their real name was Makela, which is Finnish for 'hill,' and they changed it to that. This area was settled by Finns.

"Well, one day in 1891 the brothers came this way on a hunting trip. From a ridge they looked down into a beautiful valley and decided to homestead here."

Vernon Hill attended the second Hamlet school, which was built in 1915. That one was closed in 1936 and students were then bused to Seaside, as Hamlet students still are. In 1935 the cemetery had its last burial, Hill said.

The school built in 1915 was now a community hall and used for such occasions as potluck dinners, celebrations, and for physical exercising by the ladies of the narrow, stream-cut, wooded valley.

"Hamlet never had more than ten families, about fifty people," said Vernon Hill. "It has about the same number of families now — but only two whose roots go back to the settling of the valley."

These two occupied the original homesteads: Vernon lived on the land of his father and Andrew Hill, Vernon's cousin, resided on the property of Henry Hill, Andrew's brother.

"Hamlet never had a store or a church or anything like that," said Vernon Hill. "Just the post office, which was in our house, and the school and the cemetery — and they're all part of the past now. But it was a nice place to grow up in — and still a good place to live in. I mean, it's a good place to get away to."

"Were your father or your uncles students of Shakespeare," I asked.

"Not that I know of," he replied. "Why?"

"I was wondering how the place got its name," I mused.

"Oh," said Vernon Hill, "it was named Hamlet because it was a hamlet, don't you see?"

And so much, alas, for our man from Stratford.

Part II

I have some rights of memory in this kingdom.

Shakespeare, *Hamlet*

That was all I knew of Hamlet until I met Marie Pottsmith, who in 1908 had taught school for eight months at the remote clearing. She was past ninety when she talked to me, and sixty-five years away from her Hamlet residency, but she remembered clearly many details, and what she could not offhand recall she read from a journal to which she had trusted her experiences. A peppery, high-humored, no-nonsense woman, Mrs. Pottsmith could look back and laugh at some uncomfortable incidents, but she also knew what she knew and brooked no quibbling with her facts. Her story of Hamlet is a precious chapter of a schoolteacher's life in a backwoods community and of the settlement itself.

You must hold in mind that the year is 1908. From her account you may sometimes drift into thinking that Marie Pottsmith is talking about the 1870s. Hamlet in the early twentieth century was more primitive than many Willamette Valley communities fifty years before.

Marie Pottsmith, born in Wisconsin and reared in Minnesota, was twenty-three and had had several years of teaching experience when she came out to Oregon in 1905 to see the Lewis and Clark Exposition. She stayed on, to teach in Salem and to continue her education. Then, to earn money to attend the University of Oregon, she applied for a job with the Hamlet School District, and was hired by the clerk, Mr. Ollers. He lived at Necanicum, which on the map did not seem far from Seaside, the home of Marie's cousin. So Marie packed her trunk and two suitcases and took the train from Salem to Portland and then on to Astoria and down to Seaside. She was then twenty-six years old.

In Seaside, where she stayed overnight with her cousin, she called at the town book store, as advised by Mr. Ollers, to obtain the details concerning her new teaching position. A group of men was there idling time away, and what they informed her came as a rude surprise.

"Necanicum was twelve miles inland from Seaside," Mrs. Pottsmith recalled for me. "I learned from these men that my school was in Hamlet, another eight miles into the mountains. Furthermore, transportation those eight miles over the Coast Range was by horseback. Shrewd Mr. Ollers had not told me that.

"Those men in the bookstore were having a lot of fun, telling this greenie what to expect." And she opened her journal and read from it. " 'The postman waited here for you as long as he could before he drove to Necanicum with the mail,' said one of the old-timers. 'They don't have any electric lights out there and they have to travel early. He wanted to get back before dark.' Another one said, 'The people in Hamlet are Russian Finns and you have to eat black bread and sour milk and maybe you've got to sleep with some of the kids, too.' With a gleam in his eyes a third declared, 'There are cougars up in those mountains.' Truly, here was something to ponder. The thought of cougars, black bread and sour milk did not disturb me very much, but the probability of having to sleep with even one child made me hesitate. Perhaps these informers were only having a little fun exaggerating for someone they thought looked like a tenderfoot. They had never seen me shuck grain or face a Dakota blizzard on the way to the little country school. I had never lived in the mountains nor among Russian Finns, but my prairie experience gave me the confidence to brace my shoulders and go on to Hamlet!" She put down her journal, looked at me, and asserted, as though I had any doubt, "Well, it did take courage."

Courtesy Oregon Historical Society

Marie Holst Pottsmith washing clothes at Hill homestead, Hamlet. Finnish bathhouse in background

Approving my acceptance of her statement, Mrs. Pottsmith continued: "Next morning I hired a liveryman to take me to Necanicum, on four wheels; it was a heavy hack, and my trunk and two suitcases in the back." And she read again from her journal: "It was pleasant to ride in the heavy open buggy behind two horses that misty morning as we followed the narrow road away from the seashore into the cedar and fir forest. Even the moss-covered logs produced their share of woodland greenery. Hemlock seedlings, huckleberries, and salal bushes grew right out of the weathered old trunks. I was entranced. I loved it. Prairie girl, why wouldn't she enjoy this?"

She turned to me. "What was at Necanicum? Nothing that I know of except the Oller residence. Mrs. Oller hadn't been out of the mountains for twenty years. She contented herself with books and magazines brought from the store at Seaside. Mr. Oller raised bees. He was called the Bee King of Clatsop County.

"Well, anyway, she had a warm meal ready for me. And the mail carrier from Hamlet was there with his horse, Nellie was her name. He brought the mail in and out of Hamlet twice a week. As soon as I finished eating, I began stuffing the older suitcase with things; oh, I had to leave my trunk there, you know. It couldn't be taken because the trail wasn't finished. Had to ride that nice horse Nellie. It was on a Sunday, and the Hamlet people knew I was coming, so the mail carrier was there.

"When Mr. Jackson, he was the mail carrier, saw how that old suitcase began bulging, he says, 'Here,' and pulled out a flour sack. And he said, 'Put some of that in here,' which I did, and maybe a few more things. Tied them together. Put them across the horse at my back, and a yellow slicker over my lap because it was in March and sleeting, raining.

"He had high rubber boots on and he walked along the trail. I wasn't a heavy weight and neither was he, but I think two of us would have been too much for Nellie on that sticky trail. As he walked alongside he gave me all the news about Hamlet.

"He said, 'Now, there are two places where you may board. At my place I have only two boys, or you may board with the Albert Hills. I'm two miles from school with only two boys and Mrs. Albert Hill has eight children and they have at least one hired man. But keep in mind that she is getting ready for you.' I said to him, 'I think I'll try to persuade her to give up the idea. Let's see if I can come to that.' 'But Mrs. Hill is getting ready for you!' he replied. And we were silent.

"After jogging some hills Mr. Jackson pointed ahead toward some distant packhorses. I asked him, 'Who are those, what are they carrying?' He said, 'That is the rest of your factory-made furniture to go into your room.' That was the first factory-made furniture ever to go into Hamlet. All the other furniture up to then was hand made.

"The first building I saw in Hamlet was that pretty little schoolhouse. It made me feel good right away. That's all the 'town' there was. Hamlet was just farms, about 160 acres each among the hills. It wasn't a prairie, they weren't leveled off. Just farmers with their homesteads of 160 acres.

"Let's see now, we're at Hamlet, and I could hardly get off that horse, I was stiff and bowlegged. Mr. Jackson helped me off and up a number of stairs — the Hill residence was up rather high. Well, I didn't even have to knock at the door; it opened, and the crowd was waiting to see the new teacher. Isn't that something? And Mrs. Hill was in the kitchen preparing, and I tried to persuade her that she was taking on too much — not that I was particular — but she already had her big family and the extra boarder. But when her tears came I threw off my coat and said to Mr. Jackson, 'I'm staying!'

"Mr. Jackson said on his way out, 'She really needs company.' I think she wanted to get away from her family, and we'd go out with that old camera of mine on Saturdays. She'd take her knitting while I took pictures. Then there was a trip that we made together, to Elsie. I let school out early.

"Oh, I must tell you," Mrs. Pottsmith alerted me with a quick thrust of a finger, "in order to make the eight months' school and get out of there to the university to start a new term I asked them if I might teach right through the summer. We started school at eight or eight-thirty and we shortened the noon and the recess period so the children could get home and help with the haying and huckleberrying." At this point Mrs. Pottsmith licked her lips and murmured, "Umm, huckleberry pudding, ah, huckleberries. . . ."

After a moment she smiled freshly and renewed her tale. "One Friday afternoon I let school out very early and Mrs. Hill and I ate a hasty lunch and went up over the hills on our two feet, we didn't have any horses, and over the fallen logs over that Elsie trail, six miles, to Elsie. She wanted to see her old friends back there. Elsie is in a beautiful valley.

"About the school? I had twenty-one students, four girls and the rest boys. Grades from the first through the seventh, and all in that lovely one-room schoolhouse.

"Of course there wasn't electricity. There was no such thing at Hamlet. No electricity, no indoor plumbing, no telephone, no city conveniences. Oh, nothing like that!

"No, I wasn't there for the Christmas party, but they told me about the one they had the year before. I remember what they said about Andrew Hill. He started out on horseback for the school with his two little girls, he had them each sitting in a sack, one on each side in front of the saddlehorn. And he had a little seat in each sack for the girls, so they could look out and see the scenery. Well, when he went in with his horse to cross the stream that flows right past the schoolhouse, the North Fork of the Necaninum, that nice little old horse slipped and fell. Word got to the people inside, and the merrymakers came out and got the girls into the schoolhouse. Mr. Hill had to go to a neighbor's to get a complete change of clothing in order to enjoy the Christmas party. So that's one of the incidents of living out there in the mountains at that time.

"What did the children do during recess? They just took care of themselves, in and out of that woods, playing out there. It was a wonderful playground for the children. What would you have done had you been one of the kids out there in that wild and wonderful woodsy place? There wasn't a playground; you couldn't play some of the games like pom-pom-pullaway or prisoner's base. The kids just turned the woods into a playground."

Mrs. Pottsmith paused and said: "You haven't asked how much

money I received for teaching in Hamlet. Everybody wants to know how much country school teachers got way back then. Well, I was paid five dollars more a month than I got in Salem, and I got fifty dollars a month in Salem. And I only paid eight dollars for room and board. So I saved money. And I didn't have to sleep with the kids either. See all I got? And nice scenery, too."

She opened her journal. "I want to read you a paragraph about education in Hamlet." And she found her page:

"The first school in Hamlet was held in the old Osvik House and was taught by Katie Osgood. Those who attended that winter term of 1899-1900 included five children and four adults. The adult Finn has always been eager to obtain an education in his adopted country. Surely in this case, attending school during the winter months must have helped to break the loneliness in the mountains."

Mrs. Pottsmith laughed. "There are some pretty good phrases there. And now I ought to tell you about the role of women. Well, let me read what I wrote when my mind was a lot fresher." And she did.

"Pioneering days in Hamlet were often sorely trying for the women, especially in the summer when the men went out to fish for a little cash. Then they had the responsibility of both farm and family. One evening Mrs. Matson left her children, a girl of four and a baby, alone in the house while she went out to bring the cows home. The cowbells sounded near and she thought it would take her only a short time. But the mist and fog overtook her and the cowbells became more and more distant. Before she realized the situation, it was dark and she was lost. Finally she crawled under a log to spend the night, worrying about her unattended children. That short summer night must have seemed long and terrifying to Mrs. Matson. As soon as daylight began to come she got her bearings and hastened home. She found her children well and happy and the cows mooing in the yard."

Mrs. Pottsmith glanced at me. I was shaking my head. "The frontier," she said. "Let me read you something else about the role of women out there. This story pertains to Mrs. Andrew Hill. There were three Hills, you know, three brothers. Here, I've found the place." And she read on.

"When as an expectant mother, she was journeying on horseback with her husband over the trail on a cold frosty morning to the hospital in Astoria. Somewhere between Necanicum and Seaside the baby arrived. Mr. Hill wrapped his wife in blankets and left her lying on the trail as he took the baby and rode to the nearest farmhouse, the Johnson home about seven miles away."

She put down her journal and remarked, "What else could the man do but put blankets down and wrap her in it and take the baby to the nearest house?" And she returned to her reading:

"While she was lying there, Mrs. Hill heard footsteps in the distance. Someone on the trail with a pack, she thought. The steps became more distinct, but slower, as if the traveler were wary and cautious. Soon a heavily bearded man peered into her face and exclaimed partly in Norwegian, 'Oh, a woman! How did you get here? You are sick.' He didn't give her any help, of course. But he spoke kindly to her and then went on with his pack. It was some time before Mr. Hill could bring back help to move her.

Finally the men arrived and using layers of sheets as a stretcher, carried her to the Johnson home, where both she and the baby were well cared for until she was able to ride her horse again."

Mrs. Pottsmith raised her chin in pondering, as though trying to remember what else there was to say about the toils and trials of women in Hamlet, but suddenly she remembered a typical morning scene. "The men got up first. And here's my room right off the kitchen, and I could hear the men slurping their coffee, you know, like this," and she made a sound that drew from her a chuckle of nostalgia. "Oh, that Finnish coffee was good. And they drank their coffee before going out to the barn to do their chores. And in the meantime I got into the kitchen and slurped some too. For cereal, there was oatmeal. Oh, they brought oatmeal in during the warm days; they packed in everything in big, big, well, big containers. Anyway, mostly oatmeal in the morning, and some nice cream and oh, Mrs. Hill toasted bread on the back of the stove. Of course they used wood. But they didn't do much chopping. There was a lot of loose stuff around."

Having mentioned her room a moment earlier, she returned to it, out of sheer delight in remembrance. "You know, they had it all dolled up for me. It had been the pantry and they moved out everything — pans, milk and what not into the milkhouse, a few steps from the back door. And then they papered the room and they had put in that new furniture we had seen on the packhorses. They must have gotten there in a hurry to get it set up. I had a single bed, nice bedspread on it, even to pillow shams."

Now Mrs. Pottsmith turned to medicine and garments, and read from her journal:

"Hamlet was not without its home remedies, such as the bitter dose of quinine, without benefit of capsules, if you please, for colds. Diluted carbolic acid for dressing wounds. Also brown soap and sugar for boils and other infections. And for stomachaches, the old-fashioned Alka Seltzer, vinegar and soda, were prescribed — it fizzed. When someone was ill at the Sarpola home — they were the elite family — sulfur was burned on the stove to fumigate the air and protect the rest of the family. For colds and other communicable diseases the children wore small bags of crystallized camphor hung on strings around their necks. Spirits of Huffman drops on cubed sugar they liked, but the hot lard and turpentine dressing on a piece of Dad's old Scotch woolens wasn't anything to transport them to fairyland. Oh, how it itched! There were no cosmetics in Hamlet aside from cow's cream and tallow to heal chapped hands and soothe the little feet during barefoot days.

"The men on their trips to Seaside and Astoria brought bolts of outing flannel, shirting, ginghams, and calicos for their wives to sew into garments for the family. Sometimes among the smaller families the bolts would be divided. The youngsters didn't mind having dresses look alike. There was no keeping up with the Joneses out there. Many an undergarment was made from flour sacks. Most of the men liked their woolen flannels for winter, and no doubt the women enjoyed the comfort of a red flannel underskirt during the cold season. Mrs. Andrew Hill had one with knitted lace around the bottom. Once a Santa Claus wore it and Hilma exclaimed, 'Why Mother, that's your petticoat!' "

Mrs. Pottsmith chuckled. And then she remembered the Saturday night sauna bath, which was twice a week at harvest time.

"I never missed one of those! I should say! The men would go out first and then the ladies. All the women, from the little tots up. We surely did undress. There was a big pile of stones and a hollow underneath of course, and the teen-aged boys would start the fire late in the afternoon and get that pile of stones good and hot. And then we would go up under the platform on the side to go up to the balcony so that steam would come up there and hit us plenty. There was a tub with cold water running into it and dripping right down on the floor through the cracks. Now, that was picturesque. Wasn't that wonderful? And on this side near the pile of stone there was a long wooden trough of hot water. Grandma would come over — Henry Hill, the bachelor, his mother lived with him, they had no bath house — just about each family had its own sauna — and they would come over and he would go with the men and Grandma with us. And Grandma would go up to the steps of the balcony and sit right opposite that pile of stones, 'cause she could take it. We each had our individual handmade tubs into which we put our feet, and the boys made nice cedar brushes, and with the water we could soap and switch ourselves. And Mrs. Hill would throw a pan of water on that pile of stones and the steam would roll up. I couldn't stay, I had to come down, even though I was farthest from the pile of stones. But I was in there for at least half an hour, and when I came out I would perspire for a long time. But Mrs. Hill would bring me a nice big glass of milk, and I think it was half cream."

The people of Hamlet sang in Finnish and English, but Mrs. Pottsmith did not remember a musical instrument there. "I rather think they just were too poor to buy any musical instrument and too busy getting settled to think of music, except to sing old songs they knew."

Twice since she left in the autumn of 1908 did Mrs. Pottsmith see Hamlet again. The first time was with her youngest daughter and son-in-law. "The trees were all green. You know, I loved that country the way I saw it. Those tall timbers and then the beautiful greenery, young growth coming in. When we went out, everything was solid green."

But not everything remained the same. On her second visit, Mrs. Pottsmith took the bus to Seaside, where she was met by Mrs. Andrew Hill's daughter, Hilma Hill, at whose house she stayed overnight. The next day Hilma drove Mrs. Pottsmith to a barbecue at the second schoolhouse in Hamlet, the one used as a community hall.

"It was a fine barbecue," recalled the old schoolteacher, "and it was good to see the students who were still alive and still around Clatsop County. But the schoolhouse — ah, but it's not as picturesque. It was bigger, yes, but not as cute as the one I taught in. Time colors everything, doesn't it, but on that I know I am right."

Maybe, thinking of the way Mrs. Pottsmith remembered her idyllic days in the remote settlement, Hamlet said it best: "And leave her to heaven."

Directions: From Necanicum (U.S. 26), turn south onto Oregon 53. 0.7 mile, Hamlet Jct. Turn east. 6 miles, Hamlet.

Baptism at Bacona

Few people turn off U.S. 26 for a look at Buxton.

Thirty-five miles west of Portland, Buxton is at least a half-century away in time. An old-fashioned grocery store, a country church, an unpretentious schoolhouse, some dwellings. But Buxton, small as it is, seems mighty big after a trip to Bacona, about nine miles north. If there weren't the local-made sign at Bacona you wouldn't know where you were when you got there.

Bacona was once a viable settlement. Now only one house can be seen from the dirt road, and that rustic residence was built in the 1930s when Bacona was skidding downhill. Coming in from the back way you can miss the sign; there isn't another at the north end.

The post office was established in 1897 and named for the pioneer-

Bacona *Ralph Friedman*

ing Bacon family. Sixteen hundred feet higher in elevation than the valley in which Buxton stands, winter comes early to Bacona. The settlers stocked up on a six-month supply of groceries and other necessities in the fall, knowing the road would not be open again until spring.

The Jeppesen ranch, half a mile below Bacona, was homesteaded before the turn of the century and is still occupied by the same family, which now operates a tree farm. A Grandma Moses farmstead painted in a swale below a crooked road, the Jeppesen place looks out to the darkling turrets of the Coast Range and, in the foreground, to the blue-haze pools of the undulating vale. But the warmly weathered house and the old barn, the latter a Gothic piece of rural architecture, date back to about the founding of Bacona.

It was at the ranch that we found our most precious treasure of Bacona, Arlena Jeppesen. She was closing in on the ranks of octogenarians but I didn't believe it. I have seen other eighty-year-olds spry, witty, outgoing and contemporary but only a few who appear able to frolic up and down slopes — and that's how Mrs. Jeppesen impressed me.

She had come into these hills as Arlena Dillinger when she was nineteen, and taught school for eight months. While here she met the Jeppesens and formed an abiding friendship with the family. After she left her teaching at Bacona she did not think she would ever return. Four years after her departure she wed Lloyd Herman Kuhn and lived in cheerful matrimony until he died in 1932. Then chance brought her back to the Jeppesens and she hitched up with one of the boys. "I hated the winters!" she said spiritedly, banging her fist on the kitchen table. "Then to think I married a man at Bacona and spent nineteen years living there!"

She recalled that in the long ago it took her a whole day to go from Bacona to Dundee, the site of her girlhood home. The trip involved mail wagon, train, bus and "red car" line. "Now," she said, "we can drive from the ranch to Dundee, where we live, in an hour and a half."

In June of 1914 Arlena Dillinger first saw Oregon, coming out from Colorado. That autumn she took her senior high school year at Newberg, where she completed a class in Pedagogy. It qualified her for a two-year teaching certificate.

No sooner had she graduated, on June 2, 1915, than she sought a job at a country school — any country school. Only country schools took high school graduates. She was hired on at Bacona, a community completely alien to her. All she knew about it was that the school had been on a list of vacancies, and she had tried them all.

Some months after we met, Mrs. Jeppesen sent me a handwritten manuscript, titled "My First Year Teaching School," and accorded me permission to use it in this book. Her story is a vivid account of a backwoods hamlet, with all the agonies, joys, fatalism, and courage found in a rude outpost. Because it is an authenic picture of an Oregon few of us know about, I am happy to share it with others. As befits the vanity of one who poses as a scribe, I have done some editing, none of which, I trust, has done harm to the narrative. I have also changed several names, on Mrs. Jeppesen's suggestion: "Some of those school kids are still living and might not like to see how *poor* they were way back then."

The story begins in August of 1915, when Arlena decided to visit "my school," which was not to open until November:

I rode on the train to Buxton. There Mr. Green met me. I was to board with them. He had a skinny little team of black horses and a kind of hack to ride in. So we started up the mountain. He said, "Oh, it ain't far." We plodded on and on and on. Every once in a while he would stop to let the poor old horses rest.

On and on we went. I wondered if we would *ever* get there. We passed a house once in a while. Finally we passed a big house, down under a hill, and Mr. Green said, "This is where the Jeppesens live." I was *so* tired. I couldn't have cared less. Now we had only five more miles to go — oh boy! Well, we finally made it. It's been so long ago I do not remember *what* we had for supper.

The Greens lived over and around and down — down — down — into kind of a hole — at least it *seems* like a hole as I look back, in a small three room house made of shakes. There was a loft above the rooms where Mr. Green slept after I moved in. There was a kitchen, a small living room, a few chairs, a *small* bedroom on one side with *no* windows and two beds — home made frames with slats layed across, with a straw tick on each bed. The six-month-old baby boy and three year old girl slept with their mother in one bed. I was to sleep with Lila, the six year old school girl, in the other bed!

Well, the school house was a mile away and Lila and I walked to it over a sort of path. The next day I think I met the other three families. Anyway, I signed my contract (fifty dollars a month I think it was and I was to pay fifteen dollars a month for board.) I was not too happy, just thankful. I do not remember how I got back to the Buxton depot.

Come November first I was back in the hills, ready to begin my teaching career. The school house was new, I was the second teacher. It was a very fine building, with a big bell which I delighted to ring every morning at eight-thirty. That was the first bell, and at nine I rang the last bell. That community was very proud of the new school house and the big bell.

My first day at school. These were my pupils. There was Lila Green, and there were Alice, Wendy, Arthur, Lionel, and Horace Weller, and Sylvia and Dorothy Preston. And there were Bobby and Alfie Mead. Their mother was dead and their dad was trying to eke out a living by some hook or crook while proving up on their homestead. All these families moved out in the hop and prune season to make enough money to buy groceries for the long winter ahead.

Little Alfie Mead was in the first grade — a very appealing child — he always looked undernourished — his shirts were always clean on Mondays but never ironed. His 14 year old brother Bobby always took good care of him. They were very proud and would never accept cookies or anything else from the others.

Alice was 16 and had boys on her mind a lot. All of the Wellers were musical and loved to sing. Lionel always had a cold and a very runny nose — he always needed a hankerchief which he *never* had. Mrs. Weller was a red-haired, quick-tempered Irish woman — pregnant with her seventh child. Mr. Weller — an easy-going sort of ne'er-do-well — likeable —

liked to sing in the evening with his kids joining in. He played a mouth-harp.

The Preston family were also homesteading. Mr. P was a carpenter and worked out, in town, and so they had more money than the Wellers. Besides Sylvia and Dorothy there were two sons, Dan and Tom. Dan worked away from home quite a lot and Tom was gone part-time; he was the same age I was.

Although I was homesick by Christmas I will never forget that yuletide. We had such a good time practicing songs and finding pieces for each child and we put on the Nativity Scene, of course. The boys cooperated very well and made dandy shepherds. I had a small gift for each child — also a book for Mrs. Weller and one for Mrs. Preston. And we had a bag of candy and nuts for each one — pupils and parents. And just as we were about ready to start our program at 7 P.M. we heard voices and lo and behold it was the other Bacona community, from three miles away. There must have been nine or ten of them. Oh me! Oh my! We didn't have bags of candy for them — what would we do? I was so embarrassed. Mrs. Preston said, "Hurry! Let's empty all of the bags into the water pail!" We did, after emptying the water first, of course. So when these young folks came in we were all set. My! I sure was flustered — wondering how they would like our poor little program. But it went over very well — for they all seemed to have a good time. And 35 years after that Christmas I saw Mrs. Preston and she told me that she still had the book I had given her. The name of it was *Beulah*. I forget the author. I think it cost me twenty-five or thirty cents.

But I was homesick, very homesick, the longest I had ever been away from home. I could hardly wait to get away and after the Christmas party I went home for a week's vacation. When I came back I found my landlady, Mrs. Green, very sick — with the flu, we thought. The neighbors came down to see her and Mrs. Weller insisted I must go over to their place while Mrs. G was so sick, so I packed my suit case and went home with her. Two nights later we were awakened by Tom Preston. He told us that Mrs. Green was dead. Mr. G had left her — dead — with the three sleeping children and he had hurried over to the Prestons to tell them! Mrs. Preston was waiting for Mrs. Weller, I think. Mr. Weller went with Mrs. Weller and they in turn picked up Mrs. Preston and went down to the Green shack to do whatever had to be done. Alice and I were left to wake up and fix breakfast. There would be no school that day. It was on a Thursday. There was no school until the following Monday.

Mrs. Weller got back home the next morning, bringing the three Green kids with her. Mr. Green stayed with his dead wife while Mr. Preston went over to the other neighbors in the other Bacona school district to get *some* one to drive clear down to Buxton to get a coffin for Mrs. Green. Mr. Green would not move her body without a coffin, no sir!

They finally got in touch with Mrs. Green's mother in Dundee and she got in touch with a well-to-do uncle in Forest Grove, and somehow or other he got a casket to Buxton. Meanwhile my Aunt Mellie who was big and husky and knew the grandma in Dundee, got on the train and came to Buxton where Mr. Hoffman, who lived in the other Bacona district, met her with a sled, for there was much snow and no one had cars then.

Mr. Hoffman loaded the casket onto the sled and put Aunt Mellie into the seat and they came nine miles up the snowy mountain road. Aunt Mellie was smart enough to bring a pair of overalls along and she needed them on that sled ride for about halfway up the hill the sled tipped over and the casket rolled 30 feet down the snow and Aunt Mellie and Mr. Hoffman landed in a snow bank. They pulled themselves up and finally got the casket to the Green home — and her body into it and back to the Hoffman house by dark.

During the day they were bringing the casket up the hill the Green baby was having convulsions every hour or so. He would roll his eyes and stiffen out and turn blue in the face but Mrs. Weller was equal to this. She kept a boiler of warm water on the stove and when the baby would go into this convulsion she would strip off his gown and diapers and dunk him into the warm water. It seemed to bring him out of these spells.

Early the next morning the men around the neighborhood loaded the coffin onto the sled once more — no doubt roping it on this time — and Aunt Mellie wrapped the sick baby in a blanket and the other two children were bundled up and, with Mr. Hoffman driving the team, headed down the mountain. Mr. Green did not even go — he seemed to be in a daze and left everything to the neighbors and her mother and her uncle from Forest Grove. I don't remember but I believe the old uncle

Courtesy Arlena Jeppesen

Arlena Dillinger Jeppesen shortly before she went to Bacona to teach.

Courtesy Arlena Jeppesen

School at Bacona where Arlena Dillinger Jeppesen taught. Her students are seated on stairs.

met the sled in Buxton and had a grave dug and somehow or other they got poor Ada Green buried. The children's grandma kept them for a year or two, until other relatives took over.

Well, the death changed things for me. I moved my trunk over to the Wellers for the rest of the year. Things quieted down and school went on. I rather enjoyed my school until Tommy Preston, the 19-year-old boy, decided he would take the eighth grade over, "just to have something to do" and devil me, I always thought. He was not a very good influence on the other boys — he smoked! And he and the other boys papered the inside of their outhouse with pictures of girls in their winter underwear — out of Montgomery Ward catalogues. I, an innocent babe, was horrified. They also took little tobacco bags and filled them with dry horse manure, which at first glance I thought was tobacco — much to the enjoyment of the boys. I kept my desk drawers under lock for I was afraid they would put in a mouse or snake or, worse yet, a water dog in my desk.

One morning Bobby brought a team of little water dogs to school. He had made a harness of string and hitched them to the insides of an old clock. I screamed and yelled and made him get rid of the water dogs — lizards to me. This country all seemed so wild and scary. Little Horace used to walk with me to school every morning, as I went much earlier than the other children. I never felt afraid when he was with me, although he was a very tiny six year old!

One Saturday afternoon that winter — it probably was in February — Mrs. Weller and I decided to take their old horse and hitch him to the pung — a kind of large sled — and drive the three miles to the Hoffmans, who had the Bacona post office, for our mail. We only got mail twice a week. It was snowing but we set out. The poor old skinny underfed horse didn't make very good time at the best and when we came to a drift around the curve on the narrow road I wanted to turn around and go back, or turn the horse loose and let him find his way home. But no, Mrs. W thought that we had better tie him to a tree while we walked on the mile and a half yet to the P.O. We were warmly dressed and even had gunny sacks over our shoes to keep our feet warm. We got to the Hoffmans, where the mail was, about 3:30 P.M. and it was by then snowing and blowing like every thing. They wanted us to stay all night but Mrs. W said, "No, we must get back to the horse." They insisted we eat supper and oh my! how delicious that hot venison, potatoes and gravy, carrots and home made bread and butter did taste.

By this time it was dark, so they loaned us a lantern and we headed back for home. The wind howled and the lantern flickered and almost went out several times. Mrs. W, who was five months pregnant, stumbled and had a hard time trying to walk in the deepening snow. On and on we went. I wondered where that miserable horse was — on and on we plodded. Finally she said, "We are lost — we are not on the road — I don't know where we are." I wondered how long before a bear would find us and tear us apart.

"Well," she said, "we should go down the hill, seems to me." So down we climbed over rocks and snowdrifts. Finally she said, "Oh, here is the road and here is old Fred." The horse whinnied and was as glad to see us as we were to see him. She untied him and led him until we finally came

Arlena Jeppesen at the age of eighty

to the Preston home. Every minute we expected to find some of the menfolk out hunting for us. It was 1 A.M. when we banged on the Preston door. It flew open and here was Mrs. Preston, in her flannel nightgown, wondering why we were out. They all supposed we would have sense enough to stay all night at the P.O. She built up the fire and gave us a cup of hot tea and some cookies. I was so tired that I could not go one more step but we had another half mile yet to go, so we left old Fred in their barn and plodded on home. She thought Jim would be walking the floor and wringing his hands worrying about us. It was by this time 2 A.M. Imagine our chagrin to find the house dark — the fire long since dead — the room cold and everyone sleeping peacefully!

The spring of 1916 was pretty tough on the folks in my school district. The Wellers had only my fifteen dollars a month to live on and with me that made nine to eat three meals a day. The Prestons did better — they had plenty of supplies plus a good milk cow, with plenty of cream and butter. But when the snow was deep, food was scarce in the Weller household. For breakfast we had oatmeal, cooked dried prunes — or a half-gallon of canned loganberries — sugar syrup and hard biscuits made mostly with flour, water and baking powder. For my lunch I often took two of these — as Mrs. W called them — "dough-god" biscuits and a half-glass of sugar syrup or a glass of prunes. For dinner in the evening we would have more dough-god biscuits, onions and potatoes sort of boiled or fried together — coffee — prunes or loganberries.

Looking back, I just don't see how I stood it. But I did. For one thing, in the spring I got acquainted with the young folks in the other district and spent Saturday and part of Sunday with them and they were all good cooks and had plenty to cook — meat, bread, butter, vegetables — cream, milk — eggs — cinnamon rolls — cookies. So I did not suffer from malnutrition but I really did worry about the Weller children and the Mead boys. I think the Mead boys lived mostly on pancakes and venison, if they got a shot at one. I was never in their shack.

There were four Danish families in the other district — the Hoffmans, Jeppesens, Petersens and Nelsons. Mr. Hoffman had a small sawmill and Mrs. H cooked for the seven or eight men who worked at the mill. In the Jep family there were six boys. Mr. J was dead. Mrs. J, a middle-aged woman, with the four sons at home, milked 8 — 10 — 15 cows. The Petersens lived a mile or so farther on. The Hoffmans, Jeps and Nelsons were related. Mrs. H and Mrs. Nelson were sisters of Mr. J. The parents had all come from Denmark and settled near each other up here in the hills, each homesteading their allotment.

These four families were very close. They had church services each Sunday in their school house and Mrs. H was their leader. Here they read the Bible, sang and visited, and after their service every one went to one of the four homes for dinner and supper. They took turns about; each time was called their "home Sunday."

In May of 1916 my mother decided to make me a visit to see how I was faring. I was very happy to see her and she spent a week around. I had told her to bring a big mess of steak when she came. She did and was thoroughly put out and mad when she saw how my landlady cooked it. It was tough and my mother could not understand why Mrs. Weller hadn't made a big skillet of good gravy along with the steak and potatoes. She could see all the kids were half-starved from our long winter of dried prunes and sugar syrup and onions and potatoes! So you will not be surprised when I tell you that from the time Mama went home until school was out she sent me a box of goodies every week: cheese — cookies — dried beef — candy!

My eight months of teaching finally ended and once more I was home — in Dundee and a bit lonesome. In Dundee I was just "Lean" — up in the mountains I was Miss Dillinger, or "Teacher."

There is a postscript I would like to add. As Mrs. Jeppesen and I exchanged parting words that golden summer day at the ranch below the Bacona sign, she paused in reflection and added: "Today is like living in a different world. I look back and wonder if it really happened. Did I teach school here, or was it a dream? Sometimes I think it was a dream, a very strange dream, but I know it was real."

Directions: From U.S. 26, turn right at Buxton Jct. 1 mile, Buxton. At forks in front of church, go right on Bacona road. 7.5 miles, side road to right. Continue straight. 0.8 mile, Jeppesen farmstead. 0.4 mile, Bacona.

The Not So Meek Joe

Let me tell ya how quiet that place was: there was this peetrified bird sittin' on a peetrified tree singin' a peetrified song.

Jim Bridger, another Mountain Man

If Joe Meek, that craggy and colorful frontiersman, were to rise from the dead and find he had been buried in a church cemetery, he might be a bit surprised but he'd take it in stride. Uncle Joe had seen too many strange things happen to be shocked by the unexpected.

With the true character of the wilderness wanderer who subsists off his wits, Joe Meek in life was ready for any situation. When a visiting young British journalist asked him what changes the old man had seen in Oregon since he arrived, Meek roared, "Changes? Wagh! When I first come to Oregon, Mount Hood were nothin' but a hole in the ground!"

Together with five other Rocky Mountain free trappers and their Indian wives, Meek and his Nez Perce bride came to the rich grasslands of the North Tualatin Plains on Christmas Day, 1840. (He was against settling in the woods; that would have involved a heavy dose of felling trees, which would have made him a drudge, and even the mere thought of that was more obnoxious than finding a skunk in his tent.) Meek was then, as he seemed to be for the next thirty years, tall, erect, full of outgoing humor, and with dark eyes twinkling from out his round, bearded face. He had the Mountain Man look about him, which he was to retain to the end: bold, hardy, fearless, and direct, as his biographer, Frances Fuller Victor described him in *The River of the West*, published when Joe was sixty.

Rude in dress and his language spiced with trapper jargon, he impressed her with his behavior and she spoke of him as having "an inborn grace and courtesy."

The fact is, Uncle Joe was a born ham. He would have made a great character actor, the Wallace Beery or Walter Brennan of his time. Mrs. Victor was captivated by his normally pleasant voice, the tones of which she found "both rich and soft, and deep too, or suddenly changing with a versatile power quite remarkable, as he gave with natural dramatic ability the perfect imitation of another's voice and manners." Like all Rocky Mountain College students who had closely observed life around them and had borrowed heavily from Indian culture, Meek loved to mimic, and was good at it. When he turned to pantomime, impressively using the sign language of the Indians he had known intimately to accompany his mimicry, Mrs. Victor was fascinated, as were other tenderfeet before her and those to follow. But the old-timers weren't taken in. They were furious at Mrs. Victor for passing off Joe Meek's yarns, which they called a pack of lies, as pure history, and she was accused of abandoning the skepticism of an historian and of confusing her literary genre. Only the philosophical, who had distilled a dram of whimsy out of their experiences, could appreciate Joe as authentic folklore and thank Mrs. Victor for having recorded him for posterity.

On the North Tualatin Plains Meek took up the occupation of a farmer but his success, and legend made him that, lay in other fields, all of them associated with the nostalgia of history. (His daughter Olive said of him: "As long as I knew him he was always perfectly willing to let someone else do the work around the place. When it came to fighting Indians, or hunting, trapping, or making long dangerous trips, there were few men as willing and as good as Father was, but he had no liking for manual labor." He would much rather spend his time, she added, making friends, which he did easily, and regaling them with his trapper yarns.) He was a sheriff, a U.S. marshal, a prime mover for Oregon joining the sisterhood of states, the "Who's for a divide?" bellower at Champoeg, and a "colonel," the title being more wry than real. He was also first man in the chow line at every get-together and the tallest tall-story-teller in all the annals of Oregon folklore.

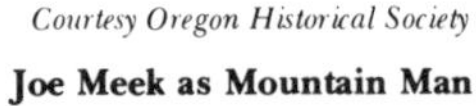

Courtesy Oregon Historical Society

Joe Meek as Mountain Man

Joe Meek was something else too: a white man who refused to desert his Indian wife, even at the insistence of many of his pious and pragmatic contemporaries who argued that he would go farther if he weren't burdened with a squaw. "I can't leave her," he once said of his Virginia, whom he renamed after his native state and who bore him five children. "It would break her heart."

Virginia survived him by twenty-five years, being eighty when she passed away, in 1900. She gave to everyone who asked about her late husband the same summing up: "No man like Joe."

Joe Meek died June 20, 1875, on his farm, four miles north of Hillsboro, and through whose land the Sunset Highway, U.S. 26, now runs from Portland to the sea.

Two days later the funeral was held. Four hundred gathered, some of them old comrades and some who had come out of curiosity. He was laid to rest under a lone tree at the northeast corner of his farm. Born in Washington County, Virginia, he was buried in Washington County, Oregon. His life had spanned a continent and the settling of the West.

Years later, when the Meek property was sold, his remains were removed to the lovely rustic cemetery of the Tualatin Plains Presbyterian Church, better known locally as "The Old Scotch Church" because its

Courtesy Oregon Historical Society

Joe Meek as Frances Fuller Victor saw him

Grave of Joe Meek

charter members came from the same area near Glasgow, Scotland. Close by Meek lie his wife and other members of the family.

Organized at Columbia Academy, four miles northwest of the present site, on November 16, 1873, the congregation moved into its new church in 1878. Remodeled in 1959, the edifice remains as it has for a century, beautiful in its simplicity and majestic as a rural sanctuary.

Like most Mountain Men, Joe Meek was not religious, at least in the conventional sense. Except for his old friend, Marcus Whitman, who had proved his worth on the trail, Meek had little use for missionaries. Most preachers were a plague to him, especially those who sneered at his marriage to Virginia and sermonized on his pungent folkways. If he was "indifferent to some of the commandments," as Mrs. Victor declared, he was equally soft on the doctrinaire sins of others. What mattered most to him were the qualities that stood him best as a trapper: loyalty, compassion, generosity, justice. Put more simply, he was not one to let a soul go hungry, or to laugh at another's wounds, or to desert a comrade, or to deny anyone a fair shake.

A year after he came to Oregon, and in a sudden, unexpected burst of redemption-seeking, the then naive and impressionable Joe, always the actor and ever eager to please friends, called out in a holiness meeting held in an oak grove, "Tell everybody you see that Joseph Meek, that old pesky Mountain sinner, has turned to the Lord." Then, having confounded and satisfied everyone present, he returned to his old beliefs.

There was something sad and funny about preachers who took life as deadly serious, thought Joe, who tended to see more humor as he grew older, treating as joke what others saw rigorously. This exasperated the preachers, who mounted ever-increasing attacks upon Meek. Joe grinned most of the sermons away, but when he was fifty-eight one assault upon his character drove him to action.

He had come to church to pay his respects to the new minister, as a gesture of community courtesy, and was shocked to hear himself vilified. When he could take no more he strode down the aisle, picked up the minister, tucked him under a powerful arm, marched outside the church, and, to the amusement of the congregation, set the trembling Bible-thumper down. Then, a smile returned to his lips, Meek went home satisfied. He had both paid a courtesy call and fulfilled his honor.

Meek never belonged to the Tualatin Plains Presbyterian Church, whose congregation was founded only two years before his passing. But if all the dead in the cemetery awakened, he would be pleased to find himself among people who took others as they came, even Mountain Men who would rather spin tall stories than work a plow.

Shaded by firs, oaks and maples, the burial ground holds the remains of illustrious pioneers. But none cut as deep into the imagination of the state as "Colonel" Meek. His wife was right. In his own way, there was "no man like Joe."

Directions: From Hillsboro, at 1st and Oregon 8, go north on Glencoe Road 4.5 miles to Scotch Church Road. Turn right. 0.5 mile, Tualatin Plains Presbyterian Church.

A Peacefulness at Pike

They swum the deep rivers and clumb the high peaks,
They rolled thro' the country for many long weeks,
Thro' all sorts of misery, dry days and wet,
If they hadn't gone on, they'd be campin' there yet.

Sweet Betsy from Pike, American Folk Song

"I guess you know all about the cemetery at Pike," a greybeard said to me some years ago.

"No," I replied. "Where's Pike?"

"Oh," he said, "some place out of Yamhill. You ought to go up and take a look at it. You might put it in a book."

That's how I learned of Pike, and at the first opportunity I set out to find it, which didn't pose too much of a problem.

The old man was right. The cemetery was worth putting in a book. I had been to hundreds of cemeteries in the state and none moved me as did this simple burial ground, where no one famous in the annals of Oregon lies. Somehow, in the rural peace and solitude, I felt the hand of poetry on the knoll. Everything I looked at seemed to come out of literature which bespoke the Western folk roots of this nation. And when I reached the weathered tombstone of William and Elizabeth Hines I could not leave it until I had visualized the epic proportions of the small, scattered hamlets which, in their prime, had been the heart of Oregon.

When forty-four-year-old William T. Hines died at Emigrant Crossing on the Snake River on August 7, 1847, his family knocked together a rude coffin, set it in their covered wagon, and plodded on.

At Pike, in Yamhill County, the fatherless Hines family came to the end of their trail. William Hines was buried on a grassy knoll away from the settlement. Elizabeth, wife of William, died seven years later, on October 24, 1854, at the age on forty-eight, and was buried next to her late spouse, with their children placing a single marker above their graves.

Named by the first settlers for their home in Missouri, Pike was a booming rural area before the now thriving town of Yamhill, five miles southeast, was born. Founded on the banks of the North Yamhill, still a lovely stream, Pike was later a station on the Carlton and Coast Railroad.

By 1915 there wasn't anything left of Pike but the railroad station and burial ground. Today, all of Pike is gone, except a nameplate, a couple of houses of recent vintage, and the cemetery, a mile off and up a gravel road.

There wasn't anybody else walking around the rise when I was there,

Ralph Friedman

A gravemarker at Pike Cemetery

but the whole place seemed to be awake with the ghosts of the men and women who had come ambitious and sure, or wondering and uncertain, into this raw land that was all tree and grass and with the mystic shadows of the Coast Range dancing as the days started and ended.

What a time it was to be alive, to feel the freshness of morning, to see the soil yield foot by foot, to watch their grain grow and their fruit trees bud and their cows fatten, to carve out a road to Yamhill, to build a school, a church, a hall, to taste the sweetness of the North Yamhill, to touch the velvet of evening, to go to bed with the wind circling the house with a guitar tune twanged out on the sloped hills across the hollows.

So they plowed and cut timber and put up fences and houses and barns and went off to school and marriage and war. And they died, one by one. There was no calamity, no dread disease, no epidemic. They died at home or in some town where they had gone off to work or in some war they felt had to be fought. And their bodies were brought from the farm and the town and the battlefield to Pike and carried to the burial ground on the hill to lie with their neighbors, schoolmates, lovers, parents, wives, husbands, children, brothers, sisters, relatives and friends.

Five generations lie here, with the grass curling green around their graves and roses wild on thickets and Scotch broom glowing at the edges. I walked among the graves and wondered what each would say if given the chance, as Edgar Lee Masters gave voice to his dead in his *Spoon River Anthology*.

What would be the words of William T. Hines, who perished 130 years ago at Emigrant Crossing on the Snake River? I listened close and I thought I heard him say: "Well, I made it that far, farther than any place I ever was to before. And Elizabeth, my wife, and the children, made it to Oregon, to across the state, to a place we called Pike, where the grass was thick and high, good place to grow cattle, and plenty of trees to build a house and barn. And Elizabeth died there, seven years after I did, but the children carried on, like we knew they would, and they settled it more, and their children spread over the hills and valleys, as was wont to happen. And so Elizabeth and I lie here, seeing some things that are good and some that trouble us, and there isn't anything more to say, except that I'm glad I started out for Oregon, and glad that my family made it good here and knowing that I'd have to be buried somewhere, Pike is as good as anywhere."

Directions: From Yamhill (Oregon 47), turn west toward Fairfield. 0.1 mile, turn right. 0.3 mile, turn left, toward Pike. 3.9 miles, turn right for Pike Cemetery. 0.8 mile, cemetery. Return to road. Turn right. 1 mile, site of Pike.

High Tide for Sam Simpson

Look homeward Angel now, and melt with ruth.

John Milton, *Lycidas*

On a rather uncertain day, typical of Portland in October, the Sons and Daughters of Oregon Pioneers gathered at Lone Fir Cemetery in Portland to dedicate a monument to one of their own, Sam L. Simpson.

But Simpson was more than a child of overlanders who came to Oregon before statehood. He was a poet, and best-known as such, and on the monument are chiseled some lines from his most notable poem, "Beautiful Willamette."

He is little remembered today — ask all about you, "Who was Sam Simpson?" and you will be met with looks of puzzlement — but in his time, though sometimes shabbily treated, he was regarded as the poet laureate of Oregon and the singer of love songs to the state. In an obituary editorial that appeared in the Portland *Oregonian* four days after Simpson's passing, Harvey Scott, the distinguished man of culture, expressing regret that the state had produced little in the realm of literary creativity, handed down his unequivocal verdict: "The death of Sam L. Simpson leaves Oregon with no poet of merit or reputation."

By 1927, when the Sons and Daughters of Oregon Pioneers met at Lone Fir Cemetery in the season of falling leaves and moaning wind, Samuel Leonidas Simpson had been dead twenty-eight years. Few of those at the dedication had known him, and none well. He had been a mystery to even his closest friends, who were so rare that none has appeared in print. There are numerous articles about his poetry, but precious few accounts of the person, and these are either patently in error — most writers have the year of his death wrong — or are in such conflict with each other that they do more to raise doubts than resolve questions. I have found only two photos of him. The earlier, probably made when he was approaching middle age, shows him to have a walrus mustache that somehow appears wistful, cheeks that seem delicate, thinning hair, a high forehead, and eyes that are both languishing and haunted.

Everyone at the dedication read the lines from Simpson's "Beautiful Willamette," and that was the only poem of his most of them knew, though he wrote hundreds, perhaps thousands. Some were popular for a week, a month, a year — but only "Beautiful Willamette" remained constant in the collective mind of Oregon. For the more than three decades that he lived after he wrote "Beautiful Willamette," all the poetry he created was compared to what the critics called his "masterpiece." It was a heavy cross to bear. So much had been made of "Beautiful Willamette" that Simpson found himself on the defensive when people discussed his poetry. "You think you must not write anything unless it is as good as 'Beautiful Willamette,'" he was told late in 1879 by a man whose cabin Simpson was sharing, and who was trying to induce the poet to resume writing. "That," replied Simpson lugubriously, "has exercised a sort of tyranny over me."

Simpson shared a common fate with William Cullen Bryant and Edwin Markham: his first poem was his best, at least his most famous. But he was most commonly compared to Edgar Allen Poe and Robert Burns, not so much because he wrote in their vein but because, like they, he suffered from alcoholism. He was once described with provincial hyperbole as "the most drunken poet, and the most poetical drunkard that ever made the Muses smile or weep."

Only one commentator saw a literary kinship between Simpson and Burns and Poe. He was Judge John Burnett, who had read law with Simpson. "Simpson is the Burns of Oregon," Burnett averred. "What Poe was to the beginning, Simpson was to the close of the century. The first singer of Oregon — preparer of the way."

Burnett's panegyric was quoted by John B. Horner in his *Oregon Literature*, published in 1902. Not to be outdone by Burnett in laudation, Horner devoted nine pages to photographically illustrate "Beautiful Willamette" and delivered himself of a eulogy the shy Simpson would have trembled to hear:

"Truly it may be said, he added to his ideal beauty of conception of nature, ever true, a classical expression and descriptive power seldom equalled, if ever excelled. His soul was set to music."

A few of the elderly Sons and Daughters of Oregon Pioneers who assembled at Lone Fir Cemetery on that October day in 1927, when a cloud scudded across a thin haze of burning leaves, remembered from their childhood Sam's parents, Benjamin and Nancy Cooper Simpson, who had come across the plains from Missouri to Oregon City in the forepart of 1846, when Sam was six months old.

Nancy Cooper Simpson was fierce in her intent that Sam get a good education, and she started early. When he was four she taught him the letters of the alphabet by "making them in the ashes upon the broad hearthstone of their pioneer home on the Clackamas River," as Horner recorded. Later he attended log-cabin schools in Polk and Marion counties, where his family lived, until he was fifteen.

Sam was ten when his parents moved to the Grand Ronde Indian Reservation, where his father built a sawmill and ran the sutler's store at Fort Yamhill. Well-liked by the officers and men of the post, to whom Sam served liquor, he returned their affection by drinking with them. It was the beginning of disaster. Fifteen years after his death, W. W. Fidler wrote in the *Oregon Historical Quarterly*, "The life failure of such a man as Samuel Leonidas Simpson should be accounted for historically and truthfully, and the cause of it all summed up in that one word we are forced to use with much reluctance — inebriate."

A number of legends have grown up regarding Sam's stay on the reservation. One was that he spoke frequently with U. S. Grant. That would have been a good trick, since Grant departed for California three years before Ben Simpson brought his family to Grand Ronde. Another is that Phil Sheridan gave Sam a book of Byron's verse, thus inspiring the lad to write poetry.

This may or may not be true. Horner thinks it is, observing "the similarity of style so noticeable in many of Simpson's poems to those of Byron" and adding that "the complaining moods of Byron are very conspicuous in Simpson's verses."

Still, Horner is not sure of the source of Sam's lamentations; he only knows they are there. "Maybe it was an inherent quality of his soul, or maybe environment," Horner philosophized in his *Oregon Literature*, "but in all Simpson's work we note the sad undertone — 'The wail in mirth's mad lay,' 'The Sad Refrain' of love, 'The thorn beneath the rose' that seemed to have pierced his heart. This thought is forcibly expressed in the following lines:

Courtesy Oregon Historical Society

Samual Simpson

The breath of immortality
But withers human thought, we love
The summer smouldering on the lea,
The mournful deathsong of the dove.

"This idea seems to have become such a passion that he exclaims —

The divinest pleasures arise and soar
On wings that are sorrow laden."

At sixteen Sam enrolled at Willamette University, at Salem, and was graduated with honors in the class of 1865. His father, anxious to further Sam's bent for writing, purchased the Salem *Statesman* the following year, but Sam was disinclined to accept the golden opportunity. He was then more interested in law than journalism and, after studying with several prominent attorneys was, at the age of twenty-one, admitted to the bar.

For several months Sam practiced with J. Quinn Thornton, a leading barrister and a controversial activist in state affairs, at Albany. He left Thornton on April 11, 1868, a week before "Beautiful Willamette" was first published. It is quite likely that in those seven days Simpson wrote what Howard McKinley Corning, himself an excellent poet in his prime, summed up as "four memorable, if not great stanzas."

"Beautiful Willamette," or *Ad Willametam*, as Simpson originally called it, appeared in the April 18, 1868 edition of the Albany *Democrat* and was signed simply S.L.S. The editor prefaced the poem with the hope that "the author will not let this be the last time he will favor us with his literary productions." We can rest assured that no money changed hands between editor and poet.

There was talk on that October day in 1927 at Lone Fir Cemetery in Portland about where Sam Simpson had stood when he wrote "Beautiful Willamette." The general agreement was that he scribbled his stanzas while standing, or sitting, just below the Albany bridge, on the west bank of the stream. But there was no doubt that Simpson had the whole of the Willamette in mind, and all of it in heart. As a small boy he had played around the wharves of Fairfield landing, where his father had opened a warehouse in the spring of 1853 and promptly advertised in the Salem *Statesman* that Ben Simpson "kept on hand a supply of dry goods and groceries for sale cheap." Sam had traveled along the river as far south as Eugene and up to Portland. So had others, but they were practical-minded and saw the Willamette only as a road of commerce. The young bard, not yet twenty-two, gave to Oregon a river it had daily looked upon but had never really seen, and certainly not through the eyeglass of an anguished soul.

Actually, "Beautiful Willamette" was not Simpson's first poetic effort to reach fruition in print. He was constantly flinging out verses while at Willamette University, and those he sent off to the *Pacific Christian Advocate* were generally accepted. But it was his first poem to catch on. Practically every paper in the state printed it, followed by the leading California papers and then by many Eastern publications. Thereafter, wherever he went, whatever he did, he was marked as the author of

"Beautiful Willamette." Had he followed up the poems with epics equal to "Paradise Lost" and "Prometheus Unbound" it is likely that Oregonians would have continued to ask him when he was going to write anything again as good as "Beautiful Willamette."

1868 was a good year for Sam Simpson. He composed his first major poem and married the lovely Julia Humphrey, whom he had met while both were students at Willamette. A glorious singer, she was Simpson's "Sweet Throated Thrush" and his "Lurlina," of whom he sang:

> Heaven flies not
> From souls it once hath blessed,
> First love may fade but dies not
> Though wounded and distressed.

"O she was fair as a red-lipped lily, a rosy marble of moulded song," he recalled her in one of his verses, and to his last days he spoke of her as his "First Love," though their marriage had long been dead. John Barleycorn had come between them when they were still starry-eyed sweethearts. Little is known of their life together, or how they felt apart from each other. Neither spoke of what was obviously a bitter situation for both, and their two sons never commented upon the difficulties which separated their parents.

Even in middle age Sam romanticized Julia in poetic allusions. Perhaps he saw his failure and her beauty through the words of Edgar Allen Poe:

> And all my days are trances,
>   And all my nightly dreams
> Are where thy grey eye glances,
>   And where thy footstep gleams —
> In what ethereal dances,
>   By what ethereal streams.

And there were moments, looking back upon his life he could count his two great loves, his poetry and the divine young months with Julia, and say with Byron:

> I die, — but first I have possess'd,
> And come what may. I *have been* bless'd.

Sam Simpson liked law but he lacked the stomach for being a lawyer. His "characteristic timidity" was no match for the brusque, holler-mouthed, aggressive lawyers of the frontier. Still, after he left J. Quinn Thornton he gave the profession another try, practicing for two years at Corvallis. Then, facing reality, he gave up law for good.

In 1870 he took up journalism and until the last years of his life made a living, such as it was, from it. With the money he had saved as an attorney and a loan from his father, Simpson purchased the Corvallis *Gazette* and became its editor.

The *Gazette* could not get out of the red; each month saw the deficit mount. Unable to bear the burden, Simpson moved down to Eugene in 1874, where his father had headquarters as United States surveyor general of Oregon. Sam lived with his father for the year he filled in for the editor of the *Oregon State Journal*, writing editorials while the editor was in the East. (After Simpson's death the editor, H. R. Kincaid, wrote of his substitute: "His writings were brilliant but irregular and could not be depended upon, as some weeks little or nothing was furnished.")

By then, at the age of twenty-nine, Sam was already addicted to drink. There were long stretches when he was not sober enough to pen a line. He made a hundred promises to break the habit, and each time broke the promise. In poems such as "Quo Me, Bacche?" and "Wreck" he bitterly bemoaned the failures wrought by the disease. And in the heart-rending "The Gorge of Avernus" he reveals in the first three stanzas his break with alcohol (temporary, as it turned out), the diabolical temptation of drink for the weak, and the hold the demon beverages clamp on their victims:

I have banished the spectre of sorrow,
    And conquered the dragon of drink;
I have torn a blank leaf from the morrow,
    And fled from the Stygian brink.

There is death in the dew of the roses
    That bloom in the blushes of wine;
There is danger where pleasure reposes,
    Though we call her a goddess divine.

For I have lingerd too long — her caresses
    Enslaved me, I could not depart;
And the shimmering gold of her tresses
    Entangled my spirit and heart.

In the last verse there is hope — a prayer of hope — that in his new-found liberation he will create again:

But lo, in this pathway of duty,
    To the past, I, at least, can be true,
And the mists that bedream it with beauty
    Some long-withered flow'r may renew.

But each reprieve led to another defeat. Every sacred vow was dissolved by drink. He could muse in anguish with Bobby Burns, whom he adored:

The best laid schemes o' mice and men
    Gang aft a–gley;
An' lea'e us nought but grief and pain,
    For promis'd joy.

Simpson worked where he could, on newspapers in Salem, Astoria, and Portland, and in middle age was for two years editor of a minor country weekly in southwestern Washington, the Ilwaco *Tribune*. That was a powerful comedown from some esteemed positions he had held on leading dailies, but even those as close to him as he would permit did not realize how much farther down the ladder he had been.

Seized by wanderlust, or perhaps by an obsession to flee himself, he knocked about, earning his way by working in small printing offices. The story, perhaps apocryphal, but certainly true to Simpson's character and to the value of art in the main street marketplace, was told of Sam coming to seek employment and told that none was available, times being slow. Sam produced several pages of manuscript and said, "Here's a poem I wrote last night. You can have it for fifty cents." The newspaper editor shook his head. Sam reached in his pocket and brought out six or seven more poems and said, "I have written these during the past week. You can surely afford to give me a dollar for the lot." The newspaper owner handed Sam fifty cents and said, "I don't publish poetry. You can keep the poems." Simpson took the half-dollar and, tearing the poems to fragments, threw them into the street, where the wind swept them into oblivion.

His poems were not published in book form until eleven years after his death. But he was involved in the making of several books. In the 1870s he prepared and edited material for the fourth and fifth school readers, which were used on the Pacific Coast from the Canadian to the Mexican borders. Simpson's work on the readers was of such high quality that the publisher, A. L. Bancroft & Company of San Francisco, employed him for some time in gathering, writing, and editing material on the *History of the Northwest Coast* at a salary of $150 a month. The publisher thought he was munificent; Sam, never one to show strength in such matters, said nothing.

In 1876 he was hired by the family and friends of Mrs. H. V. Stitzel to complete and edit a novel, *What Come of It*, left unfinished at her death. In the courtly, self-effacing manner he exhibited all his life, Simpson wrote in the preface: "The author herself, had her life been spared, had undoubtedly made a better book of it. . . ."

The last book he was associated with was the forty-four-page *The Guide*, published in September 1894, and priced at twenty-five cents. As many as 20,000 copies may have been sold. Simpson's contributions were a rhymed preface and eight poems whose masked privacy made them ambiguous to readers.

Once, asked why he did not publish his poems in book form and gain from the volume the fame (and perhaps money) he deserved, Simpson replied: "I have not even a copy of my poems. I have never written anything that satisfied me. There are so many half-way poets deluging the world with so-called poetry that I am disgusted, and do not wish to add to the burdens of the long-suffering public. I believe my sister has most of my writings, but they shall never be published while I am alive."

But there was a time, according to William W. Fidler, when Simpson did prepare a book for publication. The story of this undertaking, perhaps the most productive in Sam's life, was told at length in the December 1914 issue of the *Oregon Historical Quarterly*. It is the only glimpse we have of the poet at work.

In the winter of 1879, while hunting in Josephine County, Simpson was persuaded by Fidler to share Fidler's bachelor quarters on Williams

Creek for the purpose of getting down to the hard labor of writing poetry. An admirer of Simpson's verse, Fidler had pasted in a scrapbook many of Sam's "choicer poems," while Simpson "did not have in his possession a single scrap of the many gems he had broadcast to our Western breezes."

Simpson spent weeks lazying about, awkwardly and ineffectually trying to help Fidler at the homesteader's work, and devouring the bachelor's small library of classics. Then the flame lit within him and Simpson took up pen and paper.

"He worked as I have seldom seen men work before or since, barely stopping long enough to eat and help with the culinary chores. Often, on going in at noon or night, I would hear him, long before I got near the house, going over his numbers to be sure they had the right sound and rhythms before he would transmit them to paper. When once he had his lines put down, they were apt to be in every way correct and as he wanted them to remain. Seldom was it that he had to interline or reconstruct a stanza after it was written, though he often threw away a good verse containing an excellent poetical idea, because of his failure to get a similar rhyme."

Eventually, at Fidler's cabin on Williams Creek, Simpson had enough poems for a volume which he titled *Dashings of Oregon*, a suggestion that came from Bryant's inspirational lines in "Thanatopsis":

> Where rolls the Oregon and hears no sound
> Save his own dashings . . .

But the volume "never saw the light of publication day," wrote Fidler. "The printing-house that undertook its publication . . . failed after it had the entire volume in print."

Poor Sam Simpson, feckless publisher, irresponsible editor, erratic journalist and unfulfilled poet. He could not win for losing. His one great, sustained effort — and for what? Thirty-one years would pass, and he long in the grave, before a volume of his poetry would appear.

But all was not shame and sorrow. He earned the respect of many of the most prominent people in the state, including the militant temperance leader, Abigail Scott Duniway, who parted with the uncompromising, unforgiving dries of Albany in her praise of Sam's poetry. (Condemning the man, they were blind to his writings.) Perhaps he was so inoffensive when intoxicated that he could be so honored when he was sober. Somehow his roles were never confused. In whatever condition, his poetry was lauded — though now practically all of it has been obscured by time. During the Spanish-American War the businessmen of Astoria passed the hat around to collect enough money to telegraph Sam's seventy-eight-line poem, "Launching of the Battleship Oregon" to San Francisco.

Every writer reading the above will probably reflect upon the irony of the situation: The telegraph tolls probably amounted to ten times the fee Simpson received for his ode.

Having survived half a century, he felt old and his life a waste, but he still had visions of great writing. He marked his fifty-first birthday with a confessional poem in the Albany *Democrat*:

Time flies! and I all listless stand
With a rusted sickle, and idle hand;
Soon must I face the gold-browned stars,
A beaten soldier in life's swift wars.

The autumn winds begin to moan
Round summer's sad, deserted throne;
What have I done? O God, to me
Must all the past a desert be?

Have I been idle all these years?
Shall I wet the stubble with useless tears
While I hear the jubilant harvest song
"To them who strive the sheaves belong?"

The rose that sweetened the summer air
And brightened a weary world of care
Has left but a faded wreath to me
And I drop it here by a dark, weird sea.

Ah, well, the tide still shoreward swings,
And ever a stormy chorus sings
Of faith and battle that seems to say:
"Awake! You are fifty-one today!"

In the last months of his life Simpson resided at the St. Charles Hotel, at the southwest corner of S.W. Front and Morrison, in downtown Portland. When the mansard-roofed inn had opened in 1871 it was hailed as "the finest and busiest in the Northwest." But, like Simpson, its glory was in the past, having long been pushed back in eminence by the Esmond Hotel, at 620 S.W. Front, which, when it was completed in 1881, had "a plush bellpull in every room." Simpson by then was seen by the young and the newcomers as "an early Oregon poet," though he remained contemporary to the old-timers, especially those whose memories extended back to "Beautiful Willamette."

Most of the time at the hotel Simpson spent in the barroom. Still witty, cordial, chivalrous and now the ready and pleasant conversationalist, he found helping friends among the men idling their hours away at the bar. Day after day he would borrow "two-bits until tomorrow," which he forthrightly exchanged for liquor while liberally partaking of the saloon's free lunch.

He had resigned himself to the past in "A View of Death," where he pathetically wrote:

Alas, it is this, only this we know:
That the musical fountain has ceased to flow. . . .

In the earthy sense we comprehend
That death, after all, is life's best friend. . . .

On Tuesday afternoon, June 12, 1899, Simpson left the St. Charles for a stroll after one drink too many. He slipped, fell, and struck the back of his head severely on the sidewalk, injuring his brain. In semi-conscious condition he was carried back to his room, where he remained during the night. The next morning he suffered an epileptic attack and was taken to Good Samaritan Hospital. He expired at 9 P.M. on Thursday, June 14, and his death made the front page of *The Oregonian*. Below the sketch of him were printed the four stanzas of "Beautiful Willamette."

Simpson lacked five months of being fifty-four when he died prematurely old. The poet had gone before then. All that remained of his lovely creativity in his last passive glide down the river of time was an occasional brightness in his dreaming eyes, the suggestion of another poem in the offing. But in the final months the light was more a radiance of what had been than a signal of what was to come.

He was buried in Lone Fir Cemetery, where his grave remained unheralded until twenty-eight years later, when the Sons and Daughters of Oregon Pioneers dedicated their monument to him.

Simpson left behind him two sons, Eugene and Claude, neither of whom, in their passing, had heirs to show for their existence. His sons were still very much alive, however, when they and Sam's sister collected his poems and sent them to J. B. Lippincott in Philadelphia. A volume of eighty-one poems was published as *The Gold-Gated West* and was edited, with an introductory preface, by one W. T. Burney. The first poem, of course, apart from the flyleaf "Salutation," was "Beautiful Willamette."

Not everyone was happy with the book. Col. R. A. Miller, prominent in the ranks of the Sons and Daughters of Oregon Pioneers, assailed Burney — who, among other fallacies, placed Simpson's death in 1900 instead of the actual 1899 — as "an alleged literary expert of the East" and charged Burney with an "over-editing" which "ruined much of Sam Simpson's work" by presenting it in "this distorted form."

But no other volume of Simpson's poetry was ever issued and, for better or for worse, the Burney-edited volume remains as Simpson's lone book.

Even before *The Gold-Gated West* appeared, in 1910, to revive interest in "Beautiful Willamette," that poem had been set to music by a Benedictine monk, Father Dominic, of Mount Angel Abbey, in Oregon, and sung by a Portland chorus in 1908 at Seattle's Alaska-Yukon Exposition. It may also have been the last performance, since no further word is heard of the composition.

More than three-quarters of a century after his death, what is the measure of Simpson's poetry? Certainly, he was not of major rank; what might have been is beside the point. Frances Fuller Victor, that perceptive student of literature, was quite correct when she observed, before the birth of the twentieth century, that Simpson "had written some of the finest lyrics contributed to local literature, though his style is uneven." To her he was no more than a regional poet — and time did not prove her wrong.

But there is something of critical importance that seems to have escaped everyone who up to now has written of Simpson. Apart from some story poems written in the style of Bret Harte and John Hay, both of whom were his contemporaries, Simpson devoted little effort to folktales and to the language and meter of the frontier. In much of his poetry the imagery is exotic: of ancient lands and classical allusions. He is more at home with Greek mythology than with American legends and his style is closer to the eighteenth century than to the nineteenth.

At a time when poets were striking social issues, Simpson remained curiously aloof. A hundred great debates must have swept by him, yet he comments on none of them. Once, in a poem not contained in *The Gold-Gated West*, he somewhat obliquely showed a sympathy for the Indian, but that is as far as his sentiment and outrage extended. He was, for his historic times an anomaly, and so, perhaps, was most of Oregon, separated by distance and a rustic work ethic from the thunder and fire of much of the rest of the nation. He possessed none of the daring and grandeur of two other Western poets of his period, Edwin Markham and Joaquin Miller, and echoed none of the sounds of that great master singer of American democracy, Walt Whitman.

Whitman roared, "I hear America singing, the varied carols I hear." Simpson did not hear the varied carols of Oregon: the mucker working on the railroad, the logger felling the giants of the forest, the deckhand throwing out a line to tie up a steamboat at a Willamette landing, the homesteader breaking the sod, the cowhand rounding up cattle, the choir in the country church, the weeping on the hilltop cemetery, the silent procession of the bereaved carrying within them a space left empty, the march of the stubborn suffragettes, the prospectors sifting for gold on every stream, the circuit rider exhorting at the baptism, the crackerbarrel yarns and the stagecoach tales.

Nor did Simpson's poetry reflect the spoken nuances of the state or of the frontier heritage being pieced together jagged bit by bit. Where Whitman, assuming an American uniqueness, called, "Come, Muse, migrate from Greece and Ionia," Simpson's poetry pilgrimaged with mystical delight to that far-off corner across the continent and beyond the Atlantic. By the time of his death, those making literature in Oregon looked upon most of Simpson's work as archaic.

What survives of Simpson is "Beautiful Willamette," and except for the poem being found in a few dated texts, the only lines are on the monument dedicated that moody October day in 1927 by the Sons and Daughters of Oregon Pioneers.

The Willamette is surely not the same today as it was when Sam Simpson rhapsodized on it, more than a century ago. But some day take these stanzas to some still quiet bend of the river and try (and try hard you must) to see the Willamette as it rolled to the sea in 1868.

BEAUTIFUL WILLAMETTE

From the Cascades' frozen gorges,
  Leaping like a child at play,
Winding, widening through the valley,
  Bright Willamette glides away;
    Onward ever,
    Lovely River,
Softly calling to the sea,
    Time, that scars us,
    Maims and mars us,
Leaves no track or trench on thee.

Here lies Sam L. Simpson

Spring's green witchery is weaving
    Braid and border for thy side;
Grace forever haunts thy journey,
    Beauty dimples on thy tide;
Through the purple gates of morning
    Now thy roseate ripples dance,
Golden then, when day, departing,
    On thy waters trails his lance.
        Waltzing, flashing,
        Tinkling, splashing,
Limpid, volatile, and free —
        Always hurried
        To be buried
In the bitter, moon-mad sea.

In thy crystal deeps inverted
    Swings a picture of the sky,
Like those wavering hopes of Aidenn,
    Dimly in our dreams that lie;
Clouded often, drowned in turmoil,
    Faint and lovely, far away —
Wreathing sunshine on the morrow,
    Breathing fragrance round today.
        Love would wander
        Here and ponder,
Hither poetry would dream;
        Life's old questions,
        Sad suggestions,
Whence and whither? throng thy stream.

On the roaring waste of ocean
    Shall thy scattered waves be tossed.
'Mid the surge's rhythmic thunder
    Shall thy silvery tongues be lost.
O! thy glimmering rush of gladness
    Mocks this turbid life of mine!
Racing to the wild Forever
    Down the sloping paths of Time.
        Onward ever,
        Lovely River,
Softly calling to the sea;
        Time that scars us,
        Maims and mars us,
Leaves no track or trench on thee.

Saga of a Gunslinger

Where have all the young men gone,
Long time passing. . . .

Pete Seeger

Until I phoned Riverview Cemetery to confirm the burial there of Northwest historian Frances Fuller Victor I did not know that a member of the most famous gun-slinging family in the annals of the Old West also lies on the Southwest Portland hill.

"Do you have any other big names?" I asked.

"Well," said the lady, "there's Virgil Earp."

"You mean the brother of Wyatt Earp?" I exclaimed.

"The same one," she replied.

"How did he get to be buried at your place?" I asked.

"I don't know," the lady said. And I had to find out.

The trail to the story of Virgil Earp's burial finally led me to his last surviving grandchild, but first I had to visit the grave, so ironically close to Frances Fuller Victor.

I found Virgil's grave in the Bertrand lot. That confused me. Who was Bertrand? And then I plowed through books, magazine articles, documents and old newspapers.

Let us begin with the birth of the one person really responsible for the presence of Virgil Earp's remains in Portland. Nellie Jane Earp came into the world on January 7, 1862, at Pella, Iowa, the daughter of teen-agers Virgil and Ellen Earp. She was not to see her father until she was thirty-seven years old, and a long way from Iowa.

Virgil and Ellen had married despite the strong objections of their parents, particularly hers, and when life became unbearable for him Virgil went back to Illinois, where his family had lived, and joined the Union Army. Word reached Ellen that Virgil was wounded, then a false report that he had been killed on a Civil War battlefield. Ellen, thinking herself free, remarried and in 1864 came to Oregon.

Virgil served until the spring of 1865. Discharged, he went West, where he became part of the peace-keeping folklore of the frontier. For a few weeks he assisted the most illustrious Earp brother, Wyatt, as town marshal of Dodge City. In 1879 he sold his half-interest in a gold mine near Prescott, Arizona to join Wyatt and the paranoid, tubercular Doc Holliday in Tombstone. Late in 1880 Virgil was appointed temporary marshal of Tombstone, already one of the wildest towns in the West. He refused to be a candidate for the regular term in Tombstone's first municipal election held January 4, 1881 but that summer, following heavy looting which came in the wake of a disastrous fire, the Tombstone vigilantes forced the resignation of the marshal and appointed Virgil to fill that incompetent's unexpired term.

Almost everything you read about in Western books happened to the tall, slender, lithe, handsome, soft-spoken, immaculately dressed, mustachioed Virgil Earp. While following the trail of three murderers on the Arizona desert, his horse dropped dead under him. He subdued dangerous characters with his bare hands, had his life threatened many times, was the target of trigger-happy mercenaries hired by his enemies, and survived shootouts and ambushes. And through it all he was courtly to the ladies, protected the weak, and prayed for the day when people would stop slaughtering each other.

He was with Wyatt, a U.S. marshal then, at the celebrated Battle of the O.K. Corral in Tombstone and caught a slug in a leg. On the night of October 28, 1882, once more on duty, Virgil was shot up by outlaws as he was silhouetted against the lighted windows of the Eagle Brewery Saloon. A load of buckshot tore a gaping hole in one side and another shattered an arm above the elbow. The serious wounds marked the end of his service as marshal of Tombstone. Early in 1883 a still weak Virgil was put on a train bound for California. His days as a lawman and gunfighter were

Grave of Virgil Earp

over. Thereafter he confined himself to more tranquil, though hardy, ventures.

Throughout the years Virgil managed to keep informed of the whereabouts and progress of Ellen and Nellie Jane but did not correspond with them. It was Nellie Jane who did the first letter writing — but more of that later.

Ellen was married three times and died in 1910. She bore Virgil no enmity but never speculated on their coming together again. Anyway, Virgil was married when he and Ellen met in Portland. His wife, Allie Stevenson, who died late in 1947, at the age of ninety-eight, is buried in Los Angeles. Allie and Virgil had no children. I have my own theory as to

Illustrations of Earp, his ex-wife, and his daughter appeared in *The Morning Oregonian*, Saturday, April 22, 1899.

why her body was not brought to Portland to be placed near that of Virgil, whom she adored, but it is not relevant to this tale.

Like her mother, Nellie Jane married young, being only eighteen when she took the vows with Levi Law in Eugene, Oregon on January 3, 1880. Nineteen years later the two were divorced. In 1901 Nellie Jane wed Louis D. Bohn. Levi Law, the father of Nellie's three children, was victimized by cancer and committed suicide at the close of 1916. Nellie Law Bohn lived on until mid-1930.

Born to Nellie Jane and Levi Law were two daughters and a son. Magdalen Katherine, called Kay, married at the age of seventeen and died, childless, less than four years later, in the spring of 1915. Pamela Maud, called Maud, married at the age of fifteen and died in the last winter weeks of 1902. Her husband was Alex Bertrand, a steamboat captain and ship carpenter. Their only child, a girl, was named Virgelena, after Virgil Earp. She too married young and, like her mother, died before she saw her twenty-second birthday. George, born in early 1886, was married in 1905 to a woman thirteen years his senior. They had no children.

Early in 1899 Nellie Jane tracked down Virgil Earp in Prescott, Arizona, and wrote to him frequently. According to a press account of the day, "When she became ill with pneumonia, he hurried to Portland." But George Law told me that it was one of his two sisters who came down sick and that Virgil traveled to Portland to be at the bedside of his granddaughter.

So early in the fourth week of April Virgil Earp arrived on his first and last visit to the Pacific Northwest. A reporter for *The Oregonian* wrote: "Earp carries a lame arm which is plugged full of lead, and can tell many reminiscences that affect the hair like a stiff sea breeze."

The meeting with Ellen, Nellie, and Nellie's three children, one of whom was five months pregnant with Virgil's great-grandchild, was a joyous experience for the old lawman, but he had to return to home and business. He never saw any of his Portland family again.

I found George Law, ninety years old in 1976, living alone, as he had since his wife passed away thirteen years earlier, in a self-described "shanty" on a quiet street in southeast Portland. A rugged-faced man who must have been very handsome in his prime, the tall, still straight-backed Law talked about Earp as he held in his lap the big family Bible his father had given his mother in 1886, the year George was born.

Law remembered his grandfather, whom he spoke of as Virgil, as "a powerful big man. He wasn't fat; he was broad-shouldered. His right arm hung like a rag."

When I remarked that a biographer of Wyatt Earp had written that in the ambuscade at the Eagle Brewery Saloon in Tombstone, the buckshot had ripped open Virgil's left side and smashed into his left arm, Law replied, "Well, I remember that it was his right arm, but I was only thirteen then."

He closed his eyes to turn back time but there was too much haze of intervening years. "Ah well," he signed. And he rested his palms on the Bible.

"What kind of a man was he?" George Law replied to a question that lifted his head. "Well, he didn't break out in a laugh. He'd just smile. And he did some things that impressed us kids.

"One day he took my mother and my sisters and me on a streetcar. He said, 'I'm not going to give that conductor my fare.' The conductor came around and collected from everyone but when Virgil looked at him the conductor kept on going. My mother asked Virgil, 'How come the conductor didn't ask you for the fare?' and he said, 'It's the way I looked at him. He was afraid of the look.' But before we got off, Virgil paid the fare. He was just trying to show us something.

"My father, Levi Law, didn't believe that Virgil was my mother's father. He thought Virgil was her boyfriend. He went berserk with jealousy. He'd get drunk and make a fool of himself. Virgil went down to bring my father home. He just put his left arm around him and led him home.

"He'd sit and talk about his experiences and about his brothers. He told a lot of stories about Wyatt but I remember only one story. When Virgil was a small boy his brothers went deer hunting and didn't take Virgil along. He decided to go anyway, and set out on his own, carrying a

George Law, grandson of Virgil Earp

stick. After he walked into the woods a ways he saw a deer crouched on the ground. 'I'm going to get that deer,' Virgil said, and he threw the stick at it. The stick hit the deer and Virgil thought, 'It doesn't move. I killed it.' Just about the time he reached the deer he saw his brothers coming out of the brush, and they were laughing. They had shot the deer."

And George Law chuckled, so that he looked younger than ninety.

"I only saw Virgil Earp for two weeks," said Law, relaxing back in his chair, his hands folded peacefully on the Bible. "And I was just a boy then — and that's been a long time back, and time can play tricks on your memory. Anyway, now you know everything I know about Virgil Earp."

Virgil joined Wyatt in the rush to the mines of Goldfield, Nevada and died there on October 20, 1905. "Virgil's wife wired Nellie Jane that if she wanted the body of her father she should come get it, and do it right away, because Wyatt Earp was claiming it," said George Law. "So her son-in-law, Alex Bertrand, sent for the body."

There is another version. Persons who knew Alex Bertrand when he was an elderly man, including a relative in whose house Bertrand lived for some years, told me that Bertrand repeatedly stated he had gone to Goldfield and returned with the casket. Newspaper accounts of that period corroborate him.

In 1902, upon the death of his wife, Maud, Bertrand had purchased a family lot at Riverview, and here Virgil Earp was buried. In 1956, at the age of ninety-two, Alex Bertrand was laid alongside Maud. In the fifty-four years he had outlived Maud he had never lost his love for her, though much had happened to him; he was only thirty-eight when death took her. He had been devoted to Nellie, too, and had cherished Virgil, whom he had met in 1899, when he and Maud had been married only three years. They had named their child for Virgil. When word reached Nellie Jane from Virgil's wife, Nellie had no one to turn to but Alex. And he responded, as he always did.

By the machination of whatever gods that be, Virgil Earp was buried only a few feet from Frances Fuller Victor. Through inquiry about her I had learned of him, and here they were, almost side by side.

Frances Fuller Victor was probably Oregon's most noted historian. She had interviewed many colorful, legendary pioneers and had woven a book around one of them, Joe Meek. Sometimes she had had to travel far to find her people. And not all of them had the time she wanted nor had she always had the time needed. And now here she is in eternity with Virgil Earp, as interesting a character as any she ever met.

Suppose the dead could speak. What questions would she be asking him? And what answers would he give? I sat on the grass at their graves and tried to imagine the conversation. But all I heard was the wind moaning in song, "Where have all the young girls gone, long time passing. . . . Where have all the young men gone, long time ago. . . ."

Kinton Has Some Little Lambs

In the enclosed yard that was once a playground, sheep munched, drowsed and ambled. Inside the frame building that had been a schoolhouse, hay was stored. This was Kinton, all there was to Kinton, except a Grange hall, bordering the yard, that came out of a Grandma Moses painting, and, on the other side of the sheeplot and across Tile Flat Road, an 1860s house with original form, tone, and gingerbread.

Throughout Oregon there are barns and toolsheds that were once schoolhouses and churches. Not many, and each different, but none in the western part of the state to match the lovely rustic scene and seasonal chemistry found at Kinton.

I first learned of Kinton through leafing the pages of the *Oregon Almanac*, published in 1915 "for the information of homeseekers, settlers

School at Kinton

and investors by the Oregon State Immigration Agent." Obviously that was before the James G. Blaine Society.

The almanac described Kinton as "Farming, dairying, fruit growing and poultry raising. Soil especially adapted to the growing of onions, wheat, oats, etc. High and public school, said to be the first organized in Washington County. Evangelical Church."

It was mention of the school that caught my eye, though I also paid heed to the church. That edifice, down the way toward Scholls a piece, sits by the side of the road as a vacant recluse. Close by is a new church building, a modest suburban product barren of rural folk feel.

I drove the wavy countryside all around Kinton and it was one calendar photo after another: a windmill, a water tower, ample houses curtained by bright flowers, a field that you know in due time will be rows of pumpkins, a barn where cows were hand-milked for decades, a quick rise that startlingly threw open a stunning view of the Coast Range, a touch of Pennsylvania's well-fed Bucks County, a cameo of Grant Wood Iowa, a middle Ohio snapshot that called for a sound track of "Bringing in the Sheaves." Each exhilarating, all delightful, but none as enchanting as where Mary went to school a century ago and now the little lambs play.

Directions: In Portland, take I-5 to Tigard turnoff, Oregon 99W. 1.7 miles past turnoff to downtown Tigard, take turnoff right to Kinton. 3.1 miles, Beef Bend Rd. Turn right. 0.8 mile, Oregon 210. Turn left. 0.9 mile, Kinton.

The Pittsburgh Dream of Lake Oswego

A hundred times my friend had driven from Portland to Marylhurst College and a hundred times back before learning of the silent smelter at Lake Oswego. One day, in casual conversation, I asked if she had already painted it. She is an artist, with an eye for historical structures.

"Where is it?" she asked.

"Just a few blocks off the road you have traveled for many months," I replied.

"Why haven't I been told before?" she demanded.

"Few outsiders seem to know of it," I explained.

"Tell me about it," she said. "Give me its background."

"I'll write of that," I promised. And here I have kept my word.

In 1865, when ground was broken at the bend of the Willamette River here, now Lake Oswego, to build the first iron furnace west of the Rockies, the shrewd businessmen who had organized the Oregon Iron Company proudly proclaimed: "We will have the Pittsburgh of the West."

Everything — well, at least almost everything — was at hand to insure success. The river bank offered good docking facilities. The waterpower would be drawn from Oswego Lake via Sucker (now Oswego) Creek, which streamed into the Willamette. All around the new industrial site were dense stands of timber to furnish charcoal for fuel to fire the furnace. And there was plenty of ore in the nearby hill that came to be known as Iron Mountain. The first mining was strip, and the ore was initially transported by oxen and then by narrow-gauge railroad.

By 1865 Oregon and the entire Pacific Coast were hungry for iron. And what was needed right away was only a fraction of what the dreamers foresaw. Iron for construction, transportation, agriculture — there could be no solid industrial development, no great society, without iron. For a moment in time the furnace at Oswego, as the town was then called, held the promise of the future.

Then it was found that some things had to be transported. Limestone, needed to unite with the impurities, was brought by sailing ship from the San Juan Islands, west of Seattle. Sand was hauled from the Sandy River, southeast of Portland. And there were changes in production planning. Hot blast gave way to cold blast after experiments with cold blast produced an iron "hard as flint, durable as steel and very tough."

August 24, 1867 was an historic day for the Oregon Iron Company. The first iron was produced. Two pigs were cast and were promptly purchased by J. C. Trullinger, who owned at least half the Oswego townsite, for street markers. One of them is still in the city at the northwest corner of Ladd and Durham Streets; the other is in the Oregon Historical Society.

Look at an object and what do you see? I stared at the slender rod so obscured outside the fine middle-class house at Lake Oswego that I could not have found it if the owner had not pointed it out, and behind the rod I saw John Corse Trullinger.

He was an earnest Hoosier who lived to create for the sake of God, Country and Himself, and if he saw the three as an indivisible trinity committed to work, purpose and profit, he could scarcely be blamed. He was from Indiana but he was Yankee to the bone, the kind that turned Oregon from a benevolent wilderness to a white man's feast. If there wasn't enough at the clambake for everyone to fill up on, that was because, as Trullinger saw it, there was only enough for those who were pious believers, took risks, and traded sharply.

There were a lot of Trullingers in Oregon. One of them was a Portland dentist who had gained peripheral recognition because his wife ran off with John Reed, the revolutionary. Maybe in later years the doctor, if he was farsighted and broad-minded, could console himself with the

Oregon Iron Company, Lake Oswego

thought that he had occupied the same bed with a woman whose lover (and later, husband) wrote the classic *Ten Days That Shook The World.*

No scandal touched the life of J. C. Trullinger. He had a good, abiding wife, he noted contentedly, in the former Hannah Boyles, who bore him eight children, and he was busy from the time he arrived overland in 1848 at the age of twenty-one until he died in 1901. He was a warehouse owner, a farmer who pioneered in sowing timothy, a flour miller, a sawmiller, a timberman, an organizer of the Republican party in Oregon, a cattleman, a town developer, and the builder and operator of Astoria's first electric light plant. In his thirties he called upon Heaven to save the nation and worked for Abraham Lincoln; in his late fifties he was certain that the incandescent bulb was a step closer to the angels.

Trullinger may not have been awed by the first pigs that came from the smelter. After all, he had his own knack for devising things. He could tinker with the best of Yankees: He had to his credit seven patented inventions, including a turbine waterwheel and a duplex axe. In his own way he was as unique as the Oregon Iron Company.

I could not resist including Trullinger — a man typical of his time — but with the purchase of the first two pigs cast on August 24, 1867, we leave him to his rest.

The next year, on March 8, the Ladd and Tilton Bank, on Portland's Front Street, received the first iron stove ever to be cast in the state. Even before then, though, Oregon pig iron was in demand in San Francisco. As early as January 1868, a steamship arrived at the city by the Golden Gate with a cargo of cast-iron water pipe from the "Pittsburgh of the West."

Despite its early successes, the company never really prospered. Financial and mechanical problems racked the firm, which changed hands often. In November of 1885, after several earlier closures, the plant was shut down for the last time. Total production for the eighteen years of its existence is estimated from 40,000-some tons to 93,000-some tons. By today's standards the smelter would be classified as cottage industry but to the mid-nineteenth century farmers and builders of the area it was a giant whose smoke had the color of money.

More than ninety years after it closed the smelter still stands. From the outside the plant looks like a miniature of an English mansion out of a Bronte novel. So appears this last relic of a great notion. All else that was part of the industrial complex was many decades ago torn down or moved away.

The river is still there, of course, and the creek too. The forests are gone and the land around the smelter, in George Rogers Park, is green grass. A steel fence keeps out the curious, as though the smelter, having done its service for the cause of Oregon, wants now only to be distinguished in memory.

Directions: From State St., in center of Lake Oswego, drive south 0.5 mile. Turn left at south end of George Rogers Park. 0.3 mile, smelter.

A Corner of History at Oregon City

All things considered, Oregon City is the state's most historic community. It can boast of many Oregon firsts, of famous and colorful characters, of critical events, of beginnings and endings. For all practical purposes it was the end of the Old Oregon Trail: More covered wagon emigrants found their way here than to any other settlement; and from Oregon City they fanned out into the Willamette Valley. Until Portland grew to size, Oregon City was the dominant community in the state.

But don't look for deep history in Oregon City today. Apart from the McLoughlin and Barclay houses, both of which have been moved from their original sites, the Ainsworth and Locust Farm houses standing where they were built; and Mountain View and Canemah cemeteries, what else is there?

Well, there is a bit more, a corner of Oregon City that few know of and fewer explore. It is the mill grounds of Publishers Paper Company.

Publishers Paper leans against the river; in the early days all interior Oregon towns started on river banks. The only roads were waterways. Before the sailing boats and the steamers, the Willamette was plied by Indian canoes and the pirogues of voyageurs. It was not uncommon to portage around the falls and accounts of traders and trappers speak eloquently of the rough going here.

Facing the river, then, or within short distance of it, the city arose. The first American hotel beyond the lower reaches of the Missouri, the Old Main Street House, a cabin measuring 14-by-17 feet, took in travelers where the industrial plant now throbs. The stockade put up by John McLoughlin to guard his Hudson's Bay Company stores stood in this vicinity. Then came the house McLoughlin built, moved in 1909 to its present location on the bench above the early town.

One of the more interesting establishments here was a mint built by the Oregon Exchange Company, a private enterprise which operated from February to September 1849 and produced $58,000 worth of five- and ten-dollar pieces known as "beaver money" because each was stamped with the likeness of a beaver.The pieces were made from dies and a press constructed from old wagon irons. Whatever you will say about the pioneers, they were innovative. Not for nothing had they learned from McGuffey's Reader that necessity is the mother of invention.

All kinds of items were used in lieu of a regular currency in the early days but "beaver money" was the most notable. A few of the pieces today would be worth a small fortune. Probably most of them were discarded

Courtesy Oregon Historical Society

Oregon City, 1845, as sketched by Henry Warre. Publishers Paper Mill stands at site of center foreground of settlement.

Plaques on grounds of Publishers Paper Mill, Oregon City

after their contemporary value ran out. It is a story often told in mirth and woe: if the old-timers could have foreseen how much the Sears, Roebuck catalogs of their youth would bring sixty years later, would they have used them up in the outhouse? The stuff a farm family threw away fifty years ago as being worthless is today sought after.

Within the present compound, as indicated by plaques, stood the first Masonic lodge this side of the Rockies, constituted on September 11, 1848; the first paper mill in the state (built long before Publishers Paper was founded); and the *Oregon Spectator*, the first newspaper in American territory west of the lower Missouri.

Although the *Oregon Spectator* did not make it to a complete decade, the fortnightly strongly influenced the political and cultural life of its time. It was avidly read by the makers and shakers of the new land, who used the organ as often as they could for their own forum.

Print extends oral declaration and it was inevitable that the Oregon Lyceum, the debating society which involved itself in early efforts to organize a government, should start thinking about a way to get its thoughts broadcast beyond the range of word of mouth. The result was formation of the Oregon Printing Association, which gave birth to the *Spectator*.

There are some scholars who believe that the OPA was a front for several prominent and ambitious persons who wanted a paper for only one reason: to publish the corporate acts of the new American territory of Oregon. Be that as it may, the Printing Association laid down a hard and fast rule, "that the press should never be used by any party for the purpose of propagating sectarian principles or doctrines, nor for the discussion of exclusive party politics."

The rule was to account for a steady turnover in editors, who were too partisan and strong-willed to be bridled, but it did not stifle the passions of men with causes, schemes, peeves and hates. No Oregon newspaper today contains language as livid and as brutally sarcastic as that expressed in the *Spectator*. Here is a scalding exchange, no more fiery than other verbal outbursts which bombarded the newspaper, between David Goff, who had been an associate of Jesse Applegate in the blazing of a wagon road into southern Oregon, and J. Quinn Thornton, who had come with the first caravan on the hellish trail and never forgave its surveyor-promoters. Goff denounced Thornton, who was then a supreme court judge of the Provisional government, as a man "whose conduct has made him so odious to the company with which he traveled that scarce a hand would have been raised to defend his life or a hole dug to hide him when dead," and added "that the quibble, subterfuge, and falsehood which might pass unnoticed in the pettifogger became conspicuous in the judge, and his present elevation, like the monkey on the pole, only shows the plainer that the role of ermine but half conceals the dog." Thornton tartly asserted in reply that "the many untruths contained in the article written over the name of David Goff" was obviously the work of another because Goff "is so exceedingly illiterate as not to be able to write his own name or even to read it when written for him."

A printing plant was obtained in New York in 1845 through the services of George Abernethy, who was to become the first and only Provisional governor of Oregon. The machinery and supplies were shipped 'round the Horn and set up at Oregon City. On August 5, 1846, the first issue was pulled from the sticky type of a Washington handpress. With a swagger typical of hearty frontier boast, the *Spectator* flaunted on its banner, "Westward the Star of Empire Takes Its Way."

The first editor was William Green T'Vault, prominent in early Oregon newspaper history. He was thirty-nine when he journeyed to Oregon in 1845 with the pain-wracked Meek's Cut-Off Party. Promptly making Oregon City his home, he was soon appointed postmaster general for Oregon. Then came the *Spectator*.

T'Vault lasted all of thirteen issues. Then, his aggressive spirit thwarted by the association's rules against political discussions, he resigned and took off for southern Oregon, where he started other journalistic enterprises.

Succeeding T'Vault was Henry A. G. Lee, a descendant of the distinguished Virginia Lees. He, too, balked at the association's prohibitions and also moved on. Following him was George L. Curry, later a Territorial governor. Like T'Vault and Lee, he could not contain his political fervor and quit to found in Oregon City the *Free Press*, Oregon's second

Building on left is said to be old Opera House, built in 1865. Building to its right is probably as old. Both are on grounds of Publishers Paper Mill, Oregon City.

newspaper. Started in March 1848, the *Free Press* gave up the ghost in October when the California Gold Rush emptied Oregon of almost all its printers.

Unlike some newspapers we see today, the *Oregon Spectator* was never dull. If at times the news lacked punch and there was a lull in the snarling and counter-snarling, the ads supplied lively content. Consider this paid bit of information which appeared in the issue of April 30, 1846. The work of a former Mountain Man who had arrived in Oregon with Joe Meek and made his own mark upon the state, this tongue-in-cheek ad by the owner of the early steamship line above the falls at Oregon City reveals how economy minded were the pioneers. One wonders what the passengers thought when they read that they would be permitted to board themselves.

PASSENGERS OWN LINE

"The subscriber begs leave to inform the public that he has well calk'd, gumm'd, and greas'd the light draft and fast running boats, Mogul and Ben. Franklin, now in port for freight or charter, which will ply regularly between Oregon City and Champoeg for the present season.

"Passage gratis, by paying 50 cents specie or $1.00 on the stores. Former rules will be observed — passengers can board with the captain, by finding their own provisions.

"N.B. Punctuality to the hour of departure is earnestly required. As time waits for no man, the boats will do the same.

Robert Newell."

From September 7 until October 12, 1848, the *Spectator* failed to appear. On the latter date the editor apologized to its readers for the paper's negligence and explained the absence: "The *Spectator*, after a temporary sickness, greets its patrons, and hopes to serve them faithfully, and as theretofore, regularly. That 'gold fever' which has swept about 3000 of her officers, lawyers, physicians, farmers and mechanics of Oregon from the plains of Oregon into the mines of California, took away our printers also — hence the temporary non-appearance of the *Spectator*."

So relatively swift was the growth of Oregon, with thousands pouring in yearly by wagon and boat, that by the time Oregon achieved statehood, in 1859, probably half the people in the state then had never seen a copy of the *Spectator* and, so fleeting is fame, many had never heard of it.

Such is the story of a small part of what happened in one modest area of the compound.

Amidst this hearth of history stood a small yellow cottage where was born in the spring of 1852 the poet Edwin Markham. Five years later he was gone, taken to California by his scholarly mother, and never to return to Oregon to live. The flood of 1861 destroyed his birthplace and there is nothing in the state to show for his family but his father's grave near Silverton. But for five years of his life he did reside here: The eye falls upon ground where the tot and little boy stumbled, found firm steps, ran in circles, loped from the cottage to the store his mother kept, and spent delightful hours, as he recalled in his *California the Wonderful*, "picking up pebbles on the shore, watching the white waterfalls, gazing on the high mysterious bluffs that look down upon the young city." He remembered John McLoughlin as "six-feet-six, handsome and impressive," and when he whom the Indians called White Headed Eagle died, "I was taken into the cathedral in Oregon City when the good man was lying in state," Markham wrote in the foreward to Richard Montgomery's biography of McLoughlin "(and) some strong man lifted me onto his shoulder that I might look down upon the face of the great dead."

Still standing are the old Opera House, built in 1865; two other buildings at least a century old; and a pioneer woolen mill that is now part of the industrial complex of Publishers Paper.

There are no historical tours of the grounds, no brochures (probably no one in the company knows all that was there), no invitations to come looking for nostalgia.

Maybe that's the beauty of the place — a corner of Oregon history that is in the shadow of our awareness.

Directions: The best time to come is on Sunday, when the plant is relatively quiet. Check in at the plant office first.

Great Day at New Era

Listen to the jingle, the rumble and the roar,
Riding thru the woodlands, to the hill and by the shore . . .

The Wabash Cannon Ball

Six miles south of Oregon City on Oregon 99E you pass a sign reading New Era and, seeing nothing there, you go on. Another marker at the same site reads Spiritualist Camp and, for those who go there, that's all there is to New Era. The camp is three-tenths of a mile up a side road and completely hidden from the highway.

But New Era takes on more meaning when you come to know that at one time stagecoaches, river boats and railroad all met here, and that for three months it was probably the most important transportation point in Oregon.

The story of how the railroad came to New Era is filled with high drama, low morals and unforgettable characters, chief of whom was Ben Holladay, a hard-driving operator whom romantic historians have turned into a gruff but sentimental legend.

By 1865 there was unanimous agreement in the great heartland of Oregon that a railroad was needed. Its overall purpose was to connect with a railroad coming up from San Francisco, thus establishing quick and efficient transportation from Portland to the Bay Area. It then took six and a half days to travel by stagecoach from Portland to Sacramento and all freight had to be carried by water transport. Too long for the burgeoning cities, especially for Portland, whose population in 1865 was an awesome 6,080, more than double the 2,917 inhabitants of 1860.

Two rival groups organized to build the railroad. Each called itself the Oregon Central Railroad Company, and both aimed their tracks at Salem. One group planned to build on the west side of the Willamette and the other on the east side of the river. To distinguish it from the "West Side" company, the east side people called their outfit the "Salem Company."

Practically all of Portland then was on the west side of the Willamette and the city, aided by some of the most prominent figures in the state, including Jesse Applegate and Joel Palmer, enthusiastically supported the west route.

Heading the west side contingent was Joseph Gaston, an ambitious lawyer and journalist who had come to Oregon from Ohio in 1862 and practiced at Jacksonville and Salem. He was only thirty-three in 1866, when his company was formed, but his sincerity, single-mindedness and clear thinking commanded the respect of older and more influential figures.

The "Salem Company" was California financed and represented, in essence, the interests of the California "Big Four" — Huntington, Stanford, Hopkins, and Crocker — who, having completed the Central Pacific as part of the first transcontinental railway, were building their line north, hoping to expand into Oregon.

At first the Oregon and California Railroad Company, as the Californians called themselves, sought to buy out the west side group. Failing that, they incorporated their own Oregon Central Railroad Company.

The east side group had muscle to spare. Its president was none other than George Lemuel Woods, governor of the state. Its secretary was the rainbow-chasing Samuel Asahel Clarke, who left his post as editor of *The Oregonian* to help organize the new company. Clarke had been swift to rush to every new gold field and he saw in the railroad the pot he had never located in his searches across the state, from the Umpqua River to Auburn.

More at stake than passenger fares and freight tariff was the federal land grant, to yield tremendous riches for the successful company. The issue appeared settled on October 10, 1866, when the state legislature designated the west side Oregon Central Railroad Company as its federal land grant choice. Unperturbed, the east-siders moved ahead with their plans.

The race began in mid-April of 1868. On the fifteenth the west side group broke ground near the head of Fourth Street, in what was known as Carruthers Addition, in Portland. The next day the "Salem Company" formally began its labor on Gideon Tibbet's farm, near the present corner of S.E. Fourth and Morrison.

Work started vigorously but was soon overshadowed by bitter court battles, in which each side accused the other of stealing its name and of fraudulent financing, and by the hot winds of rhetoric and ceaseless legislative maneuverings.

Then into the fray stepped Ben Holladay, recruited by the "Salem Company," which he took over as he had taken over everything else he had put his grabby hands upon.

Ben Holladay was two months short of his forty-ninth birthday when he arrived in Portland in August 1868, to take command of the east-siders. He was well prepared for the skullduggery, the shouting and the in-fighting. From the time he entered the contest until he departed, a decade later, he dominated "not only the railroad situation in the state but its politics as well, by methods then novel to the community," wrote Charles Henry Carey in his *History of Oregon*.

A man of the frontier, Holladay had the instincts of a horse trader, the shrewdness of a land speculator, the jugular-vein aim of a high-rolling gambler, and the morality of a highwayman. Compared to him, Jesse James was a two-bit piker. Had he been around to know Bonnie and Clyde, Holladay would probably have dismissed them as messy amateurs.

Born in the prickly hills of Kentucky in 1819, he was brought up in a rough country store, where he early learned to swap, bargain, water the whiskey, and outfox the farmers. At seventeen he came to St. Louis, where he picked up the tricks of the border country. Three years later he had worked and traded his way across the state and found employment clerking at Weston, on the east bank of the Missouri River. Soon he purchased a hotel, then became postmaster. Within ten years after he landed in Weston he had been a druggist, a proprietor of a general store and, with a brother, had owned a factory.

At the start of the Mexican War in 1846, Holladay lifted his eyes to brighter financial horizons. He took the first of his many steps in the transportation field, delivering freight to the army of General Kearney. In 1849 he brought a wagon train of goods to Salt Lake City, where he unloaded the merchandise at a hefty profit. Brigham Young gave Holladay his blessings and asked him to bring more freight to the Mormons.

Expanding his business, Holladay stretched his freight-hauling as far west as California and made enough money to lend some of his surplus cash to the pioneer stagecoach line of Russell, Majors and Waddell, which had become famous through its Pony Express.

The loan was not given in love. Before long the firm of Russell, Majors and Waddell was deep in hock to Holladay. In 1862, when the company failed to meet its obligations, it was taken over by Holladay, who held a first mortgage on the business.

Joseph Gaston, Holladay's unfriendly rival in the Oregon railroad war, offered another version of the dealings in his four-volume *Centennial History of Oregon*. He stated that Russell, Majors and Waddell "fell into financial trouble, and in order to tide over their affairs and force a cheap settlement with their creditors, as related to the author by Mr. Russell himself, the firm delivered to Holladay as their friend $600,000 of government vouchers the firm had rendered, under an agreement that when they settled with their creditors Holladay should return them the $600,000. Holladay took the vouchers, collected the money and when requested to return it to the confiding firm he repudiated not only the agreement to do so but also all knowledge of the transaction. . . . On this plunder Holladay came to the Pacific Coast, bought the line of ships to Oregon and got into the Oregon Railroad."

(Holladay's callousness and primordial acquisitiveness seemed to run in the family. His brother, Joseph, frugal where Ben was profligate, would not lend Ben money without getting a solid note for compound interest.)

Holladay changed the name of Russell, Majors, and Waddell's company to the Overland Stage Line, upgraded animals, equipment and services, pushed into the Pacific Northwest, and secured more and fatter government contracts. Then by purchasing a competing line, in a manner that would have filled later transportation moguls with buccaneer respect, Holladay blocked the plans of the foremost stage operator, Wells, Fargo and Company, from expanding to the East.

By now Holladay was living in a palatial mansion on the Hudson, occupying an opulent office in downtown New York, and dining routinely at Delmonico's, the royalty of epicureanism. And his stagecoach empire had been renamed the Holladay Overland Mail and Express Company.

Both Holladay and Wells Fargo knew that a struggle between the two giants would be too costly for either to emerge unscarred. In addition, Holladay was afraid that a transcontinental railroad would put him out of business. Negotiations followed. On November 1, 1866, Wells Fargo purchased Holladay's entire stagecoach holdings for $1,500,000 in cash and $400,000 in Wells Fargo stock.

So up from California, where he was running a successful steamship line, came Ben Holladay. His first move, after asserting complete control

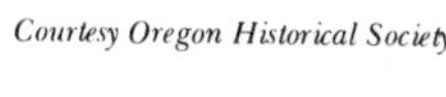

Courtesy Oregon Historical Society

Ben Holladay

over the "Salem Company," was to persuade the state legislators to rescind their resolution supporting a federal land grant for the "West." This he did by a strong and costly newspaper campaign, hiring speakers to proclaim his cause, and, more importantly, the winning over of legislators. He dined them lavishly, bestowed gifts upon them, and openly bribed the shameless and subtly seduced the modest.

Turning to Congress, Holladay induced that august body to extend the time of the Land Grant Act. A bill stated that the company that should first complete twenty miles of road would be the recipient of the grant. There was one hitch: Congress had set a time limit — December 25, 1869.

The eyes of Oregon were now focused upon Ben Holladay. No one could be neutral about him. Those who liked him found him tireless and adventurous and the one hope to pull Oregon out of its sagging economy. The dislikers belittled him as basically uncivilized and completely unscrupulous.

Henry Villard, the journalist and financier who followed Holladay as the railroad king of Oregon, thought Ben "illiterate, coarse, pretentious, boastful, false and cunning." But John Hailey, the Idaho historian, bespoke other sentiments. To him Holladay was "sociable, generous, energetic, open and frank."

Within a few months it was evident that the "West" could not complete its task. Legal tricks and treachery ground Gaston and his associates to a standstill. It wasn't that they were more honest than Holladay; it was simply that they lacked experience in employing their thumbs and knees to neutralize their opponents with gouging and well-placed kicks. As gentlemen called each other crooks and as their society wives broke off social contact with the women of the foe, Holladay swaggered on. He knew that brains and prestige could be purchased as easily as bread, and he did a lot of buying.

The question now came to the deadline: Could Holladay beat it? Could his Oregon Central Railroad Company get to Parrott Creek by Christmas Day of 1869?

Provincial Portlanders asked where Parrott Creek was and for whom it was named. The newspapers were soon telling them. It was about six miles south of Oregon City and was named for Joseph Parrott, a pioneer of 1844. Apart from having a steamboat landing, the area had a small reputation for its potato growing. A county road that led to the landing was lined with potato cellars.

There was never any guarantee that Holladay would meet the deadline. Sickness plagued his men, fights erupted, high waters dashed work schedules. Holladay spurred the men on: He could talk as tough and profane as any roughneck. The muckers and blasters responded to his entreaties and commands. The guff the gandy dancers would not take from any dude they cheerfully swallowed from the stocky, fierce-eyed, country-boy-flavored Holladay, who wasn't afraid to get his boots muddy or too high-falutin' to share a smoke with the help.

The last section of track was laid on December 24, 1869 — one day before the deadline. The first twenty miles of the Oregon Central Railroad had been completed. Holladay had won the fat federal land grant.

On the afternoon of Christmas Day a train pulled out from Portland. It pushed through heavy rain and biting wind down the east side to Oregon City. There the cliffs echoed the whistle of the locomotive. At Canemah, whose walls looked down upon the thundering falls of the Willamette, the whistle wailed again. Beyond the palisades the iron horse snorted on, throwing back a trail of smoke to mark its passage. It was dark when the train pulled into the "terminal" at Parrott Creek. A handful of farmers and construction workers, stamping their feet in the mud as they huddled together, hats pulled down and collars turned up to hold off as much of the rain and wind as they could, cheered once, then cheered again, louder now, as out from the last car stepped Ben Holladay, a cigar thrust cockily toward the world from his smiling lips and his grizzled beard seeming to bristle with success.

It may have been his finest hour. As the line expanded he was to go on to greater glories, but with each triumph came more litigation. In December of 1872 Holladay completed the line as far as Roseburg, but that was the end. Financial difficulties forced him to quit and in 1876 he was succeeded by German-born Henry Villard, who had been an American newspaper correspondent during the Civil War.

All through the winter the terminal at Parrott Creek bustled with activity. The railroad made it possible for Willamette River boats to stop there and deliver their cargo. No more boats would have to go to the falls below, at Oregon City, to receive and put off freight from Portland. Now the goods came direct by railroad to the steamboat landing, ushering in a new era in integrated transportation.

In the spring construction began anew and the importance of Parrott Creek swiftly and drastically declined. But trains stopped there every day for many years and as late as 1915, according to the *Oregon Almanac* issued then, there were "daily steamboats on the Willamette River."

One of the farmers waiting for Ben Holladay that late December evening in 1869 was Joseph Parrott, who in his own way established as durable an institution as any conceived by Holladay.

In 1873 Parrott founded the Spiritual Society of the Pacific Northwest and named it New Era, for a visionary publication of the day. It was the first organization of its kind in the United States. A campground was laid out in 1886 and a hotel built in 1890.

Three years after Parrott started the Spiritual Society he platted the town of New Era. It was never very large — perhaps a hundred people at most. Among farmers it was known for its bee culture and breeding of high-class poultry. And apart from the Spiritual Camp it had at its height only a sawmill, flour mill, public school, Catholic Church, Grange hall, and store.

There isn't much to New Era today — but what remains is a short discovery trip off the highway.

Two-tenths of a mile up the road from Oregon 99E, and near what was the center of town, is the old Herman Anthony farm. The house, water tower, barn, prune dryer and bee house were all built in 1880. A tenth of a mile further is the New Era Spiritual Camp, still going strong more than a century after the founding of the Society. The hotel continues to be occupied during the summer by visiting Society members, as it has every year since it was opened a decade before the start of this century.

Just about everyone who comes to New Era these days goes there for the Spiritual Camp. Despite the mysticism attached to it, it is a friendly place. Visitors are welcomed at Sunday service and at the potluck (or minimal charge) luncheon which follows. Sometimes on a hot day I leave the highway to rest in a shady spot on the campground and to date no one has challenged my being there or regarded me as an intruding outsider. Unfortunately, I have never taken the time to find out what the Spiritualists believe in, but from what I have seen they are pretty nice people.

Diagonally across the hotel sits what was the New Era Grange hall when it was put up in 1889. It is now a residence. The gravel lane in front of the house has for more than a hundred years been a county road.

Down this road, lined with potato cellars, plodded the farmers wagoning their produce to the steamboat landing. What a great day it was when the railroad arrived and they knew that henceforth they could get their crops delivered faster and cheaper to Portland and Oregon City. How they must have huzzahed for Ben Holladay! Maybe he was the biggest crook in the state, or west of the Rockies, or the whole blamed country, for that matter, but he had brought them the railroad, and any man who did that couldn't be all bad.

Ben Holladay is a vague name in New Era today. But he had his applause on December 25, 1869, when he gave the people on Parrott Creek the best Christmas present they ever received.

New Era Spiritual Camp hotel, built 1890

Battle Hymn of Abigail

I am bound for the promised land;
I am bound for the promised land:
O who will come and go with me?
I am bound for the promised land.

A favorite hymn of black slaves

Abigail Scott Duniway, Oregon's prominent suffragist, and her husband, Ben, lived in a dozen or so homes, but only one still exists. It sits on a hill west of Lafayette, about a mile past the town's Pioneer Cemetery.

This frame dwelling, overlooking the Willamette and Yamhill valleys, was probably built by the Duniways in 1858, five years after they were married and when they already had two children.

Here Abigail, who was to become more influential than anyone else in obtaining the vote for Oregon women, was busy from early morn until she was too weary to stand.

She tended the chickens, planted rosebushes, seeded a flower bed, turned the virgin earth into a vegetable garden, helped her husband with his farm chores, kept house (with all its multitudinous tasks), cared for her youngsters, and still found time to write.

It wasn't proper then for women to be literary so Abigail wrote a letter to the *Oregon Argus* signed "Jenny Glen, Sunny Hill Side," and when it was printed she was so thrilled that she followed up with a poem advising marriage to lovers in doubt. When that appeared she submitted more poetry. Finally, in a preface to a forty-line poem titled "To Viola," the editor commented: "We publish the following to please the writer. We think 'Jenny Glen' could write a very fair prose article, and would suggest that she try her hand on that kind of composition hereafter."

Abigail wasn't outraged but the friends and relatives of "Viola," a farmer's wife whose real name was Susan Isabella Walker Cooke, were, and the editor vowed to be kinder to "Jenny Glen" in the future. As now, editors then were more sensitive to their readers than to their writers.

The industrious Mrs. Duniway also penned letters to the *Oregon Farmer*, signing herself, "A Farmer's Wife," which was fair enough. And, somehow, she finished a novel, *Captain Gray's Company, or Crossing the Plains and Living in Oregon*, using her own diary of the trip from Illinois, recollections she had not noted in her journal, and her budding ideas about woman's place in the home.

There in the house on the knoll she began her long apprenticeship that was to lead to a prominent writing career, for she was more than suffragist; she became a fair poet and an excellent essayist as well.

A biographer of Abigail had given me some random directions on finding the Duniway house.

"It's on a hill, is near an orchard, and has a circular porch that was added on after the Duniways left, and there are mobile homes around," she said.

But she hadn't been there for five years and wasn't sure if the house still stood.

We spent several hours traveling all over those hills. (I didn't know they could be so deep and rough and have so many dirt traces slicing into them.) We must have stopped at no fewer than twenty homes to make inquiry. No one had heard of Abigail Scott Duniway; not a soul knew the whereabouts of a house with a circular porch. The typical remark was: "I've only been here six months." Sometimes we were directed to an "old-timer." "He knows everything; he's been here for ages." It turned out that "ages" was no more than five years.

I can't say that I didn't meet some interesting people. I remember one in particular: a crisp, strong-faced, mid-thirtyish, English-accented, casual-mannered woman in rough farm clothing who invited me inside while she telephoned around. After striking out on every call, she suggested: "Why not try the town pub? Some bloke is bound to know a thing or two."

Finally we did meet someone who had heard of Mrs. Duniway and, better yet, had a rough idea of where the house was located. By a combination of following his map and guessing lucky, we found the house — at least I think we did.

I mean, the house looked more than a hundred years old. It stood on a knoll, the remains of a circular porch were there, and mobile homes were close by.

We asked a young woman who, with her husband, occupied the residence, whether the place was really the Duniway House, and she said she didn't know.

"We've only been here a few months," she said. "The place must have had a hundred owners and renters."

But she did know that until recently there had been an orchard close by and that there were still some cherry trees around.

"I think," she said, while we were wondering whether we had located our goal, "that this must have been a famous house because when we came here I found a picture postcard of it, and some old man told me that there was something important about the house. But," and she shrugged, "I'm not up on history. It's just a place to live in. We're redoing the whole inside."

As we were about to leave the hill I stopped at a mobile home to ask a man if he knew anything about Abigail Scott Duniway. "Doesn't ring a bell," he replied. "She doesn't live around here."

"She does now," I said, and went off satisfied.

Though I had long been interested in Abigail Scott Duniway, finding the home above Lafayette fired my enthusiasm to a greater peak, and in my lecturing on Oregon I often spoke of her. Not to my surprise, few listeners had heard of her; far fewer knew anything but the barebone details of her life.

Abigail Jane Scott was seventeen, tall, spindling, and bright blue-eyed when her family left their farm near Peoria, Illinois for Oregon in the early spring of 1852. En route she kept a diary, and in it are entries which show the moral indignation that was to mark her in the public mind as a strong and controversial person in later years, and passages which reveal a sentimentality and starry-eyed lyricism which were obscured by her political activities.

On April 15, 1852, she inscribed in her journal: "Saw a man today who said he owned seven slaves of a good stock — he had raised them himself and two of them were worth one thousand dollars apiece; but he had not got enough work out of them yet, and in a few years they would be worth more. May none of us ever be guilty of buying and selling the souls and bodies of our fellow creatures. Slavery is a withering blight upon the prospects, happiness, and freedom of our Nation."

On June 20 her mother passed away. The next day Abigail poured forth her grief in a rush of poetic prose. "We this morning dispatched our breakfast in silence and with sorrowful hearts prepared to pay the last tribute of respect to the remains of the beloved lamented dead. She now rests in peace. . . . The place of her interment is a romantic one and which

Duniway House, above Lafayette *Ralph Friedman*

seems fitted for the last resting place of a lover of rural scenery such as she when in good health always delighted in. The grave is situated on a eminence which overlooks a ravine intersected with groves of small pine and cedar trees. In about the centre of this ravine or rather basin, there wells forth from a kind of bank a spring of icy coldness, clear as crystal. In the outskirts of this basin clusters of wild roses and various other wild flowers grow in abundance. And from an eminence where all this can be viewed at a single glance, reposes the last earthly remains of my mother."

She was to weep for the dead again late in August, when her youngest brother died. "Two months and seven days this morning since our beloved mother was called to bid this world adieu, and the ruthless monster death not yet content, has once more entered our fold & taken in his icy grasp the treasure of our hearts! Last night our darling Willie was called from earth to vie with angels around the throne of God. . . ."

All this sensitivity to language from a girl whose learning consisted chiefly of a five-month term in an Illinois academy. The seed to create in prose was within her on the Oregon Trail, though she thought the yearning came later. In the introduction of her *From the West to the West*, a syrupy novel which is an exercise in fantasy on Abigail's crossing the plains to Oregon, published in 1905, she reminisced on her first serious literary effort:

"Fifty years ago, as an illiterate, inexperienced settler, a busy overworked child-mother and housewife, an impulse to write was born within me, inherited from my Scottish ancestry, which no lack of an education or opportunity could allay. So I wrote a little book. . . .

"Measured by time and distance as now computed, that was ages ago. The iron horse and the telegraph had not crossed the Mississippi; the telephone and the electric light were not; and there were no cables under the sea.

"Life's twilight shadows are around me now. The good husband who shaped my destiny in childhood has passed to the skies; my beloved, beautiful, and only daughter has also risen; my faithful sons have founded homes and families of their own. Sitting alone in my deserted but not lonely home, I have yielded to a demand that for several years has been reaching me by person, post, and telephone, requesting the republication of my first little story, which passed rapidly through two editions, and for forty years has been out of print. In its stead I have written this historical novel."

She spent her first Oregon winter at Lafayette, then took a teaching job in Polk County at Cincinnati, later called Eola. "It was here," she recalled, "that I met my fate in the person of Mr. Ben C. Duniway, a young rancher of Clackamas County, who took me, a bride, to his bachelor ranch, where we lived for four years."

Benjamin Charles Duniway was regarded as "the best catch in the county" and he was devoted to Abigail, and supportive of her, but his business judgment was poor. Five years after moving to the farm on the hill above Lafayette they were forced to sell, so that Ben could pay security notes he had signed despite Abigail's opposition.

The worst was yet to come. Soon after the farm was lost Ben was disabled in an accident with a runaway team and the entire burden of earning a livelihood fell upon Abigail. She started a boarding school in her Lafayette home, then moved the family to Albany, where she taught school until she thought she had enough money to open a millinery shop. She didn't, but she found a benefactor in Jacob Mayer, a leading Portland wholesaler. He selected a stock of goods that came to twelve hundred dollars, and Abigail paled. "I'm afraid to risk it," she quivered, showing Mayer her little wad of thirty dollars. "Never mind," he assured her, "you'll need that money to get some articles at Van Fridagh's retail store. Take this stock home and do the best you can with it. Then come back and get some more."

What follows is told in her *Path Breaking*, subtitled *An Autobiographical History of the Equal Suffrage Movement in the Pacific Coast States*, published a year before her death:

"I was back in three weeks and paid the debt in full. My next account was for three thousand dollars; and from that day to this, I have not known extreme poverty; though I am not wealthy and never can be. I have earned and expended over forty-two thousand dollars in my long-drawn struggle for Equal Rights for Women, which if I had used in trade, or invested in real estate, would have made me several times a millionaire."

By 1871, when the Duniways moved to Portland, Abigail was convinced of her future. It was to carry on an unrelenting battle for liberating women from second-class citizenship. That she stopped only with the vote is unfortunate, but at least she did that much.

"I was not an easy convert to Equal Suffrage," she frankly declared. "I had been led from childhood to believe that women who demanded 'rights' were man-haters, of whom I certainly was not one. But a long train of varied pioneer experiences led me at last into the light."

In Portland, Mrs. Duniway founded *The New Northwest*, a weekly that ran from 1871 to 1887.

"THE NEW NORTHWEST," she asserted in unmistakable tone, "is not a Women's Rights but a Human Rights organ, devoted to whatever policy may be necessary to secure the greatest good to the greatest number. It knows no sex, no politics, no religion, no party, no color, no creed. Its foundation is fastened upon the rock of Eternal Liberty, Universal Emancipation and Untrammeled Progression." Yet it was evident even before the first issue came off the press that *The New Northwest* was to be Duniway's express vehicle for women's suffrage.

Despite lack of advertising revenue, the paper persisted, and the issues of a hundred years back read today as contemporary as many current publications.

The New Northwest had been publishing for two years when Mrs. Duniway organized the Oregon State Equalization Society. "She was then a woman around forty, strong of body and limb, firm of jaw and sound of mind," wrote Oswald West in the December 1949 issue of the *Oregon Historical Quarterly*. "She was a woman of ardent convictions, and possessed the courage and intellectual power to defend them. It has been said: ' 'Tis the business of small minds to shrink, but those whose hearts are firm, and whose conscience approves their conduct, will pursue their principles unto death.' This truly applied to Mrs. Duniway."

Two-thirds of a century after it happened, West recalled the first time he saw Abigail Scott Duniway.

"In the summer of 1883, when Mrs. Duniway was around fifty and I was ten years of age, she spoke on 'woman's rights' at a meeting to be held in the Marion Square, on North Commercial Street, in Salem. The 'Square' was a good-weather meeting place for those holding patriotic, political and similar speaking events. My home was just across the street.

"Noticing a small gathering of women — young and old — around the speakers' stand which nestled under the tall firs, I decided to learn what it was all about. So, barefoot and curious, and with ragged straw hat in hand, I found a seat on one of the rough planks which served as seats for the public.

"The speaker introduced was Mrs. Duniway, who discussed many matters which were far over my head. But a question she put — and she happened to be looking in my direction when she put it — struck home and never left me all down through the years. This was it: 'Don't you consider your mother as good, if not better, than an ordinary Salem saloon bum?' My answer in sotto voice was: 'Sure I do.' I cherished great love and respect for my mother, and much contempt for the city's saloon bums — all of whom I knew by their first names.

"I had noticed the gathering of these saloon bums in the feed yard at Bob Ford's livery stable on election day. There, from a box stall, each would be handed a party ticket and two dollars to cover carrying charges to the poll. This was before the coming of the Australian ballot.

"Who would have thought that a question put by a strange woman to a ragged kid would live with him down through the years and color his political life?

"Who could have foreseen that ragged kid, as Governor of our state, would be standing by her side, giving aid and comfort in her last great and successful battle for women's rights?"

There can be no doubt about Mrs. Duniway's prime role in the Suffrage movement. Her brother, Harvey W. Scott, long the distinguished editor of *The Oregonian*, a paper which opposed the vote for women, placed his sister in correct perspective when he wrote on August 20, 1906:

"The agitation was begun by Mrs. Duniway, and has been carried on by her unceasingly; and whatever progress it has made has been due to her, more than to all other agencies together. But for her, indeed the subject would scarcely have been mentioned in Oregon to this day, and little considered. The progress it has made is an extraordinary tribute to one woman's energy."

But two small matters ought to be cleared up. Abigail Scott Duniway did not organize the first group dedicated to suffrage in Oregon. Before she launched upon her campaigns she learned that an Equal Suffrage Society was in existence in Salem, with Col. C. A. Reed as president and Judge G. W. Lawson as secretary. At her request, the two men appointed her their delegate to the California Woman Suffrage convention at Sacramento.

There is also some belief that all men were opposed to suffrage and all women for it. That's not the way it was. The hardest workers for suffrage were women but many looked upon the "suffragettes" as radicals

Courtesy Oregon Historical Society

Abigail Scott Duniway, in center, after voting in first election in Oregon open to women

and malcontents. In the beginning, and for many years afterward, most men ridiculed the movement or were indifferent to it, but Duniway and her compatriots had powerful friends in such as Jacob Mayer; Solomon Hirsch, U.S. minister to Turkey; U.S. Senators Joseph N. Dolph, John H. Mitchell, and George E. Chamberlain; William U'Ren, author of the Initiative and the Referedum; bankers and judges, ministers and merchants, industrialists and transportation tycoons; the venerable Jesse Applegate; famed rancher William Hanley; Charles Erskine Scott Wood, the great friend of Chief Joseph; and a host of others.

Abigail Scott Duniway was also active in obtaining suffrage for Idaho and Washington but she is most closely identified with Oregon, where she played a leading role in five of the six campaigns that eventually won the vote for Oregon women.

No other state voted as many times: South Dakota came closest, with five. It is one of the contradictions and ironies of history that the person who did the most to advance the cause of equal rights also did the most, unwittingly, to hinder it. The very strengths of Mrs. Duniway eroded into factors which antagonized other feminists and drove away men who would be her friends. Her tremendous drive could become overbearing, her organizing ability dictatorial; the wit upon which she prided herself could turn to scathing sarcasm, and pettiness sometimes reduced her to a torrent of abuse. Having carried so much of the load herself, she developed a complex that seemed to her loyal supporters to hover between martyrdom and the messianic and to those who did not know her well her vanity was outlandish. Forced much of her life to make so many decisions herself, she found it hard to take counsel from those who did not have the same leadership status, and she developed an unhappy knack for alienating those not in complete accord with her. She lacked the depth, the humor and the broad-mindedness of Elizabeth Cady Stanton, the almost ascetic humility of Susan Anthony, and the forgiving soul of Lucy Stone. But none of these distinguished suffragists had had to pull themselves up by their bootstraps, as Abigail did, and none, however harrassed back East, had the rough times experienced by the Oregon feminist.

Tireless, witty, unexcelled in extemporaneous oratory, quick to feel and understand the mood of every audience, gifted with the ability to turn any situation into a platform with open-eared listeners eager to hear her mixture of burning idealism, down-to-earth stories and piercing repartee, Abigail Scott Duniway was a natural in the campaign for a good cause. That she made mistakes and, worse yet, did not profit from them in her campaigning, ought not to detract from her historic contribution.

A major illness forced her withdrawal from the final drive in 1912, in which suffrage carried by a vote of 61,265 to 57,104. But the state recognized passage not only as a breakthrough for women but as a personal triumph for Abigail Scott Duniway. Gov. Oswald West, facing the duty of issuing a proclamation declaring the Equal Suffrage Amendment to the Oregon Constitution in effect, assigned the task of drawing up the document to Mrs. Duniway. "This she did with proud, but trembling hand and pen," he recorded.

Three years later, on October 11, 1915, she died, eleven days short of reaching her eighty-first birthday.

Few writers have probed Mrs. Duniway beyond her public life and what she made plain in her books. So much the pity, for she was a vessel of contradictions, as straight-laced in some ways as she was liberal in others, and as far-out as she was realistic. She was for total abstinence, yet she could be charitable to alcoholics touched with genius. She championed women whom she thought had been done wrong by their men, but she put a limit to self-pity and she abhored turning betrayal into exploitation. She heralded women who had the courage to seek divorce but, "concerning free love, we are too intensely disgusted to speak." She was too ladylike to even hint at the mildest profanity but at a Progressive party rally she applauded a Kansas woman who urged farmers to "raise less corn and more hell." She had a romantic streak in her a yard wide and all glitter. She strongly believed in spiritualism and was in close touch with psychics; it was a sore point with some of her family. She loved clothes and dressed handsomely; she could be as elegant in a simple schoolhouse as in a celebrated hall. Despite the freshness and perceptiveness of *The New Northwest* she was too single-minded to really reflect upon, let alone involve herself in, other burning issues. Many of her compatriots, women and men, had greater social vision, and in the last three years of her life she was looked upon as an old warrior who had completed her battle.

Some years after she was buried at Riverview Cemetery, in Portland, her body was disinterred and cremated, and her ashes were placed in the same grave as the ashes of her only daughter and first child, Clara Belle Duniway Stearns, who died in 1886 at the age of thirty-two. As a girl Clara could not comprehend her mother, resented being in her mother's shadow, and for a while all but broke with Abigail, who spoke none but the tenderest words of her darling. And now the ashes of the two are united as when, in life, Clara was an infant in the arms of her twenty-year-old mother.

Nearby sleep three of Abigail's five sons and her husband, Ben, whom she survived by nineteen years. She never forgot that summer of 1896. " 'Good night, Mother!' he said to me, at midnight, on the day of his passing. 'You must have some rest. Don't worry; we'll meet again in the morning.' But when morning came he had lapsed into unconsciousness, from which he did not rally; and never since, through all the mornings of (the) vanished years, have I awakened, whether from a dreamless or a dreaming sleep, failing to quote a sentence in his memory, from a dear old-fashioned hymn:

> Here in the body pent,
>   Absent from him I roam,
> Yet nightly pitch my moving tent,
>   A day's march nearer home."

Joint grave of Abigail Scott Duniway and her only daughter, Clara

Long Road to the Cook House

We have heard it said a thousand times, "If this house could talk, what a story it could tell!"

But look at it another way: The story of many an old house began before the first tree was cut for lumber or the first brick laid.

Come to the Amos Cook house, half a mile off the main stem of Lafayette, and if you are told that it was built in 1850, you look upon it with respect and take note of its pioneer dimensions. The same with the Francis Fletcher house, a mile past the Cook house, and constructed in the same period.

Your interest may heighten when you learn that both Cook and Fletcher were members of the Peoria Party, both arriving in Oregon in 1840; that both settled in Yamhill County; and that the two participated in the famous May 2, 1843 Provisional government founding meeting at Champoeg.

The finding of the Duniway house, on a hill above Lafayette, eventually led me to the Cook house, across the Yamhill River, and my curiosity in the Cook house lured me down the thorny, often frustrating, and sometimes exhilarating path of history.

You could start with Amos Cook and Francis Fletcher, but that isn't the real beginning. You could tell a linear tale, but by staying to the highroad of the story you would miss many of the bypaths that give drama to what otherwise would be a dry recital of facts. In essence, a story begins wherever the storyteller wants it to. For me, the narrative of the Cook and Fletcher houses starts in 1838, with Jason Lee's trip across the continent.

Jason Lee, as you recall, was the first missionary in the Oregon Country. He arrived in 1834 to Christianize the Indians and make a white heaven of the Willamette Valley. By 1838 he was in trouble, sorely in lack of means and personnel to implement his plans. So he went East to secure physical and financial support for his work.

Lee left the Oregon Country with two Indian youths, Thomas Adams and William Brooks, his prize exhibits in attracting audiences and in soliciting contributions to pay for his speaking tour and to support his Methodist mission station. Thousands flocked to see the "soul-saved aboriginals" from the western wilderness, and when the curious saw them garbed in white men's clothes and heard them speak English and quote the Scriptures, the beneficial labors of the servants of the Lord were obvious, and the collection plates filled up.

Eighty-three appeals were delivered by Lee on this circuit run, William Brooks always at his side. Brooks could be funny but he could be profoundly moving, too. After observing a blind black man at a turnout in Baltimore, Brooks testified, as related by C. J. Brosnan in his *Jason Lee, Prophet of the New Oregon*:

"I saw something. I never forget. He colored man. Can't read. Can't see nothin', but he see Jesus Christ. He be very happy. Oh, I love that old man because he love Jesus Christ. Some rich man die, and where they go? That old man go to Heaven. I shall never forget him again."

And the fifteen-year-old peak-headed Chinook could be caustic, as well, especially when he spoke of whites who inflicted whiskey upon Indians:

"One thing, my friends, I must put in paper that no more these Americans they carry rum in my country — spoil all Indians. He make it himself, he must drink it himself! — these Yankees."

And he could render a simple lesson in cultural anthropology to those who regarded him as quaint. When a white-is-God believing woman expressed outrage at the "outlandish practice of head-flattening," William replied:

"All people have this fashion. Chinese make little his foot. Indian make flat his head. You," and he tried to encircle his waist with his hands while looking at her corsetted hourglass figure, "you make small here."

The last rally was scheduled for Schenectady, New York. Thomas Adams, who had been detained in Illinois by poor health for six months, had just arrived and the two lads were warmly reunited. But Brooks said few words that night. He was sick, gravely sick, and Lee, who had become attached to the young Indian, stayed with him to the end.

On May 29, 1839, Brooks whispered weakly, "I want to go home."

"You will," Lee assured him, "to your home in Oregon."

But Brooks was closer to what Lee preached. "No," he corrected feebly, "my heavenly home." And his body was brought to New York City, where it was laid to rest in the cemetery of the Bedford Street Church.

Thomas Adams had come down ill in Peoria, shortly after Jason Lee pitched a rousing plea for God, Salvation, Civilization and Manifest Destiny on September 30, 1838, in the Main Street Presbyterian Church. Lee was moving, as always. Without his speech, no "On to Oregon" fire would have been ignited in the hearts of adventurous Peorians. But without the stay of Tom Adams, Lee's oratory would have ended as just one more inspirational message.

Tom was too sick for Lee to take along on the road east. In the name of the Good Samaritan, Lee sought care for Adams and several members of the congregation responded. Tom was too weak to travel after he got out of bed and since there was nothing else for him to do while regaining strength, he became a familiar figure — a fixture, some would say — at the wagon and cooper shop run by Joe Holman, a lively, imaginative twenty-four-year-old who wanted to see more of the world than Peoria, Illinois.

Joe was intrigued by the casually spun tales Thomas Adams wove daily in his clumsy English. Back where he came from, Tom said, with the understatement of daily fact which astonishes people to whom the common-place of the faraway can be miraculous, the Columbia River was full of salmon and you could catch all you wanted without any trouble. Drying and storing them was easily done. The Indians, said Tom, caught and dried and stored so many salmon that they could eat salmon the whole year around. And listening to Thomas Adams, Joe Holman could see himself making a fortune by shipping barrels of pickled salmon to the East Coast, to Europe, and even to Asia.

Holman was the first of the Peorians to become ablaze for the distant country. Soon enough, though, he had interested some chums, and the venture was all they could talk about. Intoxicated by their own illusions, they foresaw themselves developing and controlling a "city at the mouth of the Columbia that should be the New York of the Pacific." When Narcissa Whitman had seen Fort Vancouver earlier she had, as she noted in her diary, the same optimism.

The plans of Holman and his friends, including Amos Cook and Francis Fletcher, drifted around loosely until hammered into shape by Thomas Jefferson Farnham, a thirty-five-year-old itching-for-glory lawyer recently moved to Peoria from Vermont. On March 28, 1839, Farnham assembled the starry-eyed in the chambers of a local judge, and after a massive dose of Farnham's golden-tongued oratory, which was to turn sour and tinny on the plains, fifteen men formed themselves into the "Oregon Dragoons." History knows them better as the "Peoria Party."

The tasks they set for themselves would have sent John McLoughlin, the power wheel of Fort Vancouver, into hysterics had he learned about them. Simply put, and they were precise in their scheme, the Oregon Dragoons would parade into the Oregon Country, defy the hegemony of Hudson's Bay Company, take up land, proclaim American sovereignty, and make a mint from shipping pickled salmon. You can argue that they were merely ahead of their time, but it would have taken more than a platoon of romantics to fulfill these goals.

Within a few days Tom Adams, who probably hadn't been invited to the meeting, perhaps on the assumption that a red man lacked a white man's savvy, departed from Peoria in search of Lee, with whom he caught up in Schenectady. He returned home to Oregon aboard the *Lausanne*, with Lee's "Great Reinforcement" on June 1, 1840, and that, for all practical significance, is the last we hear of him. Everyone else in that party of fifty-one was noted by biographers and historians, but Thomas Adams was just an Indian.

The former Eliza Woodson Burhams, who had become Mrs. Farnham three years before her husband caught the Oregon fever, joined in the fun. She designed and made a flag for the Dragoons and on it stitched *Oregon or the Grave*. Then, in fine spirits, she accompanied them for three days before returning to home and offspring.

Altogether, with the men they picked up en route, the Dragoons numbered nineteen at their peak. Three turned homeward on the rim of the plains, three others did later; there were desertions; and several men opted to go elsewhere.

The Dragoons started with a wagon, each man having his own riding horse and some pack stock. On the plains they sold their wagon so they could catch up, for safety sake, with a freight caravan bound for Santa Fe. (Theirs was a roundabout way.) With the sale money from the wagon they purchased a mule to pack their powder and a tent big enough for all of them to sleep in.

Only Farnham seemed to have more in mind than reaching the promised land. He carried buckled and strapped to his back a huge "blank-book" and every night he jotted down his impressions. These were later enlarged into *Travels in the Great Western Prairies*, a not completely accurate book which brought Farnham modest fame and wealth.

From the onset the Dragoons were beset by bad leadership, an excess of individuality, bumbling, bickering, brawling, and plain stupidity. The party finally split at Bent's Fort, on the Arkansas River in southeastern Colorado.

Eventually nine men reached Oregon — eight of them Peorians and the other a fifty-six-year-old handyman who had been with the Santa Fe-bound caravan.

It would take ten times the space I have alloted myself to tell this tale to report on what happened to each of the nineteen and to describe the ludicrous pathos, selfishness, generosity, courage, cowardice, wisdom, meanness, pettiness and insanities that the Dragoons acted out. A troop of cub scouts would be more efficient and show greater solidarity and compassion. So, because of space limitations, let us talk only of those who made it to Oregon.

At Bent's Fort, Farnham was charged with inebriation, fraud, incompetency and wastefulness, stripped of his captaincy, and with four others kicked out of the band. Unruffled, Farnham and the four hired a Mountain Man to guide them across the Rockies to Fort Davy Crockett, in Brown's Hole, up in the northwestern corner of Colorado.

Two of the Dragoons turned back for home at Fort Davy Crockett, which its occupants called Fort Misery because it was as mangy a hovel as anyone could sorrow to see. Everyone was subsisting on dog meat and the weak-hearted Dragoons called it quits when they were told by a Mountain Man who said he knew the Oregon Country that life out there was just as bad. Moreover, he said, the Willamette Valley farms were seas of mud in winter and parched cropless in summer and there wasn't a time of year when settlers weren't plagued by fevers and pestered half out of their minds by fleas. Having wandered so deep into a mare's nest, the two Peorians quickly retreated.

Together with Sidney Smith and William Blair, the old wagoner, Farnham continued west. It hurt Smith to ride and he limped when he walked. He had been accidentally shot near present-day Larned, Kansas when someone bumped a loaded gun while the Dragoons were hurling epithets at each other while striking their tent. Smith was first placed in a carriage but when the Santa Fe-bound caravan and the Peorians parted ways at the edge of the old Oklahoma Panhandle, the wounded man had to be dragged on a litter from camp to camp until he was strong enough to stand up and hobble along.

All the way from Bent's Fort to Oregon, Farnham and his companions encountered trappers and traders. Shrewdly, Farnham described the most colorful. At Bear River, in southeastern Idaho, Farnham saw his Indian guide, Jim, who had ridden ahead upon spotting a horseman coming up the trail, heartily shake the newcomer's hand, and a few moments later Farnham was face-to-face with Joe Meek.

Meek had all the cultural characteristics of an Indian, Farnham thought, "the same wild, unsettled, watchful expression of the eye, the same unnatural gesticulation in conversation, the same unwillingness to use words when a sign, a contortion of the face or body, or movement of the hand will manifest thought; in standing, walking, reading, in all but complexion, he was an Indian."

Like all Mountain Men who had worked for the American Fur Company, Meek was bitter about the short end he had received and could reel off woeful stories of being exploited.

"Meek evidently was very poor," Farnham narrated in *Travel in the Great Western Prairies*. "He had scarcely clothing enough to cover his body. And while talking with us the frosty winds which sucked up the valley made him shiver like an aspen leaf. He reverted to his destitute situation and complained of the injustice of his former employers; the little remuneration he had received from the toils and dangers he had endured on their account, etc.; a complaint which I had heard from every trapper whom I had met on my journey."

One more byway on the road to the Cook and Fletcher houses in Lafayette.

As for Smith, little did he dream that he and Meek would get to know each other well in Oregon and that both would be in on the history-making at Champoeg on May 2, 1843.

In September, Farnham, Smith and Blair reached Whitman's Mission, near present Walla Walla, Washington. A month later Farnham and Smith arrived in the Willamette Valley. Blair stayed sheltered under the congenial hospitality of the Whitmans until the following spring. Then, after looking over Oregon, he continued to California.

Smith jumped into history with both feet when he landed in Oregon. He worked for Ewing Young, one of the great men of early white settlement, and upon Young's death in mid-February 1841, purchased Young's ranch, which took up practically the whole Chehalem Valley, and all his unbranded cattle, for less than three hundred dollars. Eight years later Smith followed the gold rush to California and returned with $3,000, to operate a store in Lafayette. He died in 1880, seventy-one years old, an age he probably never thought he would see when he was shot on the Kansas plain.

Farnham, being a lawyer, helped the Willamette Valley settlers draw up a petition addressed to Congress (not the first or the last to be penned by the Americans) asking to be placed under the sovereignty of the United States. Then, as he shook in the rain, he decided that the Mountain Man back at Fort Davy Crockett was right; Oregon was not a fit place for the sane. So he boarded a ship for the Sandwich (Hawaiian) Islands on December 3, taking the petition with him. In Hawaii, while the ship unloaded and took on cargo, he spent so much time writing letters to U.S. newspapers denouncing the "Oregon Bubble Burst" that he was left with little leisure time for loafing in the semi-tropical sun. (One wonders why he did not fling the petition into the sea; perhaps he felt that Oregon was ideal for fools and that wise men such as he were entrusted by Providence to humor idiots.) When he reached New York he was at it again, and doubtless he convinced some aspirants to forego their Oregon ambitions. But there was something in the lure of the West that took Farnham back, and he died in San Francisco.

Robert Shortess, who had quarreled bitterly with Farnham, whom he regarded as having a "low, intriguing disposition," arrived alone in the Willlamette Valley in the spring of 1840, having wintered at Fort Walla Walla. He was active in the forming of an American government, contributed to the founding of Oregon Institute, which led to the establishment of Willamette University, married a Nez Perce, and died in 1878, at the age of eighty-one, in Clatsop County, where he had lived for a third of a century and had been a judge and Indian sub-agent.

Robert Moore, who also came alone, was the founder of Linn City, first called Robin's Nest, and now West Linn, and another enterprising man of politics. He was fifty-eight when he left a wife and ten children behind in Peoria (she died in Missouri) and was seventy-six when he passed away, in 1857.

(The divisions on the plains extended to Oregon; Shortess hated John McLoughlin and left no stone unturned to assail him; Moore spoke openly for the rights of McLoughlin, in public and in his *Oregon Spectator*, which he published in 1850-51.)

Ralph Kilbourne, Joseph Holman, Francis Fletcher and Amos Cook wintered together in Wyoming and reached Oregon in April 1840. Kilbourne is best remembered as one of the "company of eight young men" who built the pioneer schooner, *Star of Oregon*, which was sailed down to Yerba Buena, as San Francisco was then called, in the spring of 1841. There it was sold and the money used to purchase cattle, which were driven north to the Willamette Valley settlements. Holman, the fellow at whose wagon and cooper shop Thomas Adams had spun out his enticing tales, cut the first timber on the site of Salem, erected business buildings there, became one of the original trustees of Willamette University, was one of the first flax-seed growers and breeders of purebred sheep, fathered the first white child born in organized Marion County, and died in 1880, at the age of sixty-five.

This leaves us with Francis Fletcher and Amos Cook, whose houses are the last physical links to the Peoria Party.

Apart from his presence at Champoeg on Divide day and his brief role as a trustee of Willamette University, the English-born Fletcher lived a relatively uneventful life. A farmer, he died at his home, a mile from the house of his friend, Amos Cook, on October 7, 1871, at the age of fifty-seven.

Amos Cook was a Lafayette merchant, home-builder, river boatman and farmer, and he died at this house on February 3, 1895, at the age of seventy-nine. But he has to be the best known of all the Peoria men who stayed in Oregon, simply because he was the brother-in-law of Abigail Scott Duniway. In 1853 Cook married Abigail's sister, Mary Frances — he was almost as old as her father — and all accounts of the famous Mrs. Duniway include passages about Amos Cook.

Tucker Scott, Cook's father-in-law, managed the Oregon Temperance House, a hotel Cook built in Lafayette; the Tucker Scott family men and Cook belonged to the Sons of Temperance; Amos and Abigail shared views on morals and politics; and the Cooks and the Duniways seemed constantly to be visiting each other.

So we have come from the Duniway house, on the hill above Lafayette, to the Cook house, across the Yamhill River. That could bring the story full circle, but there is one element missing — Jason Lee. Without him, Amos Cook and Abigail Scott Duniway would probably never have met.

Lee returned to Oregon in 1840 but four years later was recalled by the Methodist Board of Missions, which had become disenchanted with him. He died March 12, 1845, in his native village of Stanstead, Quebec, succumbing to tuberculosis and stricture of the liver. Sixty-one years later, in 1906, his remains were brought to Salem, and he lies in a circular plot in Jason Lee Cemetery.

Before Lee took leave of Oregon for the second and last time he probably knew some of the Peorians. Everyone in the Willamette Valley seemed to know everyone else then. It is doubtful that he recalled a single face from his Peorian meeting, but all the Peorians remembered him. Ah, well they did, and Tom Adams, too, and that long, bizarre journey to Oregon.

And all of this is what I think of when now I stand before the Cook house, only thirty miles from where Jason Lee set out for the East in 1838. All this — or at least a part of it.

Directions: In Lafayette, turn on 3rd and Madison. 0.5 mile, on right, Amos Cook house. 1.1 miles farther, on right, Francis Fletcher house.

Amos Cook House, Lafayette

The Search for Jennyopolis

Friend: "What place are you looking for now?"
Ralph Friedman: "Jennyopolis."
Friend: "What was that?"
Friedman: "A settlement."
Friend: "You're putting me on! There couldn't be a town with a name like that! Not in Oregon!"
Friedman: "But there was."
Friend: "Where is it?"
Friedman: "I don't exactly know, but I'm going to find it."
Friend: "When you do, let me know. I'd like to go there myself, even if there's nothing there."

Everyone ought to be entitled to an occasional harmless obsession. For more than two years mine was Jennyopolis.

Somewhere I came across the name and thereafter it haunted me. There were hundreds of Oregon settlements that drifted off with the wind, and while scores of them have caught my fancy, none so impaled me as did Jennyopolis.

I suppose it was the name. Run Jennyopolis through the swirl of your imagination and you conjure up pictures of a happy river boat landing or of a homesteader village with a big dream or of a rude cluster of homes on the fringe of the wilderness. Once, thinking about the name, I saw a freckle-faced girl with long blonde hair falling over the shoulders of her gingham dress swishing through tall rye grass as the wind fiddled music to her mood. Another time I observed a dusty traveler ride up the one street, look around, and mutter, "This place has got more letters in its name than people."

Only one thing I knew at the start, that Jennyopolis was in Benton County. But where? *Preston's Sectional and County Map of Oregon and Washington West of the Cascade Mountains*, published in 1856, showed Jennyopolis, and above the name, "P.O." (Oddly, Habersham's map of 1878 also listed the settlement, twenty years after its expiration.) So from the map I knew that Jennyopolis was south of Corvallis and later I read that it was near Monroe. I wrote to William Carpenter, an old-timer, and he replied, "I have lived in Monroe for eighty-two years and never heard of Jennyopolis."

Neither the Horner Museum at Oregon State University nor the Oregon State Library could pinpoint where Jennyopolis was sited. Nor could the Oregon Historical Society or the archivist for Benton County. (Indeed, the name was new to all of them.) Then one day, at the Multnomah County Library, in downtown Portland, I tracked down a publication titled *Government Field Notes, Benton County*. And in Volume A of the *County Court Journal* I found the following, though the name has an extra "e":

"Other attempts were made in the early days to develop towns in the southern part of the county. One of the earliest of these was Jenneyopolis at the western foot of Winkle Butte in section 22, township 13 south, range 5 west of the Willamette Meridian. On September 5, 1853, the county court ordered that 'License be granted Robert Irwin to keep a Grocery at Jenneyopolis for the term of one year from the date of the expiration of his first license, for the sum of fifty dollars.' A post office was established at Jenneyopolis on March 24, 1852, with Richard Irwin as postmaster. It was discontinued April 19, 1857. On April 3, 1854, the county court created precinct No. 5 and named Jenneyopolis 'the place of holding elections for the same.' "

Now I could zero in on the location of Jennyopolis. But I first wanted to know something about the hamlet. Volume 2 of *Government Field Notes, Benton County*, told me that "There is a flouring mill in the western portion of the township, and a postoffice, store, and grocery at the Buttes (Winkle Buttes) on the main road from Marysville [the early name of Corvallis] to the mines."

So Jennyopolis stood astride the pike that led from the supply centers of the Willamette Valley to the southern mines. Since the state highway from Corvallis to Monroe is practically the same route as was "the main road from Marysville to the mines," I knew that the site of what was Jennyopolis had to be close to the pavement.

But back to the town. There is some evidence that in its last two years Jennyopolis had a blacksmith shop — but there is no record of the smith's name. The flouring mill was owned by a woman, Elizabeth Herbert, probably the only woman flour miller of that period. She is little remembered in the county annals. Richard Irwin, the first postmaster, fares much better. Irish-born, he came to the United States in 1832 at the age of nineteen and promptly went into the mercantile business. Within the next eighteen years he operated stores in New York, Ohio, Illinois and Iowa. He and Louise Kompp were just one day married when they set out west with an outfit costing $5,000 and a copious stock of provisions. Being a generous fellow, he shared his affluence with the hungry, the sick and the ill-clothed he encountered on the plains so that by the time he and Louise reached The Dalles, in the autumn of 1850, they were broke and themselves in need of food. But Irwin was too enterprising to stay down. A year later, after working for a Portland mercantile firm, he opened a store in Corvallis. There was greater wealth in land, he reckoned, so a few months more and we have him locating 640 acres on a donation land claim that came to be regarded as part of the Jennyopolis precinct. Eventually, by buying up land from disenchanted settlers, he owned 922 acres of Benton County's most fertile estate. A hill was named for him too but

Where Jennyopolis stood

later it was called Winkle Butte, for his neighbor Wilkey Winkle, who got his mail from Richard Irwin.

This Irwin — Richard not Robert, the storekeeper — was postmaster from March 24, 1852, to the late summer of 1855. He was succeeded by John E. Porter, who served about a year before turning over the business to William J. Robertson. (I learned about this from the National Archives and Records Service, which added: "The records of the Post Office Department in the National Archives do not include any geographical site location reports relating to this office, or the applications of the postmasters, or explain why the office at Jennyopolis was closed.")

A brief obituary in the July 22, 1876 issue of *The Oregonian* tells of the last of the Jennyopolis people to appear in print: "On Beaver Creek, Benton County, July 13, Robert Irwin, aged seventy-seven years." He had run the grocery.

I took the geographic data I found in *Government Field Notes, Benton County*, to Ralph Mason, then the assistant state geologist, and together we mapped where Jennyopolis had lived: about 1.65 miles south of Greenberry Road and probably on the east side of the highway.

"It shouldn't be hard to find," said Ralph Mason. "Just ask for Winkle Butte. People in the area ought to be familiar with it."

It wasn't that simple, as I learned from Richard Mengler, a circuit court judge of Benton and Linn counties.

Our acquaintance started with: "Dear Mr. Friedman: Your recent letter to the Archives has somehow found its way to me. This occurred because I am known to have more than a casual interest in the historical trivia of the area."

A month later, together with my wife, Phoebe, and three friends — Roy Lucier, Edna Riddle and Pat Kimoto — I traveled to Corvallis, phoned Richard Mengler, and he and his wife, Mary, met our group at the Benton Hotel and we all piled into Roy Lucier's car in pursuit of Jennyopolis.

"You wouldn't get very far asking for Winkle Butte," said Mengler. "It's much better known as Wagner's Butte, because the Wagner family lived there for many years. The land is now owned by Lon Jensen, a Corvallis dentist."

With Richard Mengler directing us, we came to Jensen's Lazy J Ranch, a mile farther south than Ralph Mason and I had calibrated the site of Jennyopolis. There was nothing but meadowland at the foot of a soft-sloping, wooded hill which the earliest pioneers called Irwin Butte. You could live here all your life and, unless told, be completely unaware that this mead below the fatty rise of land had held a settlement, and that for five years everyone who came up or down the pike knew full well where Jennyopolis was.

A horse munching on the green grass of early spring looked us over and then wheeled, peering in every direction, as though to ask, "What's the fuss about? Am I missing something?"

No, old friend, Jennyopolis doesn't mean anything to you. But it did to me that gloriously warm day. I had come to precisely where the pioneer settlement had stood. My long search was over; an obsession had been fulfilled.

Directions: From Benton County Courthouse in Corvallis, take Oregon 99W south for 10.9 miles, on left, to Jensen's Lazy J Ranch. Below the hill and touching the road is the site of the long-extinct village of Jennyopolis.

Irish Bend Nightmare

I say, thou madder March hare.

John Skelton

The commissioner didn't know how many covered bridges were still standing in Benton County. "I should," he mumbled, a bit distressed. "I'm interested in historical places."

So from his office in the Benton County Courthouse he summoned his assistant. That worthy was as befuddled as his boss. Another man was called in and he too confessed ignorance of such matters.

By now the commissioner was in a state of anxiety. "I'll check it out myself," I said, hoping to relieve the tension. He had other things to do. Several citizens, each looking quite concerned, were waiting for him to solve their problems.

"No, no!" exclaimed the commissioner. "I want to know for myself." And he dispatched his assistant to the county engineer.

About thirty minutes later the flustered aide returned with the information. There was only one covered bridge I had not found earlier: the one at Irish Bend.

"Here's how you get there," he said, and jotted down directions. They turned out to be hopelessly wrong. But fortunately, after knocking at several farm doors, I chanced upon a child whose school bus took her near enough the covered bridge to see it, and while her guidance wasn't precise, it put us on the right track.

The very name of Irish Bend is enough to whet your curiosity. If there were a town there, you can be sure it would have an authentic Western flavor. But, so much the pity for it, there was never even a post office. About 1860 a few Irish families settled just west of where the Willamette makes a strong eastward bend, and after a while the area between the Willamette and the Long Tom River became known as Irish Bend. Today the rural neighborhood, as marked by road signs, lies between Oregon 99W and the Willamette. And if you're looking for anything as romantic as the name of Irish Bend, forget it. The land is flat and given chiefly to wheat; the houses look like most other farm homes throughout Western Oregon; a significant number of the occupants are relative newcomers; rare is a descendant of a pioneer family. Only the covered bridge stands out.

Spanning a slough, the bridge is one of the most inconspicuous roofed crossings in the state. It is part of a dirt backcountry farmroad probably used by less than a dozen vehicles a day.

At Monroe, a few miles southwest of the Irish Bend district, we met a fellow who had once farmed near the bridge and was now in construction work. He told us of a mad idea he had, and just the thought of it doubled him over in laughter.

"You know how many cars — hundreds, thousands maybe — come up to Corvallis from Eugene during a football game between Oregon and Oregon State," he began, outlining his maniacal scheme. "Well, I've had this thought for years. While the game was underway I'd put up a lot of detour signs that would point all those motorists to the bridge at Irish Bend. It would be the biggest traffic jam in the history of the state, damn if it wouldn't! By the time somebody wised up, the cars would be bumper-to-bumper two miles long. That bridge is one-way and you can just imagine what would go on there when the cars would start going back. They have to go over the bridge, there's no other road out there. Maybe I'd put up a sign about a hundred yards past the bridge, reading, 'End of detour. Return to highway.' That ought to split a few livers."

"How come you haven't tried it?" I asked.

"I dunno," he smiled, cooling from his enthusiastic scenario. "I guess I'm just not cruel enough."

At any rate, be forewarned. If you are driving south on Oregon 99W

Irish Bend Covered Bridge

after a football game between Oregon and Oregon State and you see painted signs reading DETOUR, make sure they're official before you turn off. A wild dream sometimes breaks out of fantasy.

There is, alas, a postscript to the above. Some weeks after it was written I read that Benton County officals had ordered the covered bridge at Irish Bend moved or demolished. At first I thought of eliminating this sketch from the book but, on consideration, decided that the detour story was worth its keeping. Any time you find a good piece of folk humor, however zany it might be, hang onto it.

Directions: From Corvallis, drive 15 miles south of Benton County Courthouse on Oregon 99W to Irish Bend-Bellfountain Jct. Turn east onto Irish Bend Rd. 1.8 miles, junction. Turn left. 0.5 mile, turn right. 1.8 miles former site of Irish Bend Covered Bridge.

The Romance Back of Latourell

Together at one Tree, oh let us brouze,
And like two Turtles roost within one house,
And like the Mullets in one River glide,
Let's still remain but one, till death divide.

Anne Bradstreet

There is more than a question-mark settlement just off the Columbia River Scenic Highway; there is a link to a tale of romance that has seldom been told.

Look upon Latourell, across the road from the north end of Talbot State Park. It still has three streets running east and west and two running north and south. Along the streets are a collapsing store structure, a dilapidated schoolhouse (built in 1888), a dwelling that was remodeled from a saloon, and several houses of yore.

With no store, gas station, post office or school, but with some persons turning the former pioneer village into a suburban retreat, is or is not Latourell a ghost town?

Few of the many thousands who yearly drive the Columbia River Scenic Highway turn off for Talbot State Park. Of these, but a handful know the history of Latourell. And only the local historians and members of the family are aware of the romance. Without it, Latourell would have had a different name — if indeed it had become a settlement.

The tale probably begins in 1805, the year Lewis and Clark came down the Columbia to set up winter camp at Fort Clatsop, near Astoria. On the way they passed an Indian village at what is now Washougal, Washington. The chief was Schlyhoush, whose name later whites corrupted to Sly Horse. His wife was Running Fawn, the daughter of a chief. And to them was born that year a girl so fair of form and so graceful in movement that her parents named her White Wing.

She grew up lithe and strong and beautiful and would have married of her people a salmon fisher proud and industrious if a bold, persevering and persuasive Englishman had not given her his heart and taken hers.

Fort Vancouver was the metropolis of the Columbia when a young, hardy mate jumped his British ship to stay "on the beach" at the Hudson's Bay Company post. The arrival of a British ship was not unique and it was not altogether uncommon for seamen to remain in the new land, but this mariner was, without knowing it, to make a bit of history.

Drawing by Henry J. Warre

Fort Vancouver from the southeast, 1845, when Richard and Betsey White Wing Ough came in occasionally for supplies.

His name was probably Richard Howe but a clerk who lacked a keen ear for the cockney habit of dropping "h's" listed the newcomer as Ough, and so his name persisted, and under it a family was started, grew, and spread throughout the Pacific Northwest.

In 1910, when she was 105 years old, White Wing, then Betsey Ough, told a newspaper reporter the story of her courtship. She can be excused for not having every detail precise — she thought she was eighteen when she met Ough, but that would have placed the year as 1823, and Fort Vancouver was not established until 1825. She was probably closer to twenty; either that or she was younger than 105 in 1910. But she could recall with remarkable clarity that day of destiny.

"We were on the river, father and I, catching salmon. I was paddling and my father was spearing them when all at once we looked up and, oh, so many canoes coming and lots of white men in them. My father and all the Indians paddled to shore as quick as they could and the chiefs say, 'Maybe we better kill those men.'

"Then one great, big man, they call McLoughlin, he come and say, 'No fight. We want to trade. You go and bring plenty good skins and see all the nice things I will give you for them. I got all pretty things what Indians like.'

"Then is the time I saw Richard. He was standing beside Dr. McLoughlin and was almost as big as him — six feet two inches and weighed 240 pounds, and oh, he look so nice!

"I look at him and he look at me and when I look again he still looking at me. Then when I start to go away with my father I look back once more and Richard and Dr. McLoughlin was looking after me and Richard started to follow me but Dr. McLoughlin put his hand on his shoulder and say, 'No! Do you want to lose your scalp?' "

When Richard departed, White Wing thought she had seen the last of him. But a month later he was back, and when the men of the fishing village came grimly out to confront him, he stood his ground. He wasn't afraid of any man, he said, and the Indians respected his courage. He had spent a restless month, unable to keep White Wing out of his head, he declared, and the villagers sensed his sincerity. He spoke at length, poetically, fervently, his tongue dipped in honey and hot wine. "Oh," remembered Betsey Ough, more than eight decades later, "he talk so nice. I can mind every word he say."

For eight days Richard and Chief Schlyhoush talked, argued, maneu-

Courtesy Oregon Historical

John McLoughlin of Hudson's Bay Company.

vered. You can write your own scenario of the father discouraging, the suitor pressing his proposal. The father dwells long on every negative aspect: Richard is white, the whites have mistreated the Indians, white men have abused Indian women, white men have taken Indian daughters from their homes, torn them from their families, carried them into alien worlds. Richard vows that he loves White Wing, he will care for her, will protect her with his life, he will not sever her from her kin. The elders of the council ponder this strange man, but it is the father's decision. White Wing is surer each day where her heart belongs, but her father must choose. So from morning until late at night and over food and drink the debate goes on. Then the father, the chief, reaches his conclusion. Richard may have his daughter if he will build a house on the river and not leave the great stream.

The triumphant Richard was ready. "I build house tomorrow; you come day after tomorrow and I got house ready," Betsey Ough recalled him saying, and he strode to his canoe and took off in a fever of paddling.

Came the day of promise and a flotilla of Indian canoes, as many as a hundred, White Wing thought, stroked the waters of the Columbia to Fort Vancouver. Richard eagerly showed off the keeping of his bargain, a "little bit of a log house." It was more than a lean-to and less than a good cabin — but it was shelter, and that is what he had pledged. He would do more soon, he vowed, and the chief nodded.

Always the diplomat quick to turn any situation to advantage, McLoughlin, the boss of the fort and the mighty power of Hudson's Bay Company in the West, used the binding of two hearts to seal peace with the fishers. He was a man of enlightenment, believing that profitable commerce came through mutual trust. To Richard's beloved, McLoughlin expounded his philosophy:

"White Wing, this man is big warrior and good man. When I make you to marry him, the red man and the white man will be brothers. They must live all the time in peace and never, never fight each other. The Indian must catch plenty of salmon and get lots of good furs and trade them to the white man. The white man must get plenty of things that Indian like and always trade fair and never cheat Indian."

There can be no doubt of McLoughlin's sympathy for White Wing and his acceptance of her. He himself was married to an Indian woman, the widow of Alexander McKay, who had been killed in the Indian attack on the *Tonquin* as that ill-fated vessel lay off the western shore of Vancouver Island. The following year, in 1812, McLoughlin married Marguerite Wadin McKay. They had four children and were parted only by his death, in 1857.

All that day and night at Fort Vancouver the torches burned bright, the feasting was gluttonous, the songs loud, the dancing seldom stopped. Then, when all had been worn down, Richard and White Wing carried their gifts into their tiny home and started life together.

White Wing was anxious to please Richard but, unsure of herself, she took her problems to McLoughlin, who savored playing counselor.

"When I first get married," Betsey Ough told the reporter, "I don't know how to cook white man's cooking. I go tell Dr. McLoughlin I am afraid my husband won't love me if I cook Indian's cooking all the time.

He laugh and say, 'Girl, you just feed him plenty all the time and he will love you, never fear. It is only a hungry man that hates his wife.' "

Richard and Betsey stayed at Fort Vancouver for eight years, Richard working for McLoughlin. They would have continued on had they not heeded McLoughlin's advice. "Some day," Betsey recalled hearing him prophesy, "all the beaver gone, no more elk, nothing for people to eat. You go take land, make house, raise cattle. By and by lots of people come here, all hungry, nothing to eat."

Back to the tribal grounds of White Wing went the couple, homesteading at present Washougal. An Englishman fed up with the rain and the wilderness sold them his farm for $45, a saddle horse, and a baking of bread, and hurried off to California.

Together the former seaman and the daughter of a chief toiled from dawn to dusk to clear the land, put in a garden, till the soil, plant crops. It was hard going and made harder because they kept so little of what they harvested and had. Every hungry Oregon-bound emigrant who came rafting down the Columbia and put in at their place was fed, and no money asked. More than sixty years after it happened, Betsey Ough still had vivid memory of one family she and her husband took in for a week.

The father was worn to a frazzle and the mother too weak and sickly to care for their two baby girls. So Betsey did, until the comers were hardy enough to continue their quest for a plot of land in Yamhill County.

"When they about ready to start," Betsey Ough said in 1910, "I see Richard walking up and down in potato patch, and I laugh and think I bet Richard thinking about them girl babies. Pretty soon he come in and tell me, 'Betsey, you think them babies gone die?' I say, 'Think so, Richard, their mother too sick.' 'Then I give them cow,' he say.

" 'What you do now?' I ask him. 'No more milk, no cattle, all gone now.' 'Oh, never mind, Betsey,' he say, 'there is lots of elk in wood.'

" 'But,' I say, 'I can't milk elk. He jump over my head, kick me in the river.' "

The babies survived and in their womanhood called themselves Betsey's cowgirls.

Betsey Ough was 106 when she died in 1911. Her last wish was that she rejoin Richard, who had passed on before her. She left behind five children, eighteen grandchildren, twenty-eight great-grandchildren, and four great-great-grandchildren.

One of her daughters, Grace, was as lively as the young White Wing and, like White Wing, had an eye for dashing men. The fellow who came closest to resembling her father was Joseph Latourell, who came 'round the Horn on a whaling ship, found his way up the Columbia, and put down roots at Rooster Rock.

Latourell, whom everyone knew as Frenchy, didn't like living alone and might have moved on, but on a trip across the river he saw Grace, was smitten by her and, as the story writers say, laid siege to her heart. She said yes in the year of Oregon statehood, 1859, and the two started a household which eventually came to be known as Latourell. He became postmaster in 1876, a few months after the office was opened, and was the leading citizen in the village when the name was changed from Roos-

Latourell street scene

ter Rock to Latourell Falls in 1887. But there never was a post office building; the mail was handled either in the Latourell home or in the store he ran. A pouch was hung out and picked up by a mechanical arm, and the reverse process was used by the trains for dropping off mail.

Joe Latourell used every trick in his bag to provide a living for Grace and their eight children. He worked as a boatman and was the first pilot to take a barge over the Cascade rapids. He operated a fish wheel, hauled, kept store, carpentered and labored on road construction. His were the toils of a typical pioneer. But it was his zest for life which endeared him to the village folk.

A fiddler man was Frenchy, bowling out notes that made feet itch. He'd sing without prompting, mostly French songs from his childhood, and when it came to jig-dancing there was no one in town who could keep pace with him, even in his fifties.

He was a hospitable man too. "What's your hurry?" he would ask a traveler who, having spent a week or two with the Latourells, showed an inclination to be off.

Grace was as touched with goodness. She kept the Indian love of family. When the wife of her son, Mason, died, she took in the three grandchildren. She also raised a nephew. Her own children went on to long life, business success, and some pioneering; her daughter, Clara, was elected mayor of Troutdale the year after women got the vote in Oregon.

So that's the story back of the question-mark place of Latourell. Is it a ghost town or a suburb? I think — because I have thought so much about them that I believe them my friends — that Joe and Grace Latourell would like it to be a ghost town. They knew there was a time for everything. And as for White Wing and Richard Ough, they were certain of it.

Directions: From Crown Point, on Columbia River Scenic Highway (off I-80N), 2.2 miles to turnoff north to Talbot State Park. 0.3 mile, turn right. Talbot State Park. Across road is what was town of Latourell Falls.

"Mighty Peak of Tremendious Hight"

Then shall this Mount
Of Paradise by might of waves be moovd.

John Milton, *Paradise Lost*

I reckon I have read at least a hundred poems about Mount Hood, and while some of them are quite professional, my favorite is by a man of scant formal education who wrote in ignorance of punctuation, spelled atrociously, and could justifiably plead innocent to the charge of understanding the forms of grammar.

This was James Clyman, one of the most fascinating, creative and discerning of the fabled Mountain Men. He was not only a chronicler of daily events — often at the close of a hard day he would scribble by light of campfire into a little notebook resting upon his knee — he was also a poet. No one knows when he started writing verse but he was active at it for the last forty years of his life and in the final days of his stay on earth he dashed off lines as though there were no tomorrow.

His prose passages are illuminated and sharpened by strokes of imagery which lift reporting to the level of good fiction. He not only saw accurately, he interpreted incisively, going beyond the fact and the utterance to the mood and the motivation. He wove people and their surroundings together in pithy commentaries that explain each in properly related setting. Having lived long in the wilderness, he knew how critical a force the environment could be in human behavior. And having dealt closely with Indians, he was well aware that different peoples see the same environment differently and act accordingly.

But it is more in his poetry than in his narratives that we find literary flame in Clyman. Somewhere, though he makes no suggestion about the point in any of the material he left behind, he must have brushed against the classics. We find him referring frequently, though sometimes casually, to Milton and the Bible, and less often, though enough to impute an acquaintanceship, with Shakespeare.

You will want to know, as I did, a bit about this most captivating fellow. His poem on Mount Hood will be the more precious for having seen a few glimpses of him.

James Clyman was born in 1792 in the foothills of the Blue Ridge Mountains, on a Virginia farm owned by President George Washington, the first of the famous men Clyman was to know in one fashion or other.

He was fifteen when his father took the family across the mountains to Ohio. There young Clyman became involved in the War of 1812. Surviving the dangers of hostilities and the drudgery of farm work, he drifted south and west, into Indiana, and then Illinois, where in 1821 he was hired by Col. William S. Hamilton, son of Alexander Hamilton, as a surveyor.

Two years later we find Clyman in St. Louis, and there his great days begin. He is employed as a clerk of a "cargo box" on a boat, at one dollar a day, by Gen. William H. Ashley, the famous fur trader and then lieutenant-governor of Missouri.

Later that year, 1823, Clyman is in a group of a dozen or so men sent into the Big Horn country by Ashley to meet a party led by Andrew Henry, Ashley's partner. The group's leader is Jedediah Smith, perhaps the most achieving and luckless of all western pathfinders. Two other men in Smith's party are also to make their mark in Western legend: Thomas Fitzpatrick, later to be known as "Broken Hand" (the prototype of many a Hollywood covered wagon scout), and William Sublette, who blazed a cutoff on the Oregon Trail and after whom a county in Wyoming was named.

Smith's route takes him through the tortuous Badlands of western South Dakota and there the bewildered men, many of them new to the West, run into more difficulties than they have been told to expect. Sometimes they find themselves in box canyons so narrow they cannot turn their horses and so close, Clyman notes they are "without room to lie down." But all this is mild inconvenience compared to what happens to Jed Smith. An aroused grizzly bear lays open his scalp, tears off an eyebrow, and leaves a slashed ear dangling. Jim Clyman is assigned the task of patching up Smith and does a pretty fair job of sewing until he comes to the ear. He is a little hesitant about trying, but since there is no one else around willing to play doctor, Clyman studies the ear and, as he records in his little notebook that night, "put in my needle stitching it through and through and over and over laying the lacerated parts together nice as I could with my hands." Ever afterward Smith wore his hair long.

In 1824, Clyman, together with Tom Fitzpatrick, explores the Platte-Sweetwater route to the central Rockies. It is their dramatic rediscovery of South Pass and the North Platte route which later becomes the main highway to the West, the Oregon-California Trail. South Pass, which unlocked the Rockies to overland travel, had been forgotten since it was used by the first white men who came this way, a party led by Robert Stuart en route in 1812 to report to John Jacob Astor on the operations of Fort Astoria.

On the homeward trek Clyman grows restless. He leaves Fitzpatrick in a bullboat on shallow Sweetwater Creek and hikes east, expecting to meet the rest of the party at whatever point the stream becomes navigable. Instead, Clyman remains separated from his companions and suffers the abuses of a pesky nature, fatigue (he is without a horse), the presence of Indian war parties, hunger, swollen streams that he is forced to swim, and the feeling of being doomed. He walks six hundred miles in sixty days — from the headwaters of the Platte to the Missouri — before he sees Fort Atkinson, the sight so shocking that "I swoned emmedietly how long I lay unconscious I do not know."

While still on the Platte River, Clyman grew so desperate for human companionship that he entered a Pawnee camp. The Indians recovered from their astonishment quickly enough to want to kill him. (The excesses of the hunters and trappers had made the Pawnees implacable foes of all white men.) One warrior, evidently a man of stature, took a shine to the paleface's hair and expressed a strong fancy for it. Jim's hair had not been cut for more than a year. He had gone bareheaded ever since losing his hat in a battle with the Arikaras many months before, and the strong sun had bleached his mane. It was this long, white hair that the brave coveted. Jim, of course, offered no protest so long as the rest of him remained alive — though he had no choice in the matter. When the warrior had finished hacking off Clyman's hair with a dull butcher knife, he turned the white man loose, and Jim departed with his scalp intact. He never again became so lonely.

Clyman, however, often had companionship. He managed to palaver with nearly every Mountain Man who stayed in the wilds long enough to get cold, hungry, and shot at. He knew most of the trappers well and sketched them clearly in bold, wry strokes of brief prose or verse, mixing romanticism with reality. One of his favorite companions was Moses Harris, better known as Black Harris, who emerges in literature as Black George in *The Prairie Flower*, the first full work of fiction written in Oregon.

Like Clyman, Harris was one of "Ashley's young men." Later he turned to make a living off emigrants, who valued his knowledge of the unknown country they had to cross. He was a guide in the party that brought the Whitmans and Spaldings west in 1836, in that momentous march which saw a wagon — even though only a light wagon — cross South Pass for the first time. Resourceful, indefatigable, recognized by his contemporaries as an expert in solitary and winter travel, Black Harris was a good guide. However unorthodox his manners, he was all discipline in hostile land; if nothing else, he valued his own skin too highly to permit others to be foolhardy. And he could relax tensions with his ability to entertain.

Black Harris was about the tallest story teller ever to come out of Rocky Mountain College. Some of his robust hyperbole was later attributed to Joe Meek, who was never too proud to turn away a donation or too shy to take what he needed. The seemingly endless repertoire of Harris delighted Narcissa Whitman, who could not get enough of his campfire yarns. Narcissa liked all the Mountain Men in the party but Harris was probably her favorite; it is certain that she never met a funnier man or a more cordial liar.

In 1844 Black Harris guided the Nathaniel Ford party to Oregon, stayed around to scout out some trails through the Cascades, and then built a cabin on the Luckiamute River, where he lived until early May 1847, when he traveled to Missouri. There he told friends he intended to return to Oregon, or go to California — the stories differ — but about two years from the day he started east from the Willamette Valley he died of cholera.

Upon hearing of Black's fate, Clyman scrawled on a slip of paper his memorial to his camerado of the glory days. It should have been the epitaph on Harris's gravestone:

> Here lies the bones of old Black Harris
> who often traveled beyond the far west
> and for the freedom of Equal rights
> He crossed the snowy mountin Hights
> was free and easy kind of soul
> Especially with a Belly full

A few years after the harrowing hike to Fort Atkinson, Clyman left the mountains and put all his savings into an Illinois store. When the Black Hawk War broke out in 1832, Clyman had to join up; after all, he was still a young man, only forty. He found himself in the same company with — who else? — Abraham Lincoln. In two score years Clyman had gone from Virginia to the Rockies, from farmboy to Mountain Man to storekeeper, from the War of 1812 to a war in 1832, from George Washington to Abraham Lincoln. It was a personal epoch, and he had more than half his time yet to live.

After the Black Hawks were subdued, Clyman went back to being a merchant but he was too much of an outdoorsman to stay cooped up forever in a store. Restive, he took off for the virgin Wisconsin prairie where he gave agriculture another try. Life was not altogether tame — during a run-in with an Indian he was shot — but farming also tied a man down, and in 1844 he started West again, joining an Oregon-bound caravan at Independence, Missouri.

At Fort Bridger Clyman and three others, having no families or wagons, went on ahead, with all their worldly goods either on them or on their pack horses. They reached Oregon City October 13, almost a month before the first wagons arrived.

Clyman wasn't happy in Oregon City. He had never seen a more discontented community, he wrote. Instead of talk about settling on the land he found people itching to move on to new and exotic places, including the Hawaiian Islands and Chile. Most of the emigrants, he observed, were of the same roving character he was; they had been disquiet back East and they weren't any more stable here. If anything, the Oregon Trail had made them even more restless; now they had the added incentive and confidence of knowing what they could withstand and achieve.

The next spring Clyman led a large contigent of the antsy down to California. A year later he was off to the States, horsebacking all the way. But the "old country" was too domesticated now and Clyman still had sand in his shoes. In 1848 he was back in California. He never set foot in Oregon again.

Married in 1848, Clyman spent the remainder of his life toiling on his farm near Napa. The many years of his nomadic existence had taken from him all his wanderlust; where before he could not reconcile himself to cultivating the land, he now applied himself with unflinching fidelity.

He died in 1881, nearing ninety, one of the last of the Mountain Men and having completely outlived his times. He had seen the vanishing of the buffalo and the beaver from the plains and the mountain streams he

Mt. Hood

knew so well. The trails he had blazed were obliterated by good wagon roads and steel rails. Could he have imagined when he came upon South Pass in 1824 that less than half a century later you could go by railroad from New York City to San Francisco Bay? Cities covered many of his once remote and dangerous campgrounds. Even California had changed! The Gold Rush had become a romanticized chapter of history; the sprawling ranches of the Mexican Land Grants were being cut up; farms were moving in on valleys that only twenty years before had been huge cattle ranches.

He had seen the coming of the steamboat, smoke signals had given way to the telegraph and the telephone, and in the year of his death the first central electric power plant in the world began operation at New York's Pearl Street. It was a time out of mind, a furious rush of events, and difficult, though hard he tried, for a man who had lived so close to the grain of nature to comprehend it all.

If we are to go by his writings, Clyman's stay in Oregon was not unpleasant, despite his observations of Oregon City. In a notation titled "Oct. 25, 1844, *Shores of the Willamette*," he wrote:

> ". . . These pools or ponds are now overgrown with several kind of vegitation and litterly and completely covered over with

water fowl of various kinds from the nobl and majestick swan down to the Teal & plover. For miles the air seemed to be darkened with the emmence flights that arose as I proceeded up the valley. The morning being still thier nois was tumultuous and grand. The hoars shrieks of the Heron intermingled with the Symphonic Swan the fine treble of the Brant answered by the strong Bass of the goose with ennumerable shreeking and Quacking of the large and Smaller duck tribe filled every evenue of Surrounding space with nois and reminded one of Some aerial battle as discribed by Milton and all though I had been on the grand pass of waterfowl on the Illinois River it will not begin to bear a comparison with thier being probably Half a Million in sight at one time and appearantly Screaming & Screeching at once."

It was a scene to delight the heart of a Mountain Man.

The inside back cover of James Clyman's Diary, 1844-46, bears this bit of verse, titled

POESY BY A NATIVE

The Firrs their length their Extreme hight
As yet remains in doubt
But tradition throws an obscur light
That many had grown Quite out of sight
Ere Hood began to Sprout.

That was the Mountain Man tongue in cheek. But there is no doubting the sincerity and fervor of the poem he scribbled on the inside front cover of the same notebook. And here it is, James Clyman's bout with the English language as he soars off in classical eloquence:

AN ADDRESS TO MOUNT HOOD

Say mighty peak of tremendious hight
What brot you forth to etherial light
From Earths inmost deepest womb
Was central earth so Jamd so pent
That thou arose to give it vent
Or for some other purpose sent
A Monumental tomb

To shew that once in Licquid heat
The Earth had flowed a burning sheet
Of melted wavering fire
That animation Flaming lay
A molten Mixed was rocks and clay
When thou a bubble rose to play
Above the funeral pyre.

That Wonderful Ingleside Farm

God forbid that I should go to any heaven in which there are no horses.

Robert B. Cunninghame-Graham

Because we asked at the Ingleside Farm how to reach a small cemetery we had spied on a hill we found a rich lode of agricultural lore and a calendar art scene of the nineteenth century.

One look and we knew we had come upon something good; a second look and we changed the good to wonderful. For me there was here the most diverse and integrated collection of old agricultural implements and horse-drawn vehicles I had seen on any farm in the state. And we met, in the Rumgay family, the kind of hard-working, cheerful, neighborly folks you mostly encounter only in farm legends.

Everything smacked of nostalgia. There was the barn: immense, solid, a sturdy grandfather glad to receive visitors, suffused with the hearty odors of hay, manure, horseflesh, the coat of rain on old wood, wheel grease, and the aging of tools. And the wagons: right out of Currier and Ives. And the implements, associated with the horse days. And the paraphernalia used for hitching horses to wagons and plows. And the draft horses themselves, powerful Belgians weighing up to a ton each. If Budweiser suggests Clydesdales, the Rumgay Belgians pointed to plows, which is what they were chiefly used for, plowing.

Overseeing all was the ever-poised, mild-mannered Monte Rumgay, who for more than fifty years plowed with, worked and trained horses and mules. He was sold on horses as the tractors of the future, as they were of the past before tractors came along.

"Just look at the simple arithmetic," he said matter-of-factly, as though telling you it might rain tomorrow. "On a small farm, say of fifty acres, two horses can do the job. For 100 acres, you need three. You can't get a good all-purpose tractor to work a small farm for less than $10,000 — and that's cheap. You might have to pay up to $15,000. For that money you can get a trained pair, or three, of Belgians, Suffolks, Shires, Clydesdales or Percherons.

"That's just the start," Rumgay went on quietly, speaking in a smile and pleased to educate his city visitors. "Fuel prices are way up. If a tractor breaks down, repair bills are high. Replacements can put you in the red. But take horses. You don't have to worry about a fuel shortage with them. They reproduce themselves; that's something a tractor can't do. If

Monte Rumgay and friends

they come down sick, they generally heal themselves. Their feed is home-grown; all the hay you see here comes from this land. And they provide fertilizer, which enriches the soil."

Rumgay waited patiently until my writing had caught up with his talking, and then he continued his lesson in farm economics:

"You can get fourteen or sixteen years' good work out of each of these horses. And with hardly any maintenance." He laughed and tugged on an overall strap. "That's pretty good, isn't it? Show me a tractor that will give the same performance."

Monte Rumgay had another reason for preferring horses over tractors. Tractors force a man's insides to speed up, to keep his system in high gear, he said, scratching the side of his baseball cap. Farmers wear out about in proportion to their equipment; they last longer with horses. Maybe it was the slower pace, or the communion with other living things, or the exercise behind the plow. Walking behind a plow exercised the whole body and gave peace of mind, Rumgay said, looking meditative. It was apparent that for him the subject of horses versus tractors was not a problem in micrology; the matters and differences were beyond the trivial and petty.

In recent years a still small but significant number of people, especially the young who have taken up farming as a back-to-nature lifestyle, have turned to horses to do the heavy work and the draft animals are at a premium. In 1970, a pair of Belgians could be bought for $500; six years later the price had jumped to as high as $5,000. Over that period of time the price for a top-grade Belgian weanling rose from $300 to $900. But even at these figures, Rumgay considered the horses far better buys than tractors.

Several times thereafter I returned to the Ingleside Farm. I always found it an inspiriting place for writers of the bucolic scene and each time I thought that a fictioneer would find this a rewarding range for horse stories. Indeed, a rather undefined vestigial honesty compels me to say that I came back for the horses above all else, including the ever-gracious, always patient, wise and good-humored Monte Rumgay and his cordial family.

The capillary attraction of the horses for me dates back to my childhood in Chicago. I remember — I actually do — horse-drawn engines racing to fires. I was quite small then, but so impressionable, too, that the sight of nostrils furiously sucking wind, foaming manes frozen in flight, and hooves clattering swiftly, desperately down the streets, some of them still cobblestoned, everlastingly seared itself into my memory.

Later, knocking around the country as a migratory worker, I as-

Two powerful Belgians thunder down cemetery road above Ingleside Farm, pulling Number 9 wagon of Seattle Fire Department built in 1909. Monte Rumgay at the reins. Passengers are sons Ken and Jim.

sociated vagabond life with such horse-related cameos as South Dakota Sioux riding in buckwagons from their reservation homes to a trading town; with windmills on the plains (in Eastern Oregon, too); with swamping rice sacks, pitching hay onto sleds, and stitching grain sacks; with loading boxes of apples on a sled the well-trained Nellie dragged through Mrs. Marsan's orchard across the Columbia from Wenatchee; with the thin, one-eyed mare that brought us fence posts to pound into holes we had dug in a small Idaho valley; with homes lit by lanterns and with party-line telephones; and with barns I curled up in, the nocturnal silence broken only by the chomping of horses.

So that's what I saw when I came to the Ingleside Farm and was greeted by the Belgians in their barn basement home, as coarse as peasants and as sleek as artistocrats. They moseyed methodically over, all good, well-behaved beauties, to inquire what was new, and after perhaps a moment of either diffidence or indifference, turned flank and lumbered back to their supper of delicious hay.

It was a delight to limn these horses: The only difficulty was to find words that hadn't been overused or, in the hands of rank and careless amateurs, abused. They were gentle, brawny heavyweights, linked to Monte Rumgay as part of the small fraternity of nature on the farm, giving back to earth what they took, and, when day was done, proud and content.

Twice Monte Rumgay hitched the horses to a dray wagon and off we went up the cemetery hill, the great horses turning corners with ballet precision and coming down the slope sure-footed, head high, ears alert, and responding quickly and easily to command.

Rumgay sought no meed of recognition for the barn or the wagons or the old catalog equipment or the horses. Fame was not his spur; wisdom alone was his inspiration and reward. He had been waist-high in the good life before others came to the fringes of it. And he knew that, for people like him, the way ahead was the road back.

Directions: At Carver, on Oregon 224, cross the Clackamas River bridge. Turn left onto County Road 28. 1.9 miles, on right, Ingleside Farm.

The Saga of Silverton Bobbie

I am quite sure he thinks that I am God –
Since he is God on whom each one depends
For life and all things that His bounty sends –
My dear old dog, most constant of all friends.

William C. Doane

Have you heard the incredible story of Silverton Bobbie?

I first did as a young boy finding adventure in a branch library in Chicago. Little did I dream that a full fifty years later I would spend an afternoon in the home of a woman whose family owned Bobbie and that I would find Bobbie's grave only a short drive from where I live in Portland.

It was in the library that I read *Bobbie, A Great Collie*, written by Charles Alexander and published in 1926. In 1976 I was loaned a manuscript upon which Alexander, a fine novelist of Albany, Oregon, partially based his book.

Let me tell you right out, simply and starkly, the bare-bone outlines of Bobbie's amazing feat. They are enough to make you doubt, reel in wonderment, and to stand your hair on end.

In the summer of 1923, when Bobbie was two years old, he was taken by Frank and Elizabeth Brazier, owners of the Reo Cafe, in Silverton, on a trip back East, where the Braziers planned to visit their families. In Wolcott, Indiana, Bobbie disappeared. After a frantic but fruitless search the Braziers gave up and continued their journey. Nine weeks after their departure from Silverton the Braziers returned home, convinced they would never see Bobbie again. Then, on a sunny midwinter day in 1924, Bobbie reappeared. He was thin, exhausted, his paws worn to the nub, and he was in pain — but he had come home.

Exhaustive research by the Oregon Humane Society proved that Bobbie had traveled 3,000 miles in his homeward quest.

The story of Bobbie's miraculous journey was flashed around the world. He was an instant celebrity and remained famous until his death. Ripley's *Believe It or Not* featured the collie in August 1924 as "Bobbie — the Prodigal Dog — Returned 3,000 miles across the continent *alone* . . ." A movie was made, starring the collie. Appropriately, it was titled *Bobbie, The Wonder Dog*. Bobbie's trek excited psychics and clairvoyants on four continents. The renowned Dr. J. B. Rhine, head of the Parapsychology Laboratory of Duke University, wanted to know everything the Braziers could tell him about their collie. To this day the mystery of how Bobbie returned home is still being pondered and explained. Other dogs, and cats, too, lost a long way from home had found their way back, but Bobbie's story remains a classic.

In the summer of 1975, while on one of my many visits to Silverton, I recalled Bobbie and set out to find where he was buried. It was a trying task. Finally, after several hours of being passed from one person to the next, I was advised to get in touch with Mrs. Leona Dickerson. A phone call quickly revealed that it was her family that had owned Bobbie and that she had much material on the dog. Since evening was setting in and I had to return to Portland, I asked if I could see her another time. Of course, she replied amiably, and invited me to lunch — "Just let me know in advance." Before we hung up I inquired, "Where is Bobbie buried?" "Oh," said Mrs. Dickerson, "in Portland, at the Oregon Humane Society."

The following day, in Portland, I drove to the Oregon Humane Society, at 1067 N.E. Columbia Boulevard, and found the grave of the collie under a marker that read: Bobbie of Silverton. Adjacent to the grave was "Bobbie's doghouse," which early in the spring of 1924 had been built for display at the Home Beautifying Exposition in the Portland Auditorium, where Bobbie was the honored guest of the Portland Realty Board. The "modern miniature bungalow" weighed about one hundred pounds and

Grave of Silverton Bobbie, in Portland

had eight windows, silk curtains, and drapes. It is doubtful that Bobbie ever used it. He was an aristocrat only in poise and appearance.

On Washington's Birthday in 1976 I was back at Silverton, to be greeted cordially in the unostentatious but comfortable home of Mrs. Dickerson and Clifton, her husband of fifty-four years. She spread upon a large table a heap of scrapbooks, none of which she had looked at for years, she said. And yet what she had was only a small fraction of the material Bobbie's family had accumulated on the collie. The remainder had been divided between Mrs. Dickerson's sister and the children and grandchildren of both women.

How do we begin with so vast an array, this fraction of the total possessed by Leona Dickerson? The best place to start, I think, is with the manuscript written for Charles Alexander. Either Alexander had returned the letter or a member of Mrs. Dickerson's family had made a copy. It seems to me the former is true.

Herein, backgrounding Bobbie's heroic and almost unbelievable migration, is the account, as written by G. F. Brazier, Mrs. Dickerson's stepfather, who married her mother when Leona was eighteen:

> We — my two stepdaughters (Nova and Leona Baumgarten), my wife (Elizabeth), and myself (Frank as I'm best known) — were living on a rented farm on the Abaque [a creek outside Silverton] when we bought Bobbie — a natural-born bob-tailed Scotch Collie who is about one-third shepherd — when he was six months old. Naturally, we all loved him as he was a full-of-fun puppie.
>
> At this time we had a small white fox terrier that we had brought with us when we came to Oregon from Indiana in July of 1919. We made this trip by auto and worshipped our little dog Toodles for his watchfulness and faithfulness during our trip, before and after. But Toodles had become paralyzed for lack of exercise while we lived in Salem, where there is an ordinance prohibiting dogs from leaving their master's grounds. We nursed Toodles back to as near health as possible. Bobbie learned to love Toodles as much as we did.
>
> The farm we lived on was hops so we all worked in the hop fields. Bobbie and Toodles had rollicking times. Bobbie was a natural heeler; when just a couple of months old he would heel anything — cats, horses, people, etc.
>
> We moved often, as we were working out-of-doors to regain health. One place we moved to, Bobbie helped bring in the horses and he heeled once a little too heavy. The horse sent Bobbie a-sailing in air but just as soon as Bobbie realized what had happened he was right after the horse again. This episode left a scar over Bobbie's eye, which we used as one of his identifications.
>
> The next place we were on was a fruit farm. They used a tractor there and they kept the ground cultivated smoother and softer than most gardens. One day Bobbie was taking a nap and the tractor came pounding over him but the ground was culti-

vated so well that it was soft and the tractor just mashed him into the ground, not hurting him much, but leaving another identification mark.

Another time he was digging for a gopher and during his battle with the gopher he broke off parts of two teeth, and this was his third identification mark.

When Bobbie was little better than a year old Toodles had another stroke and we had to have him chloroformed and we buried him on the farm. About this time we bought the Reo Cafe in Silverton, and realizing we had no place to keep a dog in town we sold Bobbie to a friend who was to live on the farm we were leaving.

Bobbie soon located us and would come in to town every weekend. Then on Monday morning he would go back to the farm.

He kept this up until August of 1923 when my wife and I decided to go back East on a visit and take Bobbie with us. We bought him back for three times the amount we had received for him and started on our way in our Overland Red Bird car, leaving Silverton August 6, 1923. Bobbie rode on the running board or in the back seat on top of the luggage. He enjoyed the trip as much or more than the Mrs. or myself. He would jump off the running board and scramper out after a rabbit, sometimes being gone for an hour or two. He loved to roam over the hills.

Wolcott, Indiana was the first place we stopped to visit. This was August 15th. I left my wife at our friends' home and Bobbie and I went up to the filling station to get tanked up. While in there I heard Bobbie give a yelp. Rushing out I just saw him rounding a corner with three or four dogs at his heels and growling and barking, but thinking he would take care of himself, as like always, I paid little attention to him. I thought he must have gone to our friends' home where the Mrs. was. But when I got there and no Bobbie we became alarmed and began looking for him and called up everybody that had a telephone, but to no avail. So we advertised in the Wolcott paper for him, leaving the advertisement in while we went farther east and through Indiana and into Ohio, but when we returned to Wolcott, homeward bound, they had not seen or heard of Bobbie. We left with the promise that they would ship Bobbie out to us if they ever found him.

That was the last we saw of Bobbie until February 15, 1924, when Nova and a girl friend were walking down the street of Silverton. All of a sudden Nova seized her girl friend by the arm and said, "Oh look — isn't that Bobbie?", and at the word Bobbie flew at Nova and lavished her with kisses.

Nova couldn't believe it but she brought Bobbie home, and when he came into the restaurant he hunted out Leona and the Mrs., out of the ten that are employed, not paying any attention to the rest of the help. But he wasn't satisfied; there was someone else, so the Mrs. and Nova brought him upstairs to my room where I was sleeping (as I was working nights in the cafe.) They called into my room, "Look who's here!" I was half sleeping. Looking up, I couldn't believe my own eyes — for there *was* Bobbie. When he saw me he bathed me with kisses. After he was through with this he fell on the rug by my bed, so tired and worn, refused to leave the room, so they let him sleep there, and when I awoke he was giving my feet, which happened out from under the sheet, a tongue licking.

I took him downstairs and he went to the door leading to the basement, where his old bed was. I took him down there and gave him a sirloin steak and a pint of cream. After this he lay in his bed and didn't want to be disturbed for days. When we would go down there he would look at a person so pitiful as if to say, "Can't you do something for me?"

He wanted to eat nothing but raw meat when he first returned, showing that he must have lived largely on raw meat of his own catches. We took him out to the farm where we formerly lived. Just drove up into the yard, he jumped off the car and went to where his old bed had been on the porch, then started to the door. All of a sudden he seemed to think of something, and he literally flew out back to the barn. We followed him and when we got back there we just gasped. What do you think we saw? Bobbie was just digging away as hard as he could, trying to get

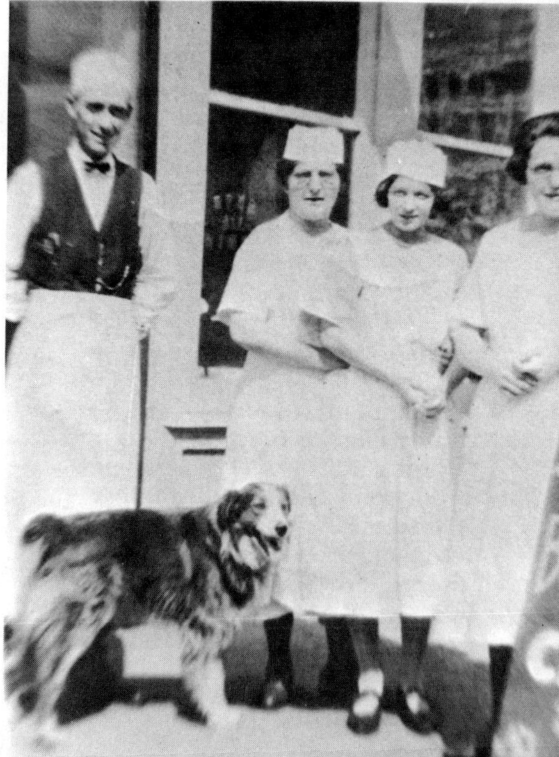

Courtesy of Leona B. Dickerson

Bobbie in front of the Reo Cafe with his family a few weeks before the Braziers began their trip. L to R: Frank Brazier, Elizabeth Brazier, Nova Baumgartner, Leona Baumgartner.

down to Toodles. If anyone could have seen that scene they never again would doubt it not being Bobbie. It certainly was heartbreaking to see him and he had such a pitiful look.

Leona Dickerson remembered the homecoming scene a bit differently:

"The sun was shining and my Sis and her friend were out walking. All of a sudden my sister stopped and said to her friend, 'Isn't that Bobbie? Bobbie!' she called. The dog came to her and jumped up on her as much as he could; he was pretty weak.

"They brought him to the restaurant. He came to me and put his paws on me. He singled me out. Then he went into the kitchen and found my mother. My mother said, 'Let's see if he can find father.' She opened the door at the bottom of the stairs that led to the apartment upstairs where the family lived and Bobbie went up and entered the room where Mr. Brazier was taking a nap and he jumped right on the bed and whined, like a dog would. Then we knew it was Bobbie for sure; it couldn't be a strange dog."

Two lumber mills were operating around the clock in Silverton, and the Reo Cafe was almost always full to capacity. That day, that hour, the place was packed. (Among the many diners may have been Clark Gable, later a movie celebrity. He was living in Silverton then and took all his meals at the Reo.)

"Well," Mrs. Dickerson said to me, "when you've got a bunch of people in the restaurant and something like this happens, the news spreads fast. Pretty soon the whole town knew it and then it was in the paper and after that it was one story after another and the mail poured in. The publicity overwhelmed us. We never dreamed so many people would be interested. As for Bobbie, he stayed close and everyone in the family kept him close."

The first burst of publicity was followed by letters from scores of people who said they had seen Bobbie on a road or in a town or had given the collie shelter and food. After intensive investigation, Charles Alexander and the Oregon Humane Society established certain facts: Bobbie did not accept rides, part of his diet came from small animals he caught (as wolves do), and someone or some ones had tried to keep him, against his will. Most important, through verifying the claims of the observers and Good Samaritans, Bobbie's long, punishing pursuit homeward was traced.

For several days he prowled around Wolcott, beleaguered by dogs of town and country, who made him their target. He survived only because of his speed, strength and fighting ability. Then, surmising that his friends had gone elsewhere, he started northeastward. At Wolcotville, eighty miles as the crow flies from Wolcott, he stayed a week at the home of a hardware clerk. As suddenly as he had come he left, heading west.

Bobbie was now threshing about blindly, as he would yet for months. Before he had gone far west he turned south and reached the rim of Indianapolis. Someone saw him swim the White River, near there, and on the western bank some hobos welcomed him to their jungle. They, too, were wanderers; they, too, had known furtive living and awakenings from hunger and a weariness so complete they could not drag themselves a step onward. They fed him out of their mulligan cans and they let him lie: They had no rules for him which they did not apply to themselves; he would go when he was ready. Later, after he had returned home, Bobbie was by chance to encounter one of the bindle stiffs who had comraded him. Recognition came easily and gratitude was fulsome.

Now he started northwest, swimming the Wabash and Tippecanoe rivers. It is possible he searched Wolcott again before veering west. There are no valid reports of him in Illinois, but Illinois he must have crossed, and somehow he made it to the other side of the Mississippi River, for he is next at Vinton, Iowa, where the familiar sound of a horn prompted him to bound into a car. He found no one he knew, but the people took him home, where Bobbie scoured the house from top to bottom. Crushed in disappointment, he crumbled, spiritless, to the floor.

The people at Vinton were kind to him; he could have stayed, but after food and a night's rest he pushed on. About a week before Thanksgiving he is in Des Moines. There he takes up temporary residence at the abode of Ida M. Plumb at 1333 Penn Avenue. He does it in his usual friendly fashion, offering his paw to shake and then quietly going to sleep.

Something is strange in Des Moines; Bobbie cannot fathom it. The next morning he finds a tourist camp only a few blocks from the Plumb home, and visits there every day for several days. Ida Plumb thinks maybe he has been lost from there. She inquires, but no one knows. Then she tries various names on him, and when she comes to Bob he responds best.

One day after breakfast Bobbie leaves as usual, and when afternoon and evening pass and he does not return Ida Plumb is sure he has left for good. But a few days later he is back. The heavy strap collar with which he came is gone; in its place is a much lighter collar, and attached to it is a fragment of rope. Someone had tried to keep Bobbie.

In Iowa the collie is trapped by the roughness of his instincts. They have not yet been sharply honed. He trots and walks at least two hundred miles out of his way before making a fresh start at Des Moines. The day after Thanksgiving Bobbie takes his final departure from the Plumb house. Six days later he is in Denver. In less than a week he has gone twice the distance west as he has traveled west in the preceding three months and three weeks. Bobbie now knows where he is headed: He has nothing to fear, though he may not sense it, except cold rivers at angry swirl, predators, high mountains deep under snow, frost that will pierce him to the marrow, and dogcatchers who will try to cage him.

His route to Denver is largely unknown. Alexander writes, perhaps fictionalizing, that, trapped on the Missouri River bridge by men who beat him and aimed to kill him, Bobbie pulled free in one last desperate effort and plunged into the river. And there is surmise that the collie crossed the North Platte by bridge, when no one was looking.

Bobbie had his own good reason for picking out 2110 Gaylord Street as an inn of hospitality in Denver. Carrie Abbee recalled: "(He) ran up to our car as we were driving into the garage and seemed very happy to see us. He went into the house, had dinner and slept in the den in the basement all night. He was a very nicely behaved dog and seemed very tired, in fact exhausted, was dusty and had burrs in his hair. We spoke of his being so tired and that he looked as though he had a long hike. We lost our fourteen-year-old collie in September, of old age, and hoped this one would stay with us, but in the morning he did not even wait for his breakfast."

From Denver it took Bobbie about six weeks to reach the Columbia River in Oregon. The best guess is that he drifted northwest across Wyoming and Idaho, crossing the Rocky Mountains and the Green River. It is fair to speculate, I think, that he found U.S. 30, the Lincoln Highway, over which the Braziers had driven on their way to Indiana.

There is no accounting for Bobbie on this stretch of the journey. He must have faced innumerable difficulties, including the weight of fatigue from long uphill climbs and churning through soft snow. Perhaps here and there he stayed a few days with a sympathetic sheepherder or rancher or a lonely couple running an outpost store. It seems inconceivable that no one along his route read the story of his odyssey. We can only conclude that the people who succored Bobbie were not the kind given to letter writing or else — and this is enough to tingle you in fear and awe — Bobbie dodged all humans and lived as best he could off the land. If we accept the latter mode of existence, he must have spent as much time hunting as he did traveling.

Somehow he crosses the Snake River, if not by bridge than by heroic swim. And he is in Oregon, and down off the Blue Mountains he finds the Columbia River. What do his eyes tell him? Does his nose remember the aroma of wheatland and sage? What is it he has stored in his memory bank to push him down the shoulder of the road?

At The Dalles he paused to solicit a meal. Beyond the Columbia River Gorge he felt the first breath of spring and knew the mountains were behind him. He was in lowland country, and somewhere in that great green expanse was home. It could not be far off, and he gritted on. But in Portland, where he turned south on 82nd Street off Sandy Boulevard, his strength gave out. At nine o'clock in the morning he crawled up to the back porch of a modest house on S.E. 75th Street.

Bobbie was lucky. With life giving out, he could not have found a better person in all Portland to care for him than Mary Elizabeth Smith, a pudgy white-haired widow who had Ireland in her soul and love in her heart. He was, right off, "Poor darling" to her, and she tended Bobbie as though he were a child of her own in misery.

He lay helpless, his legs swollen, cut and gashed; the toe pads worn away so that the bone was exposed; the feet bloody. His coat was ragged and matted with dirt, his eyes swollen. All day she nursed him, soaking and cleaning his paws and then layering them with warm paraffin, washing his eyes, soothing his coat, cuddling his as she would a child, stroking him and singing to him Irish lullabies. He was too feverish for food; he wanted only water, and she kept the bowl full. At dusk Bobbie arose stiffly, hobbled to the door, and looked up. Mrs. Smith understood. She opened the door and watched Bobbie limp down the path and turn south.

She was to see her adored stranger once after that. It was at the Portland Auditorium, where Bobbie was on display at the Home Beautifying Exposition. Back among the thousands stood an ailing Mrs. Smith, telling a friend that she knew Bobbie, that he had come to her house.

Somehow the friend cleared a way and guided Mrs. Smith past the woven wire barricade put up to protect the collie from the throngs who pushed to pet and pinch him. (So many had that he was sore.) Bobbie was tired of the crowds; he had not recovered; his stamina was of short duration. One wonders what stupidity, or pressure, or greed or hunger for publicity had driven Frank Brazier to place the dog in such a vulnerable and torturous position. Mrs. Dickerson told me that Brazier was paid only a hundred dollars for the ordeal Bobbie suffered. He did not need the money; he was about to sell the cafe at a fine price. Bobbie wanted nothing more than to escape his tormentors; he looked at them with eyes of weariness and fear, but when he saw Mrs. Smith he flew to her, barking shrilly, and as the Good Samaritan held him in her arms, muttering through choked throat, "Poor darling," they sobbed together.

It took the great collie two weeks to make it from Mrs. Smith's home in Portland to Silverton. Very probably he followed in reverse the route the Braziers had taken: through Oregon City, New Era, Canby, Barlow, Aurora, Hubbard, Woodburn, Townsend, McKee and Mount Angel. Six months to the day he last saw the Braziers back in Wolcott, Indiana he heard Nova call his name.

The first wave of acclaim was followed by a seemingly never-ending high tide of publicity. Those who gave Bobbie medals were repaid by

Courtesy Mrs. Leona Dickerson

Bobbie on luggage rack of Overland Red Bird the day Mr. and Mrs. Brazier took off for Indiana, where Bobbie was lost.

reams of press coverage that gold couldn't have bought. The officials of Silverton presented Bobbie with the key to the city and saw to it that photos of the ceremony were distributed far and wide. The naïve Frank Brazier and the suffering dog were handled as commodities on the stock market. It actually cost Brazier good money to have the collie star in the movie, *Bobbie, The Wonder Dog,* an undertaking Brazier did not ask for and was conned into helping make.

Practically every newspaper in the United States, from the most prestigious dailies to obscure weeklies tucked away between a bayou and a cotton patch, ran stories on the phenomenal homing instinct of Bobbie. Around the rest of the world the coverage was almost as great. A flood of requests for photos swamped the Braziers. Typical was one from an editor of the New York *Evening Journal*: "Will you please rush me special delivery a picture of your dog 'Bob.' " Some people sent money to cover the cost of the photos desired. Mrs. Dickerson showed me an uncashed check for fifty cents.

A broad spectrum of magazines, from *Popular Mechanics* to religious organs, carried stories on Bobbie. Some writers practically made a vocation of the subject, grinding out copy day and night to cash in on the demand. (As late as 1976 stories on Bobbie were still appearing. By then most had the facts twisted, but that didn't dampen reader interest.)

Letters arrived from every part of every state in the Union and from all continents. Some were addressed to Brazier; others to "Bobbie The Wonder Dog Silverton, Oregon"; and even those that bore no other address but Bobbie, Oregon, found their way to Silverton, so renowned had his name become. Thousands of children wrote, some of them vowing they would have taken the long journey with him. And among the "correspondents" were pets who "asked" to become pen pals. Bobbie had proxies of friendship from the owners of dogs, cats, parrots, goldfish, goats and calves.

Some people wrote prayers, others hosannas, and quite a lot of poetry turned up. All kinds of gifts arrived, including a package of dried flowers from Australia.

Quickly Bobbie grew into more than a story. He became a creed of courage, an example of perseverance, an inspirational message for the starry-eyed and heart-fallen. Sermons were given on Bobbie's devotion and unconquerable spirit; scriptures were cited to illustrate the moral of his fidelity and tenacity. Schoolteachers read aloud to their students from articles written about Bobbie. People whose dogs didn't show proper affection or couldn't find their way home from the nearest mailbox would plaintively ask, "Why can't you be like Bobbie?"

Times were not altogether bad for the collie. He romped with his family in the woods and the fields, always vigilant and sensitive. On one outing he pointed to the body of a suicide obscured in a clump of underbrush. No one suspected a corpse was there until Bobbie's urgent barks and furious diggings finally moved someone to suspicion. He sired fifteen sons and daughters, some every bit as handsome as he. But his life ended far sooner than it should have.

Early in March of 1927 he came down sick and was taken to Rose City Veterinary Hospital in Portland. There Brazier was told that the strain of the arduous journey had finally caught up with Bobbie. He died on April 6 and was buried on the grounds of the Oregon Humane Society.

Mrs. Dickerson still thought the Humane Society "wanted him for political purposes." Thus, even in death Bobbie was, real or fanciful, a pawn of publicity-seekers.

From the sorrowful mail that descended upon Silverton you would have thought that a great human being had passed away. Well, a great heart did stop beating — and for thousands there was anguish. Bobbie had come to mean more to some people, who never saw him, than anyone knew. Perhaps the best example of the tearful sentiments was a heart-rending poem I found in a scrapbook:

IN MEMORY OF BOBBIE

Dead, and my heart's died with him.
Buried, what love lies there.
Gone forever and ever,
No longer my life to share.

Only a dog; yes! only
Yet these are bitter tears.
Weary and heartsick and lonely,
I turn to the coming years.

Bobbie, who always loved me,
Bobbie, whom I could trust,
Bobbie who soothed and cheered me,
Lies mouldering here to dust.

When I started to track down the saga of Bobbie I found that only the old-timers of Silverton had heard of the collie, and no one knew where he was buried until I was directed to Mrs. Dickerson. A few people who had lived in Silverton for ten or fifteen years had heard vaguely of Bobbie. None of the newer residents knew of the epic tale.

"There are so many new faces in town," said Mrs. Dickerson. "We hardly know anybody now. When we walk downtown we feel like we're strangers. Silverton has changed so much in the last five or six years."

Her husband, Clifton, shook his head sadly and added: "Maybe letters still come, but we don't get them. I don't think the people in the post office ever heard of Bobbie."

A Requiem for Homer

This be the verse you 'grave for me:
Here he lies where he long'd to be.

Robert Louis Stevenson, *Requiem*

Homer Calvin Davenport, Oregon's cartoonist and the only Oregon cartoonist to achieve an international reputation, was a perfect example of the old saw, "You can take the boy of the country but you can't take the country out of the boy." All his life Davenport had an abiding passion for the small town and the gentle rural area he knew as a youth.

Courtesy Oregon Historical Society
Homer Davenport

Homer Davenport panel in Geer House

Once he wrote: "The strangest part of Silverton is that it never releases me a day from its hold. A day never passes that I don't hurry over its streets, see its remaining pioneers and in my vision replace those that have gone. . . . I have thought of it while seated in the ruins of the Coloseum at Rome, thought of it in London and Paris and Constantinople, thought of it while resting in the deathlike silence and shadow of the Sphinx, and told it near the Euphrates River in Arabia, while among the wild tribes of Anzeh."

He scribbled an even more poignant sentiment on a slab of lumber which is inserted on the west side of the Geer Crest Home, as it is formally called:

"I want to say that from this old porch I see my *favorite* view of all that the earth affords, it was the favorite of my dear Mother and her parents and of my Father and why shoudent it be the same to me its where my happiest hours have been spent. Homer Davenport. Apr 11-1904."

The view today is one of an undulating sea of gracefully contoured mounds that have been given the name of Waldo Hills, after Daniel Waldo, who settled in these parts late in 1843. When the land is green, a rich, shimmering green, and you can see the valley roll before you, as a billowy sea under a light breeze, the immense beauty and serenity of the scene is both piercing and softly fulfilling. How much keener the beauty must have been in Davenport's boyhood, before telephone poles and automobiles and airplanes and seed burning.

Riding Whip Tree

Homer was born in 1867 in a house which lasted a hundred years longer before being devoured by flames in 1972. He spent much of his growing up in the home of his grandparents, the Geers, about half a mile from his birthplace.

The Geer house had been built on an 1847 land grant by Ralph Carey Geer, an uncle of Theodore Thurston Geer, the tenth — and first Oregon-born — governor of the state. Homer's mother was Ralph's daughter. She married T. W. "Tim" Davenport, a promising young man who had been born in New York, practiced medicine in Ohio, and arrived in Oregon in 1851. (By coincidence, this was the same year Ralph C. Geer built his house and T. T. Geer was born.) Davenport made a name for himself in his new home, becoming a successful farmer, Marion County surveyor, two-term state representative, state senator, state land agent, and writer.

In 1853, when Homer's mother, Florinda, whom the family called Flora, was a young lady, she went off to a camp meeting at Turner. Coming home, her beau dismounted and cut off a branch of a balm of Gilead tree and gave it to Flora to use on her horse, who saw no point in moving faster than a slow shuffle. Then he cut off a branch for himself. When the couple reached her home they planted the branches by an irrigation ditch. Her father yanked out the branch her beau planted but let hers stand. Today the Riding Whip Tree is more than eighty feet tall.

Alongside the youthful tree Homer played and later, when he gained fame and returned to visit, he liked to rest in its shade. It was another strong touch of home and family.

Davenport, who died in New York City at the age of forty-five, is buried in the Silverton Cemetery. The inscription on his tombstone bears the adoring tribute: "Erected by his friends in the memory of Oregon's world-renowned Cartoonist."

Maybe Homer would have had it otherwise. Being a simple fellow and free of vanity, and being one of the people and an offspring of pioneers, he might have wanted an epitaph that read:

Far and wide did I roam
But now I'm glad I'm home.

Directions: From downtown Silverton, follow East Main St. out on county road bound for Sublimity. 5.1 miles, Sunnyview Rd. Turn right. 0.2 mile, lane to Geer house.

A Name for Opal Creek Falls

They have no names. They cannot be found on any map. No trails lead to them.

These are the waterfalls I first heard about from Ray Haines, who had found them while stumbling through the woods in search of a good fishing hole.

"If there wasn't any water," he wrote me, "I think the lava flow that created the falls is something to see."

My friends at the U.S. Forest Service regional headquarters in Portland knew nothing of the falls. Neither did the people in charge of Willamette National Forest, where the falls are located. The head of the Detroit Ranger Station, not too far from the falls, had never been to them, nor had any of his men.

So concealed are the falls, probably the most inaccessible in the state, that I doubt that more than a dozen people have looked upon them.

It would be rather difficult to reach the falls, wrote Ray Haines. "Due to the high altitude and rough going I would not advise anyone to make the trip that was not in good shape." So I gathered some stalwarts to accompany me on the safari: Chuck Allen, Marc Krieger, Pat Horrocks and her husky football-playing son, Scott, and Pat Kimoto, all of whom had exhibited stamina, perseverance, and high spirits as past members of my Oregon for the Curious class. My wife came along, too, but her legs had been hurting for some days, and she did not take the plunge into the wilderness.

At his home in Salem we took aboard Ray Haines, a tall, broad-shouldered, slightly stooped, gentle man of eighty-four. All his life he had worked with his hands, mostly out of doors, and he had all the signs of a man close to nature and familiar with toil. "I'm all set and ready to go," he smiled. And he had with him a rope, because we would have to go down a steep, almost vertical incline, to reach the middle of the three falls. He also thought he might use it for measuring. He and a friend had measured the middle falls with a rope but Ray wanted to be exact about the vertical height, and that was one reason he was glad to show us the way. "I would need more help to get it right," he had written me. "I would have to set a level on top of the cliff and send up a balloon from the bottom." (At my suggestion Chuck Allen also brought a rope, of nylon, which we used in crossing some bogs.)

East of Elkhorn we stopped on a dirt road and made our last preparations. I had been here before, to hike to Phantom Natural Bridge, to

The exploring party for the falls of Opal Creek. Left to right: Ray Haines, Scott Horrocks, Marc Krieger, Chuck Allen, Pat Kimoto, Ralph Friedman and Pat Horrocks.

the south, and from near here I had gone to Dog Tooth Rock, both minor landmarks of interest in the forest, but never had I been to the falls or even to Opal Lake, a blue shimmer in a green basin to the north.

We started carefree down a scuffed-out path that dropped precipitously into a maw of trees that shook their branches in welcome, like friendly puppies ecstatic in greeting any stranger who comes to the door. We would remember that naked steep slope when, in the heat of later afternoon, we had to pause for rest.

It took us thirty minutes to reach Opal Lake, and we did not dally. A dry thread of a path through the woods grew moist and then was swallowed up in marshland. Still, we could tell where others had disturbed the wild. Exuberant, we arrived at Opal Lake yet fresh.

Three young people were rafting on the lake and when they came close we called out, "Which way to the falls?" "What falls?" they replied. They had not gone further than Opal Lake.

"We'll find them," Ray Haines said firmly. He was using a limb as a cane now, to steady himself. But before we left the lake he wanted to tell us something about the falls. Opal Creek arises from a spring in the hills east of the basin, flows through Opal Lake, and erupts into the three-level falls. About five miles from the lower falls, Opal Creek unites with Battleaxe Creek to form the Little North Santiam River.

(You can take the process onward: The Little North Santiam empties into the North Santiam, the Santiam — comprised of the North and South forks — into the Willamette, the Willamette into the Columbia, the Columbia into the Pacific Ocean.)

From the left, or west side, of the lake, we had to push and slither our way through the thick, underbrush-heavy forest, everyone stumbling at least once or twice, and Ray Haines coming down hard several times. Each time he apologized, more concerned about our concern for him than for himself. It was not his age, he said. He still put in a good day's work, five days a week, and on the sixth chopped wood for the winter. On the seventh he went fishing or hiking. Two years ago he and a companion had made it to the falls and done fine; he did not know why the going was more strenuous today.

We tusseled through uncut stands of Douglas fir (some of the giant trees at least 400 years old, Ray Haines said), hemlock, cedar, Noble fir, anemone, rhododendron, fireweed, wild Canterbury bells, huckleberry bushes, Devil's club and salmonberry. "There is the way," Ray Haines spoke up, bent over now more than ever, but full of quiet confidence, and that is the way we went.

Opal Lake

Ralph Friedman

The upper falls of Opal Creek

At a huge outcropping of granite, a ponderous rock covered by a hairpiece of damp moss, Ray said, "We'll have to find a way over or around it." We did, through footwork that was not always deft and by using knobs of the rocky mass to pivot ourselves forward, and followed the dim chatter of the creek to the upper falls.

It seemed to some of us that the upper falls had a greater descent than the thirty-five or forty feet estimated by Ray Haines, but we were content to take his word. The water came leaping down, slapping and swishing and skipping down a scalloped cliff, free and without pose, an elfin heart performing for its own pleasure and to the delight of the forest animals who sipped from the creek.

I saw it another way too: as a trapeze artist warming up for the longer, more complicated leaps. Sixty feet from the bottom of the upper falls, the creek flung itself off a ledge and dived 225 feet, the way Ray measured, into a pool. From there, he said, it riffled 65 feet to another ledge, from which it catapulted another 225 feet or more, into a frothy basin. Then the stream shook itself out, regained its balance, and went swimming toward its union with Battleaxe Creek.

We saw the middle forks from above, clinging to trees that afforded us a vista and inching one by one out to the ledge, where we were held by a rope anchored to a friend on the bank above the trough at the bottom of the upper falls. Some of us crept and sidled as far along the knife-edge of a ridge as we could, and heard the thunder of the lower falls.

"Might as well get down to the big falls," said Ray, but as we started, expecting to backward crawl and rope our way down, for we could see there was no easy way to descend, Ray tumbled heavily, smashing a hand on a rock. The skin looked like bloody pulp and we wanted to bandage it but he shook off our entreaties. "It'll mend," he said. "Let's go."

We might have gone on — I was having second thoughts — if Ray had not twice more tripped, once to his knees and once stretched out. That was it. There was no point risking serious injury. We could have left him behind, but I was afraid. Someone could have kept him company, but if we continued it would be at least two more hours before we started back. I did not know what the two hours would do to him nor what he, restless still in spirit, would attempt. So I aborted the mission, and after Ray had stumbled a few times on the way back I put Marc Krieger in front of him and Scott Horrocks behind. By the time we reached the car, though, Ray was in great shape and talking about trying it again soon.

There was time for me to do some meditating on the hike back. What an unusual man I had met in Ray Haines. He was in the true mold of the American pioneer: the rangy trailblazer who had found a gap in the Appalachians to open up Kentucky and Tennessee, and broken the Santa Fe Trail, had discovered the open gate of South Pass through whose portals the caravans to Oregon and California had wheeled, and had quietly and anonymously changed the face of the nation. And he had seen eighty-four summers come and go — never forget that. At a time when most other men his age were waiting for a gust of wind to tip over the last slender reed of life in a nursing home, this man was still taking long steps, still exploring, still talking of undiscovered places and asking who was stout enough of heart to go with him. No, death would not easily carry him off; he would be a tiger to the end. "Before I go," he would say, pushing off the dark angel, "there is a creek deep in the woods nobody has followed from end to end, and I mean to do it."

Back on the road, we spoke of naming the falls. "I suggest Topaz, as there are two other names of semi-precious stones in the area, Pearl Creek and Opal Creek," said Ray. "That is a multiple fall and I believe the Topaz is a multicolored stone."

By the time you read this I'll probably have returned to the area, and this time climbed down to the middle and lower falls. I'll call them Haines — even if no one but me accepts the name. Topaz is fine, but the greatness of a man should be better remembered than a stone.

Directions: East from Mehama Jct. on Oregon 22. 0.8 mile, Elkhorn Jct. Turn north. 16.8 miles, forks. Take right, toward Opal Lake. 5.4 miles, forks. Turn left. 0.7 mile, forks. Take right. 4.3 miles, parking for Opal Lake. Take path on left, or north, for lake.

No More Elephants in the Bohemia

("Seeing the elephant" was a common expression during the California Gold Rush. It was used by luckless miners who despaired of ever striking it rich. Transported to California from the Southwest, the phrase was best defined by George Wilkins Kendall in his *Narrative of the Texas Santa Fé Expedition*, published in 1844: "When a man is disappointed in anything he undertakes, when he has seen enough, when he gets sick and tired of any job he may have set himself about, he has seen the elephant." The expression, though intimately identified with the California Mother Lode, did drift about the West and was still in occasional use well into this century.)

At the start of every term of the Oregon for the Curious class I teach for Portland Community College I discuss the interesting trips taken in the past. When I come to Bohemia, confusion descends on almost every face. At least half of each class consists of lifelong Oregonians and most of these people feel they have traveled widely around the state, yet it is an unusual class in which I find more than one person who has been to Bohemia.

Practically all the roads in the Bohemia mining district are dirt, and most of them narrow, and several of such sharp incline that some cars have a devil of a time making it — and yet the roads today are freeways compared to my first journey into those mountains.

I think I came to Bohemia the first time simply because I was young, foot-loose, high-spirited, unemployed, unafraid to go anywhere, and was offered the opportunity. It came about this way: I was hitchhiking through Cottage Grove one morning and, passing a filling station, stopped to ask a small, wiry man checking the frayed tires of his battered pickup if he was headed for Drain.

"Naw," he said, "I'm goin' up to Bohemia to bring my partner some victuals."

"Bohemia?" I asked. "Where's that?"

He pointed to a haze of mountains southwest. "Up there."

The spirit of adventure triggered my next question. "It is interesting?"

"Just old mining country," he replied, spitting out a wad of tobacco juice. "See for yourself if you want to."

I wanted to.

"Won't have much of a look," he warned. "I'm comin' right back."

"O.K. by me," I said. And we were off.

He was an out-of-work machinist, he told me, as he drove toward the hills. "Thirty years at it an' now I'm just garbage," he said bitterly. He and a friend were working an old mine and making wages, nothing more. "Some days we see the elephant but it beats starving."

That's what he told me. For all I know he may have been a bootlegger — but I was ready to take his word. By then I had learned that thousands of unemployed had gone into the deserted mining country of the West to scratch for beans and flapjacks. There was a time when I was ready to try it myself — but I gave it up for a cannery job, which was probably more profitable.

That overdriven, scarred pickup, that seemed to be held together by rusty wire and flabby rubber bands wheezed and stuttered and strained and coughed and balked and lunged as the driver cursed and wooed it up the grades.

Still, as I learned later, what we were bumping over was certainly an improvement on the original stage road. Early in the history of the Bohemia mining district the road ended at the Hawley Ranch, down below, and from there a pack trail plodded into the mines.

As late as 1898 it required travelers three days to reach the Musick Mine from Cottage Grove. They had to leave early in the morning to make the Hawley Ranch by nightfall of the first day. The second day they hauled themselves to Mineral. And on the third day they made the hard pull up Hardscrabble Grade, arriving exhausted.

Even today the six miles between Mineral and Bohemia Saddle, a mile from the Musick Mine, is known as Hardscrabble Grade. It took the early miners and freighters from four to eight hours to ascend this steep slope. (Coming down was faster but not much easier and even more dangerous.) Only four horses were needed to pull freight wagons from Cottage Grove to Mineral, but six- or eight-horse spans were required to get up Hardscrabble. The grade was one of the most difficult stretches of mountain road in all the mining West.

On one trip I led into Bohemia, a passenger looked out of her car window and, seeing nothing to the side of her but a ravine hundreds of feet below, almost fainted. For the next few miles she rode with her eyes closed. And I heard of a man who froze at the wheel on the hairpin curve of a precipice and had to give way to his wife, who up to then had driven the car only in the city. But it was do or die — and she did.

I thought of my friend the prospector and my daredevil ride with him when that one woman in our group came near panicking. If she had been with us that first day I think she would have left the car and crawled back to level ground. There were times when I could not tell whether we were completely on the road or had two wheels off it. Where there weren't any shoulders, such as rocky walls or trees or mine tailings, all I could see in looking out and down was the floor of the woods, at the other end of the world. My pilot, to whom despite its many problems the road was old hat, offered me a chew of his tobacco when he glanced at my pale and rigid face. One more suicidal curve and I would have taken it.

The history of the mining district goes back to 1858, when three Cottage Grove settlers discovered some placer dirt on Sharps Creek. The

Ralph Friedman

Lundberg Stage House, Bohemia

next year they returned, installed a sluice box, and made about as much money as they would have running a grocery store.

Gold-bearing quartz was not discovered until 1863 and then, of course, by accident. The finders were George Ramsey and James (sometimes referred to as John or Frank) Johnson, a native of Bohemia, which is how the mountain got its name. Supposedly fleeing from Roseburg after killing an Indian — legend and history are so confused and hazy here as to make "supposedly" the only honest word I know in this circumstance — Ramsey and Johnson groped their way into the wild, uninhabited Calapooya Mountains, traveling by way of the North Umpqua River and Steamboat and City creeks.

One day, while dressing a deer, Johnson's eye was caught by the glitter of gold. Picking up a chunk of the quartz he returned excitedly to join Ramsey at their makeshift camp. Neither man knew whether the stuff was genuine or just fool's gold. Putting aside fear of capture, if there was such, they determined to find out. The closest assay office was at Cottage Grove. Treading warily down the slopes they found the Coast Fork of the Willamette and followed it to town.

Sure enough, the ore was gold — and Cottage Grove was in a frenzy. No one thought of apprehending Johnson now, if indeed he was wanted;

gold outweighed murder. By the summer of 1864 prospectors were working a route along creeks and up the lower rises of the hills. By 1865 the big gold rush was on, with Argonauts huffing and puffing in from every direction.

Three years later Bohemia City had sprung up. It consisted of a hotel, a saloon, a recorder's office, and a scatter of cabins. It became the "step-off" place for the siting of claims, the locations fixed as to how far the claims were from Bohemia City. Soon the rude settlement in the wilderness was headquarters for miners who were sure they had found their bonanza. More than 2,000 separate claims were filed here. And anyone who called these hills the Calapooyas instead of the Bohemia Mountains was regarded as a rank greenhorn.

Still, it was not until 1890 that gold mining became big business. To their sorrow, prospectors discovered that the gold was not the kind found in rivers but was in mountain ledges of solid rock. A pick and shovel might bring a man a day's wages but not the sought-after fortune. Roads had to be built into the hills and over them was moved the machinery and equipment to get the ore out and reduce it to gold and other precious minerals.

From 1890 to 1910 many mines were opened and they boomed, assaying up to $30,000 a ton. Those were the two great decades. From then on, the going was downhill.

Looked at nationally, the Bohemia district was never a major mining field, even if the output of gold may have amounted to $11 million, eleven times as much as U.S. Mint figures estimated were extracted. (The difference between the two figures is simple to explain: Many mine owners never reported their gold at the assay office, but they did keep records of what they took out.)

The Bohemia country today is a rage of woods veined by cold creeks, a vast parade ground of wild flowers, terrain that catches at the throat, an infinity of panoramas, the rusty, rotting bits of the mining past (most of them off the road and reached only by four-wheel-drive vehicles), hillsides pockmarked by abandoned mines and, as you would expect, the usual tales of lost mines.

For what is actually still a primitive area, the Bohemia district has been well-marked with historical signs by the U.S. Forest Service. In addition, there are picnic areas, each of which gives you a feeling of Daniel Boone in the wilderness.

The Forest Service encourages visitors to "allow yourself a full day for the 70-mile trip so you can stop along the way and really enjoy your tour."

The best time to come is from mid-May to early October. Sometimes, though, there may be deep snow on the road as late as June and as early as September. I have known the touring season to be as short as three months, or less. If that bothers you, think how the miners felt.

Two places on the route attract most persons. Each is a bit off the main road and only about a mile from the other. From Fairview Peak you can on a clear day see the Three Sisters to the east, the Coast Range to the west, and, to the south, the mountains which rim the caldera of Crater Lake. And look closer, at Fairview Mountain itself. No less than 106 species of flora have been found on this craggy upthrust. Who would have thought you could meet here such shy darlings as celery-leaved lovage, owl's clover, curlybloom, northern wild licorice, meadow rue, St. John's wort, one-sided pyrola, golden chinquapin, elephant trunk and broad-leaved stonecrop?

There were once several settlements in the Bohemia district. The vestige of only one remains, at the Musick Mine, whose vein was discovered in 1891. After the mine was opened a narrow-gauge electric railroad ran between the Musick Mine and the ore mills at the head of Champion Grade. The auto road goes over part of the railroad. All that's left of the mine and the second Bohemia City are a mine shaft, a sagging cabin that may have already tumbled, an ore cart, some pilings, and the Lundberg Stage House, built in 1902.

The Lundberg place was home base for Alex Lundberg, who for many years hauled mail and freight to the Bohemia mines. In summer, wagons brought the freight here and pack horses took it on to the outlying areas. In winter the mail came in on skis. Here meals were served, beds were available upstairs, and the old-timers of the area congregated in the evening to swap small talk and tall tales.

Returning to Cottage Grove on that long-ago day with the lean prospector, I asked him about his philosophy of life. (I was young then and was always asking such deep questions, which I later learned were irrelevant in getting people to explain their behavior.) The driver was a good union man and had been in many a tough labor struggle. "I tell you," he said out of the corner of his mouth as he maneuvered the reluctant pick-up down a curvy, shivery grade, "some days I see the elephant but the way I figure it, there's only one way to live — take it easy, but take it."

And that's the best advice I can give in driving up and down and through and over the Bohemia mining district.

Directions: From Cottage Grove, go east on Main St. Follow street signs directing to Dorena Dam. 14.3 miles, Culp. 2 miles, Red Bridge Site. Turn right and follow historical markers.

Pioneers! O Pioneers!

Has the night descended?
Was the road of late so toilsome? did we stop discouraged nodding
on our way?
Yet a passing hour I yield you in your tracks to pause oblivious,
Pioneers! O pioneers!

Walt Whitman

About halfway between Drain and Yoncalla, on Oregon 99, there stands a historical marker about Jesse Applegate.

Anyone with even the most casual knowledge of Oregon history has heard of Jesse Applegate. From the time he came here, in 1843, at the age of thirty-two, until he faded from the limelight many years later, he was a man of force and prominence.

For some romanticists, Applegate is best identified with the Great Migration, probably because his long chronicle, "A Day with the Cow Column," which he wrote when his hair was graying, is regarded as a classic on the Oregon Trail. But that piece of writing about a most unusual wagon train is only a footnote to his life. In his prime he was one of the foremost movers and shakers of the state. His advice was sought on the monumental issues of the day and if his opinions were not entreated he gave them anyway. No one ever accused him of being reticient.

Three years after Applegate arrived in Oregon he was instrumental in blazing the Southern Route, now remembered as the Applegate Trail, from Fort Hall to the Willamette Valley. Initially it was a disaster, but as the road was improved its traffic increased. Thousands of emigrants chose it over the northern route, the Old Oregon Trail.

For some people that was Jesse Applegate's chief contribution to the state. But they discount his position as first surveyor general, in 1844, and they do not reckon with his role in politics.

From 1844 to 1849 he was a leader in the Provisional government and was influential in shaping the development of Oregon as a Territory of the United States. In 1857 he was a delegate to the State Constitutional Convention. Later he aided in securing Lincoln's election. And in 1876 he almost made it to the U.S. Senate.

He was a nineteenth century liberal of the frontier: opposed to slavery, favorable to women's suffrage, for free expansion of commerce, an advocate of limited economic planning, anti-monopolistic, a champion of individual rights, and prone to avoid battle with compromise.

In 1849 Applegate left his Polk County farm and mill to move south, settling on a land claim in the Umpqua Valley. Here, at the foot of a hill, he built a large house that in his time was to become the most famous in Southern Oregon. But more of that later.

The hill was so thick with wildlife that within two years after arrival Applegate killed two bears and more than forty deer on it, as well as many game birds. What the coming of the whites did to the Indians is graphically detailed by Jesse's daughter, Roselle Applegate Putnam, in a letter dated January 22, 1852:

"The hill is called after a chief who with a numerous tribe once inhabited these valleys — among the few remaining survivors of this tribe that occasionally came to beg a crust of bread or an old garment that is getting worse for the wear — there are some old ones who remember the chief, say that he was a great physician and skilled in witchcraft — which is a belief still prevalent among them — his men hunted bear and deer on this hill and caught salmon in the streams around it and the women dug roots in the valleys and gathered nuts and berries on the hill — they were a numerous and happy nation — but the busy multitudes are low and still — the dense forest whose echoes were then only awakened by the war song and the wolf's howl are now half demolished by their enterprising successors — the game is frightened away by the sound of the axe and the crack of the whip — the acorns, nuts and roots are yearly harvested by their hogs so that if these ancient owners were still living they would be deprived of their means of sustenance."

A village was founded and six months after the opening of the Yon-

Grave of Jesse Applegate

calla post office, in mid-March 1851, Jesse Applegate became postmaster. But his real interests were farming, politics and philosophy, the last-named a category for the social and economic questions of the day.

On his ranch he raised beef cattle and in his home he entertained the famous and the humble alike with a heartfelt hospitality that lured travelers many miles out of their way. His first house is regarded as having historical significance because it was used as the first court of the southern district of the Provisional government. In his microscopic diary — this entry posted on September 13, 1877 — the Pepysian federal judge, Matthew P. Deady, who had taken the train to Yoncalla, recorded finding Applegate "camped under a shed with his wife and engaged in building a new house and I suppose his final home on earth and above ground. The spot is a lovely and picturesque one at the head of a cove filled with a beautiful and untouched grove of black oak."

From here Applegate expressed himself on so many subjects that his admirers dubbed him The Sage of Yoncalla. Practically every newspaper in the state was bombarded with his epistles; in all of Oregon he was the most copious contributor to Letters to the Editor.

As the years went by, his views, while retaining his independence of mind, showed him to be growing more inflexible. Never able to be a follower, he found it increasingly difficult to attract a following. Each year saw a further waning of his influence.

The declining of his popularity was accompanied by a sense of isolation and a touch of paranoia. On January 2, 1878, Judge Deady noted: "Got an interesting letter from Jesse A written on Xmas evening, in which he says I am the only one of his friends who has kept close to him in misfortune and poverty." But five years later the friendship of thirty years was broken, never to be resumed. Deady scrawled angrily in his diary on May 5, 1883: "Had a very mean letter from J A this week. . . . I don't think I shall ever recognize him again."

Toward the end of his life his mind began to wander and he was institutionalized. But he fully recovered, as is manifest in an item which appeared in the *Oregonian* of July 31, 1887:

"In mentioning the condidtion of Uncle Jesse Applegate, the Roseburg *Plaindealer* says: 'Hon. Jesse Applegate, who has been released from the asylum, was on our streets Friday, and seemed quite cheerful; entered into conversations with his old-time friends and seemed to enjoy himself calling up old reminiscences of the early settlers' lives and trials and cracked jokes, indicating that his mind had resumed its wonted sanity to a very great degree, which fact his many friends throughout the country will be pleased to hear.' "

The historical marker states that the house stood half a mile west of this spot, but where was Applegate buried? In the Yoncalla Cemetery, we thought, so there we drove and spent several hours prowling the sweeping burial ground on the plateau above town. We found the grave of Jesse's oldest brother, Charles (whose home, three miles from the marker, was still intact and occupied), and several generations of Applegates, but no Jesse. So we hied ourselves to the Yoncalla store and sought directions.

The lady tending the store was very helpful. "You'll see a gate across a cattle guard near the marker. You open the gate. Then you go through another gate. Don't turn right or you'll go to the ranch house. Now, at this point, where you'd go to the house if you turned right, just look straight ahead and you'll see a cemetery on the side of the hill. It's simple to get there; not far, either. Just take the road that goes up the hill."

We did as she instructed and wound up far off, following a high shoulder until we overlooked a road crew hacking a pike through the woods. None of the men had heard of the cemetery so we backtracked and made for the house. Naturally, no one was home. So, after again looking in vain for the burial ground we returned to the store.

The lady was irritated with me. Any fool could find the cemetery, her eyes declaimed. She did not know that I was a special kind of fool. "Everybody knows about it!" she argued, and called to all in the store to verify her pronouncement. But most people there hadn't heard of Jesse Applegate and of those who had only one knew that the cemetery was west of the marker, and that was the extent of his knowledge.

"I see I'm not getting through to you," the lady said and strongly recommended that we call upon a couple of old-timers. "They're in their seventies or eighties and they've lived here all their life and they can tell you exactly where the cemetery is."

We followed her suggestion and knocked on the door of the old-timers. "I've heard of the Applegate Cemetery but I've never been there and I don't know where it's at," the woman replied, "but let me call my husband. He surely knows." He didn't. He had heard tell of it, but that was a long time ago.

Twilight was stealing in through the woods. Our plans had been to go on to Portland but there was this mystery to be solved. That night we bunked down at a Rice Hill motel and early next morning we were back at the marker.

"We've got ten hours of good daylight," I said to friend wife, "and we'll use every minute of it, if necessary, to find Applegate's grave." Sometimes I do not give up easily.

We opened the gate, drove across the cattle guard, closed the gate, drove to the right fork that led to the ranch house, and took it. Again no one was home, but this time I spied a fellow out near the barn, pitching hay. He was a hired man familiar with the country.

"It's up that way," and he pointed to a knoll. "When you get past the second gate you'll see a sort of trail winding off to the left and up toward the hill. You ought to see the cemetery from the trail. It's in a sort of clearing in the woods."

We backtracked to the start of the fork, turned right, opened the second gate, drove through, closed the gate, and just a few yards ahead we spotted a dim tire trace swinging off leftward. So we followed it and two-tenths of a mile on we reached the cemetery. Here, among weeds and raggedy brush and wild flowers that seemed to be born old, we found the graves of Jesse Applegate, his wife, Cynthia Ann, and some others. Entangled in thick underbrush up the slope were second-growth fir, oak and hazel; below, where Applegate's house had stood, the pastureland was caked.

I returned to the Yoncalla store to boast of our find. The lady was not there and no one was impressed. A fellow about thirty asked, "Who was Jesse Applegate?" I informed him. He nodded vacantly and headed for the beer case, muttering, "That was before my time."

So maybe Jesse Applegate is where he belongs, on a knoll that can't be seen from the freeway and seems a long way from old 99. It is better that he be there, on the ground he hunted and farmed, secreted from all but those who search him out, than be topped by a tall marble shaft in a well-kept, conspicuous cemetery. He was a pioneer to the end and he lies in a pioneer plot.

Directions: From Yoncalla store, 2.4 miles north on Oregon 99 to historical marker.

Sunny Valley Scene

When first I saw Radio Park Store at Sunny Valley I thought immediately of what the American novelist Winston Churchill had written of a New Hampshire store, "a platform so high that a man may step off his horse directly on it."

Thinking of the community around, that held mining camps and stagecoach houses and a fort, you could believe that the barnlike store, with its broad porch reached by a rambling flight of wooden stairs, was put up in the last century or early in this one. The ore basket at the foot of the stairs came from the Almeda Mine on the Rogue River, near Galice, and the other mining equipment nearby was even older, and somehow it seemed that the store as well as the artifacts were of pioneer vintage, when people rode in on horseback.

The illusion of age was carried forth inside: a potbellied stove, out of which welcome heat poured in the cold months; a counter scale made in 1904; and lanterns that illumined the cabins of miners and homesteaders. Yet the building was as recent as the early 1930s, when it was put up as a

Store at Sunny Valley

dance hall. Since it had the only radio in the valley, folks came from miles around to listen to all the wonderful music and comedy crackling from million-mile-away places such as New York, Chicago, and Los Angeles. And that — the radio and the recreation — was how it got the name of Radio Park.

When the dance hall folded it was succeeded by a mercantile establishment which kept the dance hall name. For some years a tavern was part of the store, and that was a legitimate improvement over the residual bootleg whiskey in the younger days of the dance hall. But the tavern, too, was of the past.

We expected to find some old-timers hanging about the place, and in the few hours we were there two or three did come by in their pickups for food and drink. But most of the patrons were the kind of young men once categorically clustered under the umbrella designation of hippies. Long-haired (some braided, knotted, banded), bearded, some shoeless, some bare to the waist, and a few who looked and swaggered and, I swear, dressed like swashbuckling pirates. They were all from Southern California, had been in these parts only a year or two, looked upon Oregon as the land of wine and honey, and were dead set against foreigners lousing up the state.

That summer we saw such young people everywhere within our boundaries, especially west of the Cascades. They had displaced the hermits and stump-ranch families back in the brush. Former ghost towns were aswarm with them and if they knew nothing of the history, so what; they would make their own. At the remains of Placer, a gold camp near Sunny Valley that was born in the last decade of the nineteenth century, I asked a young mother in a big house trailer if anybody had told her any legends about Placer. "I didn't even know there was a town here," she replied in surprise. "Was there? I'm interested in the future — and this is a nice place for the future, isn't it?"

So many of the country stores around the state were now owned by folks from elsewhere, particularly from the Los Angeles and San Francisco areas. Ex-stockbrokers, insurance salesmen, garage owners, factory managers, teachers and others were running the stores that in the 1960s were owned by couples in their fifties and up. Maybe the older people — those who hadn't died — had gone south and the younger ones come north. A fair exchange, maybe, but the newcomers operated the stores like suburban shops instead of as crossroads gossip counters pungent with the smell of clover, cheesewheels and crushed blackberries.

We had turned off Interstate 5, five miles south of Wolf Creek, to photograph a lovely covered bridge over Grave Creek, a short distance from the store. With its gallery of windows on both sides the bridge was calendar art. And it probably stood in the midst of more history than any other roofed span in Oregon.

The stream was named for the grave of a fourteen-year-old girl who was a member of the first wagon train to enter Oregon from the south, on the Applegate Trail, in 1846. She was buried in a spot covered by the paved road. No one, of course, could point to the spot, nor could anyone vouch for the legend which holds that five Indians killed in 1853 were

Grave Creek Covered Bridge at Sunny Valley

buried in the same grave, which is why the stream has sometimes been called Graves Creek.

We crossed the bridge and faced northwest. In the space before our eyes ran out of land was fought the Battle of Hungry Hill — also known as the Battle of Bloody Springs — where on October 30, 1855, red and white men clashed. Supposedly six Oregon Volunteers and three regulars were slain. County historians say that five soldiers lie in graves near here, but no one knows the unmarked locations. There is no mention of what happened to the Indians slain.

Close, too, was the site of Fort Leland, a post used during the Rogue River Indian uprising of 1855-56. ("Where did it stand?" I asked a seventy-year-old whose father had been a settler in these parts. "Somewhere yonder," he drawled, not deeply interested, and waved toward the grass.)

Just beyond the bridge and a hundred yards to the northeast had stood the Harkness and Twogood Stage House, built in 1857. Among its guests were President Hayes and General Sherman. Not a trace of the inn remains. Probably Fort Leland stood nearby for, like many other forts, it was originally a stockade put up to protect settlers. It may have been an extension of the Grave Creek House, built earlier by Harkness and Twogood.

We had some soda pop at the Radio Park Store before we continued on our way. One of the pirates was there, buying a loaf of bread, a chunk of bologna, and a six-pack of beer. "You guys are dropouts," I jested. "No way!" he shot back amiably. "We're drop-ins! And we're staying."

Driving north I said to friend wife: "The Oregon Trail is as lively as ever."

"Now I think I know how the Indians felt," she replied.

Directions: From Wolf Creek, exit on I-5. South, 5.2 miles to Sunny Valley exit. Covered bridge is 0.3 mile north of store.

Bridge Over Evans Creek

Draped around a curve, Wimer looked like the print of a New England outcountry hamlet. But, unlike most such quick-seen villages, Wimer had something else, a very attractive covered bridge — about which I got involved in argument.

Pointing to a document issued by the Great State of Oregon, I asked an elderly lady if she had been in Wimer when the bridge was built, in 1927. "It wasn't built in 1927!" she protested. "That's when it was repaired."

"But here is an official list of covered bridges," I insisted, pointing to the document, "and it has this one as built in 1927."

"It was built in 1892," she repeated. "I know, because my father told me, and he worked on it. I was a child then and I wouldn't remember but my father told me, and I know he told the truth." I checked with a few other old-timers I tracked down and they all agreed that at least part of the bridge was the original, which had been put up long before 1927. One aged fellow thought a fire had done great damage to the bridge but the others said the villain had been a flood. "I remember that high water well," recalled a man born around Wimer fifteen years before the twentieth century arrived. "Just about swept the bridge away. Had to get across by boat for a while."

Covered Bridge over Evans Creek

The first lady had something to say about the people who had drawn up the document. "What do they know?" she snorted. "They're state people. We're country folks. We live here!"

If the old-timers were right, then the span across Evans Creek at Wimer was very likey the oldest standing covered bridge in the state. I don't know for sure but I'll tell you one thing: I'm not quoting the Great State of Oregon any more to the folks at Wimer.

Directions: From the city of Rogue River (I-5, Oregon 99), take Pine St. North. It becomes E. Evans Creek Rd. 8.3 miles — from downtown — Jct. Turn right for Wimer. 0.6 mile, Wimer and Evans Creek Covered Bridge.

A Grave Marker to Ponder On

BILL BRADLEY, EARLY PIONEER LIVED HERE ALONE FOR TWENTY EIGHT YEARS.

WHILE ATTEMPTING TO SUBDUE A WILD HORSE 200 YARDS EAST OF THIS SPOT IN NOVEMBER 1909 HE WAS MORTALLY INJURED. HE DIED A FEW DAYS LATER IN HIS CABIN LOCATED 50 FEET SOUTH OF THIS SPOT.

BECAUSE OF THE REMOTENESS OF THIS AREA AT THAT TIME — 35 MILES TO THE NEAREST WAGON ROAD — HE DIED BEFORE PROFESSIONAL HELP COULD REACH HIM.

HE WAS BURIED HERE BY DR. E. B. STEWART,
"BILL" SMITH, AND PERRY J. WRIGHT.

Inscription on grave marker of Bill Bradley

It was while on my way to the Dog Creek Indian Cave, three miles of strenuous climb up the hill back of the Dry Creek Store, that I passed the grave of William "Bill" Bradley, at the foot of the trail that leads to the ancient shelter.

It gives you some pause to read the words on the burial stone. They provide a better perspective of Oregon history. At a time when Portland was already a big city, there were still many areas in the state roadless, very sparsely populated, and primitive, with the frontierspeople a long way from the nearest settlements.

Bill Bradley was twenty years old, restless, energetic and self-sufficient when he came out here, in 1881. He lived alone for almost three decades, most of the time in a cabin he built with his own hands. He raised horses — and trapped, hunted, cut wood, and saw few people. You can easily drive from Roseburg to the Dry Creek Store now, over the excellent Umpqua River Highway, in less than an hour, but for most of his life here Bill Bradley lived a solitary, rough and dangerous a life as had the fabled Mountain Men sixty years before he chose this place to settle down.

One November day in 1909, when Bill Bradley was a middle-aged man, but still strong and sinewy, and as wise as he had ever been, and with vast experience on the frontier, he attempted to break a wild horse. The horse won.

Two friends who found him placed Bill on the bed in his cabin and went for a doctor. But the nearest road was thirty-five miles away and Bradley was dead when competent medical help arrived several days later.

The year Bill Bradley gasped his last breath the population of Portland was nearing the quarter-million mark and even Roseburg could boast of almost 6,000 people. Yet even into the twentieth century there were areas in Oregon, some of whose people today cannot live without television, that were almost as untouched as before the arrival of the covered wagons.

That's what I thought about when I read the inscription on the gravestone back of the Dry Creek Store.

Directions: From Steamboat (Oregon 138), 9 miles east to Dry Creek Store.

Grave of Bill Bradley

The Log Town Rose

In 1909, many years after their former home had fallen into decay and the old settlement was no more, their grandchildren took John and Maryum McKee to revisit the site. "Look!" cried Maryum. "Oh look! The old rose is still alive!"

And so it still was when last we were there — the Log Town Rose, clinging to life along the east side of Oregon 238, about a quarter of a mile north of the Log Town Cemetery gate.

Together with the cemetery, which had its first burial in 1862, an old well, and the corner of a rail fence, the yellow rose was all that was left of Log Town, a rip-roaring, crowded gold rush camp of the feverish mining years in Jackson County.

The rose, however, preceded the town, the cemetery, the well and the rail fence. It survived as a mirror of pioneer life and the ghosts of the pioneers.

John and Maryum McKee crossed the plains to Oregon in 1852. With them was Maryum's stepmother, Roxy Ann Bowen, who carried with her all the way from Missouri a yellow rosebush — classified as the Harrison yellow rose originally from England.

The family's first home was at the foot of a butte the McKees called Roxy Ann. Here the rose was planted. When the famly moved to a mining claim on Poor Man's Creek the rose was taken along and replanted.

It fell to Maryum to tend the rose. This she did faithfully, through twelve children, along with chores that kept her busy from dawn to bedtime — nursing her sickly neighbors, midwifing, and otherwise leading so busy a life that years afterward she could only marvel that she had been able to do so much.

No one seems to know when Log Town was established. It was never incorporated. Like Topsy, it wasn't born; it just grew. People were living on the site as early as 1857 but in the 1860s it made its impact on the area. Located near the confluence of Poor Man's (later spelled Poorman's and Poormans) and Jackass (later Forest) Creeks, about six miles southwest of Jacksonville, it was on the main mining road from Jacksonville to Crescent City, California, and was the supply point for the many mines located along Jackass Creek. Legend has it that for a time the creek was so rich that a man shoveling into a sluice box could make $100 a day. More legend declares a prospector reported that "After taking ten million dollars out of it in gold they called it Forest Creek." But a more accurate version may be that the name was changed after Jackass Creek had run out of rich color and the time had come for the circumspect moderns to prettify the lusty names the uninhibited pioneers had given.

Log Town, almost as frequently known as Logtown, was also recorded as Logg Town, after Francis A. Logg, who had a farm on Jackass Creek. In the 1860s it had a population of 250 whites and 450 Chinese and numbered two blacksmith shops, a livery stable, a general store, two meat markets, a hotel, a schoolhouse, two Chinese stores, three saloons, a church, and a dense sprawl of dwellings.

The Chinese, who lived in huts across Jackass Creek, worked the mines diligently — too diligently for their own good. Miners returning from the Idaho fields noted how well the Chinese were doing and drove them out, burning their stores and houses and killing at least one Chinese who protested. The Chinese were vulnerable — mining laws then prohibited them from holding claims unless they held citizenship, and few did. But even if all the Chinese had been citizens, bigotry was so rampant, the drive for acquisition so overriding, and government protection so feeble, that the result would likely not have been otherwise.

Life in Log Town was as primitive as anywhere on the frontier. Mrs. Jennie Young, whose childhood was spent in Log Town, recalled upon her

Log Town Cemetery and site of Log Town Rose

Log Town Rose

Courtesy Southern Oregon Historical Society

ninetieth birthday some years ago that the log cabins were without floors and that it was the custom to dig a hole in one corner to bury gold. She spoke of baking biscuits in a fourteen-inch Dutch oven set in a bed of oak coals. The lid was put on, and coals heaped on top. By this method cookies were also baked.

John McKee built a large log cabin with a porch across the front and in this home Maryum gave birth to all but the oldest of her twelve children. One of the blacksmith shops belonged to McKee. Being innovative, he invented the "strap-eyed" pick, which became popular with the miners. One of them is now on display at the Jackson County Museum in Jacksonville.

An early riser, McKee could make five dollars before breakfast almost any day by sharpening the miners' picks. But the McKees had to be as self-sufficient as other Log Town families. For pork and mutton they raised pigs and sheep. Venison and bear came from hunting.

"The family did the washing in a big kettle down by the creek," wrote Maud Ziegler for the Jackson County Museum, after transcribing the recollections of Mrs. John Higginbotham, a former McKee girl, when she was eighty-four. "They heated the water there in a big barrel, and when there was bedding to be done the children got in the barrel barefooted and jumped up and down.

"At night there were no lights but the candles, and 'kicking up the fire' would always make it real bright in the room.

"There was no stove, just the fireplace. That is where all the cooking was done in big kettles hung on brass bars, or in a Dutch oven. They made their own cornmeal and flour and the bread baked in that fireplace was the best. Folks didn't know what white bread was.

"Sometimes they went out in the grain field and stayed all day, because Indians might come to the house. Two squaws were digging camas one time, and came into the house. The mother could see them in the mirror, and how one held an axe to show that she could strike with it. But they only wanted bread and made themselves some corn cakes.

"Maryum McKee washed fleece, carded wool and spun it into yarn, then knitted the socks and stockings for the family. Oak bark boiled in water made pretty brown dyes. Mrs. Higginbotham was thirteen before she had any 'boughten' stockings.

"They had a Chinese cook, but he didn't want to wash the diapers. The father gave dancing lessons, and there was one big bedroom, where they could have two sets of quadrille, as well as schottisches, polkas and waltzes. Folks came from far outside the village for their Saturday night 'hoe down.' " Maryum rode her little pony on her errands of mercy but when families went visiting they hitched up the same oxen that were used for hauling logs and other work.

As mining declined, so did Log Town. People moved away and buildings came down. The last remaining house was destroyed about 1910. Somehow the yellow rosebush remained, long after any trace of store or home had rotted away. It survived lonely and unheralded until newfound friends came to praise and protect it. A granite marker was put up to commemorate the yellow rose, which was encirled by rocks and sentineled by white-painted posts, and in Oregon's Centennial Year of 1959 the Applegate Valley Garden Club planted sixty of the rose's plants as a decorative hedge at the front of the cemetery. But perhaps the greatest tribute to the yellow rose, which almost miraculously held a small foothold near the highway, was a verse penned by Fred M. Law, a grand-nephew of Maryum McKee.

It seems to me that not all of Law's statements are precise — I say this of necessity because I have indicated otherwise in my narrative — but the sentiment is clear enough, and we have here a genuine and fine folk poem. With the permission of the good people at the Jackson County Museum, who sent it to me for printing in this book, I give you:

THE LOG TOWN ROSE

To the young and the old and one who knows,
Let me tell you the story of the Log Town Rose.
It's the emblem of beauty that does display
The old pioneer of an early day.

It was back in the year of '63
When to Forest Creek came John McKee,
And then his friends that gathered around
Cut logs for his home in old Log Town.

When his home was built, it was snug and warm;
It protected his children through winter storm.
Aunt Maryum spun yarn to make socks and hose,
And once in spare time planted a yellow rose.

It was a beautiful flower of yellowish hue
And over 50 years it weathered through.
To live as it did you would never suppose
But it really did, the Log Town Rose.

Now the nails that they used have turned to rust,
And the logs that once stood there have turned to dust,
But remaining there, waving as winter wind blows
On a historic spot stands the Log Town Rose.

Protect it, friends. As you pass by
Give it a drink, don't let it die
In the earth so dry, from the sun so hot,
Please let the rose live on this sacred spot.

Place some strong posts deep in the ground
And spike strong boards all around.
Protect it from those who may pass by
That would trample it down and let it die.

It's a friend of the family of John McKee
And also a friend to that old oak tree,
But too far away from the shade it gives
Through the summer heat so it may live.

So take care of it, friends, and do it soon,
And in a very short time for you it'll bloom.
You see, my friends, it cannot cry;
It can only bloom and say goodbye.

Its breath is sweet, its heart is gold —
Now this is the story as I've been told,
And long may it wave in sweet repose,
And bloom for you all — the Log Town Rose.

Directions: Log Town Cemetery is 6 miles westbound from Jacksonville on Oregon 238.

Portrait of Van Gilder

While browsing around Wasco, we were put on the trail of a diary, then eighty years old, written by a simple, hard-working man who neither sought fame nor had it thrust upon him.

Milton Van Gilder was born November 4, 1854 and in 1889 moved from New York State to Oregon, where he settled on a piece of grassland a few miles from Wasco. He hired out, as many new and poor farmers did, taking whatever jobs he could find — all types of farm labor, road building, house building, draying. He was a spartan and puritanical man, the prototype of the stubborn, independent, thrifty, grass-roots, root-hog-or-die son of the soil, equalitarian because he wanted his economic place in the sun, and not given to light or sentimental pursuits.

His diary for 1893 shows Van Gilder to be ever mindful of the weather, proud to be a Mason, and intent on constructing a house for himself and his young family. Around 1901 he completed a two-story structure on which he had long toiled. It burned down in 1960, long after his death. A ranch-style house, in the modern motif, was built on the exact spot by his grandson, Raymond Van Gilder, who had lived in the 1901 dwelling with his family. It was there that the trail from Wasco brought us to the diary.

Van Gilder was caught up in the Populist spirit and was a strong supporter of William Jennings Bryan, after whom he named a son. There is scarcely a word in this diary of his family and small inkling that he went to socials, in country or town. He is concerned only with hard facts. Apart from the Masons and his military group, his whole life seems to be centered around work. Yet, as befitted a good citizen, he took time to participate in elections.

The entries that follow are those I selected as typical of the complete year of 1893, the year of the diary.

Jan. 1. Cut wood. Piled up wheat. Rained all day.

Jan. 2. Went to Wasco to the public installation Masonic.

Jan. 5. Went to Wasco. Cold.

Jan. 8. Helped A Poetes saw wood.

Jan. 13. Went to Wasco to military drill.

Jan. 16. Worked to Cicheldufers. Finished the smoke house $2.00. [The $2.00 were Van Gilder's wages for the day.]

Jan. 18. Went to Wm Kings and got a pig. Went to Wasco.

Jan. 20. Snowed all day. Paid A. S. Poetes 27.00 dollar.

Feb. 1. Split wood all day.

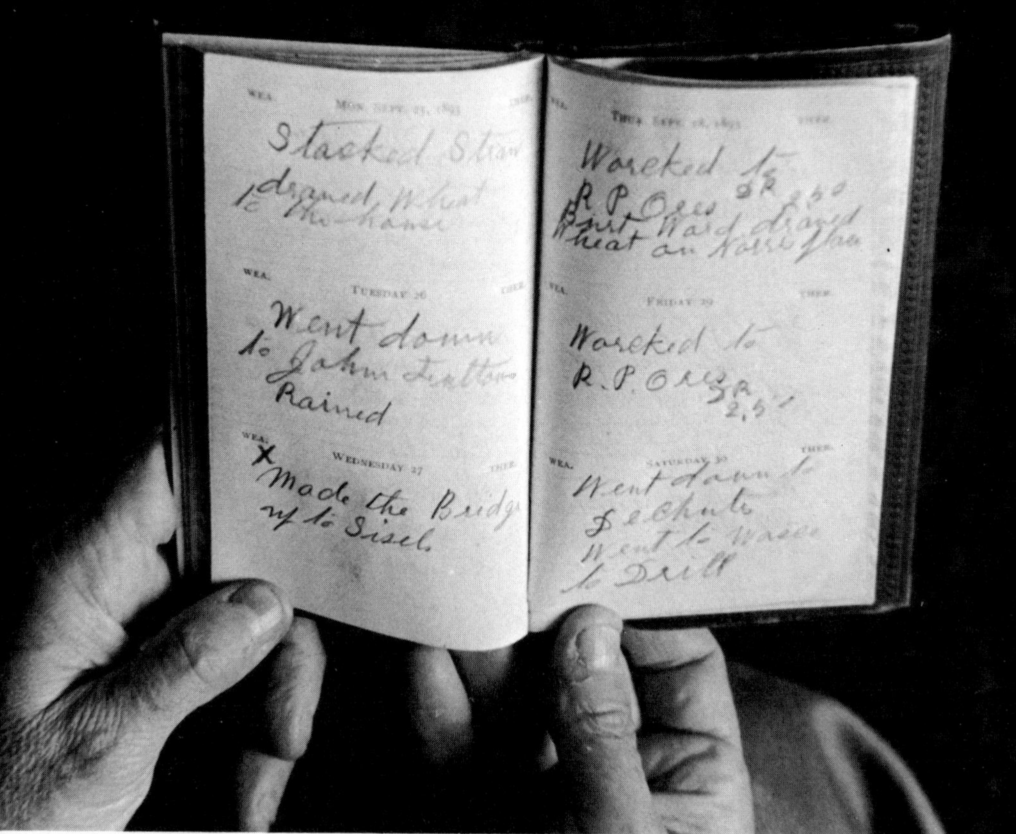

Van Gilder diary

Feb. 7. Worked on J. Bloss bed wagon. Went to Lodge.
Feb. 11. Went to Childrens Day to the Grange.
Feb. 20. Staid at home. Fixed the chairs. Cold.
Feb. 26. Went to Church.
March 1. Worked to Henry Krause.
March 4. Went to Wasco to the Peoples Party Primary.
April 7. Harrowed on the Richie place.
April 17. Sowed wheat on the Richie place.
May 5. Plowed and planted potatoes. Went to Wasco.
May 22. Drained stream and planted potatoes.
June 2. Worked in the garden.
June 4. Went to Election. One of the Judges.
June 12. Went to Deschutes and got a load wood.
June 15. Worked on the road at Biggs.
June 18. Floated wheat. The wind blew hard.
July 25. Commenced heading. All hands work one-half day.
August 5. All hands worked ½ day. Got through on my place.
Sept. 11. Worked on the Fulton Canyon with two teams.
Sept. 13. Went to Wasco. Got the horses shod.
Sept. 29. Worked to R. P. Ores. D.R. 2.50.

Oct. 2. Staid at home. Sharpened tools and fixed the wagon. Bought pig of D Radly for $2.50.

Oct. 14. Worked on the House all day.

Oct. 27. Worked on the house at Deschutes. Went to Wasco to drill.

Nov. 20. Worked to John Hendericks all day.

Nov. 23. Sowed wheat on my place.

Dec. 1. Fixed the cellar and buryed potatoes.

Dec. 2. Went to Wasco. Got some shoes. Cold and snowed.

Dec. 9. Went to Wasco. Worked on the pig narm.

Dec. 13. Worked on the hen house.

Dec. 18. Worked on Henry Krons stable. 2.00.

Dec. 25. Drayed a load of lumber to H Krause. Went to Wasco to the Christmas there. Went down to the Wordsworth School house to the Christmas tree.

Dec. 30. Worked to H Krause on the fence. Got through.

A Tolling Bell at Boyd

You can go somewhere ten times and see only the superficial, and on the eleventh visit you will discover the depth and feel of the place. Sometimes it takes a fresh look or a little more patience or someone met there to perceive the special nature of this "nothing" place. That's how it was with us and Boyd. It was not until the summer of 1972 that, through Lewis Hanna, Boyd became a map point on our minds. He and his wife were among the few people who lived in Boyd, but he could recall with clarity when the town was much larger.

"When I was a young man," he said, weakly and with much effort, "Boyd had a good church, a school, a store and a post office. You could buy anything you wanted; all kinds of machinery.

"Boyd had one hundred fifty or two hundred when I was young. Now there's six at one end and six at the other." And he started to chuckle, but the laughter sputtered out in a wheezy cough.

He couldn't remember when the schoolhouse, the church and the store had been torn down or when the post office had been closed. It was too far back — but his mind could hanker around the bend of time to the pleasures of his youth. "In the old days I'd saddle a horse and go clear to Mill Creek, other side of The Dalles, to go to a dance. Hell, I wouldn't cross the road to go to one now. Couldn't. I was a pretty good caller, yes sir, but not any more."

Head slumped by age and disease, he twisted in a slow, breath-heaving pull to straighten as he pointed across the county road, as empty as the future he knew for himself.

"I've seen snow here that was five feet on the level. Snow clear up to the fence. I went up to Grandpa's place when I was a kid and the snow was five feet thick. Then it rained and it crusted and the cows just walked over the ice and we got them out. Don't know what we would-a-done if they'd-a-broke through. But we don't get those winters anymore. Sometimes we don't get enough to make a snowball."

And somehow, with this old man bent by my side on the silent plain, I thought of two lines of poetry written by Thomas Hardy when Lewis Hanna had the world in his hand, but applicable to him and Boyd now:

Around the house the flakes fly faster,
And all the berries now are gone.

He lifted a limp-hung arm toward a scarecrow clapboard shack about fifty yards to the east and we moved toward it. Lewis Hanna trudged gamely and trying hard to carefully pick his way until we came to a ditch that marked the limit of his property.

"That's the old Charlie Nicholson place over there. That's about a hundred years old. I packed Charlie Nicholson out of there. He wasn't dead but we took him to a hospital. Cleaned him up first. He was covered with bedbugs. His mustache was so bad with them that they had to cut it off. It's no disgrace to be lousy but it's bad to pack them. I was lousy twice in my life but I got rid of them. There was a tramp came into a sheep camp when I was thirteen, fourteen, and he loused up the whole camp."

Lewis Hanna had been born in Wasco County and he furrowed the land with his toil. "I've done everything — herded sheep, put a year in the service, worked on farms. I put in fifteen years on the Miller Ranch here; that's a long time to stay in one place. And I worked thirteen years for a sheep outfit."

He couldn't come up with any folklore for a transient reporter to carry home. "I used to know fellers who could tell stories all night but I can't remember any of them. I don't remember anything anymore."

Lewis Hanna of Boyd

Bent, in pain, hard of hearing, and memory rusted by time, he did not regret having gone so far down the road at the time he did. "We lived the best part of life. These young folks, they're got a lot of hell ahead."

He paused to sum up his life, eighty-five years of living, in an epitaph carved on the wind. "I was raised right and I tried to raise my kids that way. I never been put in jail, never been arrested. That's somethin' to say after all these years, ain't it? That tells a lot about a man's life."

Hanna invited us into his house. His wife arose stiffly to say hello. She told us, her flat voice washboarding over groans, that she and Hanna were both sickly, "bad with arthritis," and they had a hard time taking care of each other. "If I fall he can't help me up anymore," she said.

"I don't see well anymore," Hanna droned. "There was a time I could see as far as any man in these parts but I can't see clear across the road now."

"We don't want to go to a nursing home," Mrs. Hanna said.

"It wouldn't be right," Hanna grumbled.

"But I don't see how we can keep on going like this," Mrs. Hanna said.

Hanna shuffled to the window and looked out, toward the hills that stretched out of reach. "I hate to leave this place," he sighed, "even if I can't see much of it no more."

A year later we returned to Boyd. We have been back several times since, but after 1973 each visit has been a vacant afterword, as though nothing had been changed to write about. I will tell you then of 1973, that rubs against my heart. The land seemed more deserted, the barns wearier, the fences sagging deeper. Here where sixty years ago there had been a village that laughed and bellowed, not even memory remained. Lewis Hanna and his wife had left. In the winter of their years they had been taken to a nursing home. And I again thought of Hardy's lines:

Around the house the flakes fly faster,
And all the berries now are gone.

Directions: From Jct., I-80 and U.S. 197, south 9.8 miles to Boyd Turnoff, 0.8 mile, Boyd.

A Dreaming at Dufur

Scanning the undulating hills that swim away north from Dufur you would not think that some of these fields of wheat were thick with apple trees less than six decades ago.

I did not think so until I chanced across an article that appeared in the now-defunct *Optimist* of The Dalles.

The article read:

> When we drive through the miles and miles of Apple orchards in the Hood River Valley, Yakima, Wenatchee and Okanogan Valleys, little do we realize that despite all those orchards, back in 1922, we, right here in Wasco County and right out in the backyard of Dufur had the LARGEST APPLE ORCHARD in the world! So when anybody commences to talk about apples, just tell them you are from an apple area where they had the largest apple orchard in the world, and we too know something about apples.
>
> This largest single apple orchard in the world was owned by the Dufur Orchard Co., which was organized in 1911 by Churchill-Matthews Co. It contained 4,000 (four thousand) acres! Half of it was planted the first year and the other half in 1912. The varieties included Newtons, Jonathans, Winter Bananas, Spitzenburgs and Blackstems. The orchard produced apples prolifically, but it proved to be so large that it was unwieldy and couldn't be efficiently handled. In 1922 it went into a receivership with A. P. Churchill in charge. He pulled out 1,600 acres of trees and reseeded the ground to wheat.
>
> However, in 1921, before those trees were pulled, 194 railroad cars were sold off this orchard and in 1922 it was estimated that they had a crop of at least 125,000 boxes! They employed 125 men regularly and in the picking season from September to November 400 pickers were employed. They kept 94 head of horses for orchard work.
>
> The balance of the trees were removed and all the place has since been planted and it is one of the best wheat ranches in Wasco County.
>
> It is located on The Dalles-Calif. highway extending north of Dufur for about four miles along the road."

Did the company really get out of the apple growing business because the orchard was "so large that it was unwieldy and couldn't be efficiently

Courtesy Oregon Historical Society

Dufur at the time the Balch Hotel was going strong

Balch Hotel, Dufur

handled?" That didn't seem to me to be good enough reason. If apples can be grown so easily up in those hills, why haven't there been many small orchards since? I did a little reseach and learned that the trees were pulled because there wasn't enough moisture to grow apples year in and year out.

My friend Ray Haines, of Salem, who had lived at Dufur in the apple years and had worked in the orchard, told me something else: "It was foreign money that was invested in the orchard, so nobody around Dufur let on that this wasn't the soil or the climate for apples."

About the time the apple company was organized, Dufur had 700 residents, two hotels, was the terminus for the Great Southern Railroad, boasted an auto stage which made two trips daily to The Dalles, and was up-to-date with a telephone and daily mail. Today Dufur has radio, television, and dial telephone, but no hotels, the railroad is gone, and the population is down to less than 600.

The swankiest of the two hotels was the Balch, which Charley Balch built in 1907. And therein hangs a tale, out of which I have spun some daydreams.

A year after Charley Balch opened his hostelry he had, through his own advocacy, gained distinction as the best-informed man in town and a fellow who never forgot anything. That was in 1908, but in 1909 a skeptical salesman from Portland, trying to inject a little humor into the boring life of a drummer, played a small prank on Balch. He left a copy of the Portland *Telegram* on a dining-room table.

It took Charley a while to get around to clearing the tables after breakfast but eventually he did, and when he saw the paper he dropped the tray of dishes he was holding and ran shouting to his wife, "Lois, Lois, the United States has declared war on Spain!"

Mrs. Balch hastened out of the kitchen to read the odd and shocking headline. Then she observed the date. "This paper was printed in 1898," she noted caustically. Charley Balch just about fainted.

The other salesmen accused Charley of unnerving them with his panic and he had to buy peace with a free box of two-for-a-quarter cigars. That was tough enough to take, but the bitterest pill was the destruction of his reputation as an unquestioned source of accurate news.

The history of Dufur is filled with such folklore, much of it found in the six big scrapbooks compiled over a chunk of years by Ed Limmeroth.

Charley Balch has been dead for decades and the hotel, still standing and still bearing his name, is now a private residence. The Portland *Telegram*, a well-known newspaper in its day, folded a long time ago. The drummer who pulled the practical joke is gone from the earth and so is Ed Limmeroth, the farmer and mechanic who devoted hundreds of hours to pasting into his scrapbooks every bit of news he could find about Dufur.

They told tall stories in the lobby of the Balch Hotel. One of them was about a Professor Strandbo, who lived up in Long Hollow with an Indian woman, whom he married "when he felt the time was ripe." The professor was a ventriloquist, who made a living of sorts operating a puppet show. He did a lot of practicing for performances but one day, as the story was bandied about, "he threw his voice so far into the hills he never got it back again."

And then there was the good-natured grousing of Bill Ragsdale, who couldn't make it all on his farm so he turned postal carrier in 1913.

"On the first trip out," he come to think of it, "I was so nervous I sold stamps at half price. There was no name on the boxes, by golly. It took seven hours with my team in the summer and thirteen in the winter. By golly!"

And when the townfolks would gather in the hotel of an evening they might chat about Dr. Larkin Vanderpool, a native of Missouri who crossed the plains in 1852 to settle in Benton County, went on to Prineville to practice medicine in 1869, and in 1884 came to Dufur as the town's first physician.

"You recall," someone might start, "that it was right here, yes sir, right here in Dufur, that Doc Larkin made up his SB cough medicine." And someone else might add: "Yeah, and what about his headache, liver and alpha pain-cure medicine? Doc had them too." "And don't forget," a third might chime in, "he was also a skin-cancer specialist. He was that; they said in The Dalles he was."

Dufur is a fifteen- to twenty-minute drive from The Dalles now, but it was much further then, and The Dalles was the big city as far as most Dufurites were concerned. Whatever The Dalles didn't know wasn't worth knowing in Portland.

Just about the time Charley Balch opened his inn some farmer came rushing into town to yell his head off about oil running out of his ground. It didn't take long to organize a stock company to drill for the stuff. The whole town waited to get rich. But after drilling failed to find any more oil, the bubble burst. It was a joke, a hoax, or something freakish, everybody agreed, and they did what came naturally, mooning about what might have been.

Now and then George Washington Peters would shyly saunter into the hotel. George was an oddity, a full Indian who actually owned land.

He had worked for Joseph Sherar, who lived at Dufur before starting a prosperous settlement at his toll bridge on the Deschutes, and when George had saved enough money he took a homestead and proved up on it.

"How's it goin', you old skunk?" some idler would holler at George Washington Peters, thudding him across the back, and the Indian would reply with proud smile, "I'm all same white feller now."

They laughed for years about how George Johnson took an involuntary bath in Fifteen Mile Creek on a spring day in 1908. When he and his companion came to where the creek divided the road, his friend left the buggy and crossed on a footbridge. But brave George didn't think the creek more than two feet deep and on he went. Before he was halfway to the other side the water had risen into the buggy. Another step and the water was up to the horse's ears and by then most of George was submerged. He made it across, somehow, but it took him quite a while to live down the story.

That, in the high noon of Dufur, was the Balch Hotel, where the locals and outlanders thickened the air with plaints and maunderings about a world not altogether generous and never precise.

I stood outside the old inn for about an hour, waiting for Ed Limmeroth or Professor Strandbo or George Washington Peters or Charley Balch himself to show up, but then I realized I had been lost in reverie, so I moved on north of town, to the wheat fields that had once been the largest apple orchard in the world.

A Friend in Time

At Dufur we chose to take the back road to Friend, never before having tried that route. It was an experience not soon forgotten.

The official state highway map showed the first five miles to be paved, but we ran out of hardtop before then. At the first fork we were lost. While we pondered our options a car came along and I gestured it down. The lady in the station wagon directed us to turn left. "At the first intersection," she said, "a marker will point to Friend." "Which way do we go from the intersection?" I asked. "Just follow the marker," she repeated, and zoomed off toward Dufur.

We turned left and drove to the first intersection. No marker there. "Friend is to the south," I said to Pat Kimoto, who was at the wheel, "so we ought to turn right." "That makes sense to me," she agreed. "If we go left now we'd be heading in the direction of Dufur."

Quickly we ran out of wheatland and soon the road was choppy dirt. "We'll stop at the first house," I said, but there weren't any houses. The road narrowed until it was practically one-way and we drifted into the strangest terrain I had ever seen in central Oregon.

Mile after mile the road wound through land that seemed to belong more to the bayous of Louisiana than to Wasco County. I had the miasmic feeling of hallucinations of the kind I had suffered during a bout with food poisoning once in Turkey. Nothing here seemed real. Where had Oregon gone? I was back in the red clay distortions of Alabama, the swamps of Mississippi, the choked pinewoods of Georgia. Sanity should have compelled us to turn back but obstinacy was stronger. Somewhere the mirage had to disappear, somewhere this sick joke of a road had to run out or be accosted by a more rational pike.

We saw no house, no barns, no hills, no fences, no signs. Nothing but the choked pines leering at us and the bayou recept dancing before our confused and stricken eyes.

The world had to come to an end, or had we somehow been transported to another planet? The road twisted so many ways we could not tell what direction had the greatest constancy. Which would we reach first, the ocean or the mountains? We could drive all day on this harebrained, sadistic trail and when we ran out of gas, where would we go?

Then around a bend huffed a dusty apparition and I cried to Pat, "Stop! Stop!" She pulled as far off the trail as she could and I waved frantically for the dust-drenched camper to halt. Out hulked a burly, bushy-bearded young giant and he lumbered toward us, his eyes hard and his lips grim. "Say, buddy," I said, as he set his huge paws on the open window frame, "can you tell us how to get to Friend?"

"You're lost," he said. It was the understatement of the year.

"We're lost," I acknowledged.

"O.K.," he said, "I'll tell you how to get there." He started, but after glancing at our strained faces he grumped, "Oh hell, just follow me."

"We don't want to put you out of your way," I apologized. "I think we can follow directions."

"That's O.K.," he lied. "I've got some business there anyway. You'll have to turn around. There's a place on the other side of the bend. I'll pull ahead of you and you can get by."

Halfway back toward the camper he paused, wheeled ponderously, and returned. "Do you people do much traveling around the state?" he asked.

"Quite a bit," we replied.

"Well," he said, frowning at our innocence, "what you ought to do is get that book, *Oregon for the Curious*. It's written by uh, uh, what's his name?"

The story could end right there. In talks on vagabonding around Oregon, that's how I close this tale. After all, everyone knows who what's-his-name is. He's the guy at the podium, pretending to be an expert.

Happily, the hirsute giant turned out to be an amiable fellow. He guided us to Friend, finding a slip of a trail we had passed by (knowing full well *that* couldn't be more than a cow meandering) and in Friend he bade us a cordial farewell assuring us that *Oregon for the Curious* was still a good book, despite the author getting lost now and then.

The story could end here, too, but since we've come this far, let me tell you something about Friend.

In the 1890s the interior of Oregon began to fill up. The nesters came by train, by wagon, by buggy, on horse alone, and sometimes even on foot. They saw the great open spaces between the mountains and they dug down to plant their future. When the homesteads reached a small cluster, somebody came in with a supply of groceries, hardware and soft goods, and a store was opened. The next step was a post office.

Almost all the homesteaders came from the East or the Middle West or from Europe, where it was traditionally understood that 160 acres would more than suffice a farm family. In many areas, 40 acres and a plow and a mule were all that was deemed necessary to support a household. And here, out in central Oregon, it was possible to get 320 acres. The honey flowed before the first bee arrived.

Great expectations ran out before the first pair of overalls needed patching. The nesters made so many mistakes it would take a book to recount them all. But two fundamental errors can be noted.

First, they treated the arid land as though it were river bottom loam — and that technique didn't work. Turning the land against them, they were in turn starved off it. But even if they had been wiser, as some of them were, they would have understood that their acreage was too small to plant crops that would thrive in this country.

Ralph Friedman

The last of Friend

What happened was inevitable. The richer farmers bought out the poorer ones, who departed; the homestead houses were abandoned and later torn down or crumpled of their own fatigue; the storekeepers closed their doors, because customers had moved away; and the post offices became relics of an earlier, more hopeful day.

George J. Friend came to this part of Wasco County in the 1890s to root hog or die. He struggled with the land and the elements and when he looked around to see a few neighbors, who had settled within eyesight, he knew he held enough poker chips to ride out the game. Early in 1903 there were enough folks around to start a community. A store was built, with a post office inside, and Theo. H. Buskuhl, who ran the store and handled the mail, proposed that the settlement be called Friend, because the store was on George J.'s homestead.

That's how the hamlet, halfway to the west between Dufur and Tygh Valley, got its name. Not because it was more cheerful or had better companions or held out a warmer arm to outlanders and travelers than other communities, but because the first postmaster had a sense of historical appreciation.

Somebody — I don't know who, and maybe it was Buskuhl himself — painted the false-front top to read: The Friendly Store. According to legend, which grew big in the tall grass, the words could be seen a mile away.

Changes came, of course. Electricity. The telephone. The automobile. It was a bountiful sight to see the light bulbs hanging from the ceiling like wayward pears, vibrating with glow, their brightness spread out over the plain and signaled the pilgrims on the dirt pikes that life was churning within their grasp. So goes another legend. And when the telephone jangled, loud enough to knock a whittling idler off the cracker barrel, everybody knew that Friend was getting mighty modern.

By-and-by a gas pump was put up, as old-fashioned now as Great-Grandma Mabel in high button shoes, but stout enough to fulfill its function. A more efficient pump followed, years later. I was there on a day — so long ago, it seems in the reckoning — when the store keeper waited until he had sliced some strips from a slab of bacon before plodding out to the wooden porch, where a dust-covered green Chevy had snuggled up to the pump.

"How much today?" the storekeeper sang out. "The usual," replied the lean-cheeked, graying driver. "Like to keep it a habit, huh?" the storekeeper asked with a bite of cheerful conversation. "Seems like it," the driver muttered vacantly, grimacing at one of his tires, so thin it didn't have enough tread left to keep the tube dry in a puddle.

When the storekeeper had finished pouring he called out in offhand briskness, "That'll be two hundred dollars."

"Yeah," grunted the driver, and handed over two very wrinkled dollar bills.

Well, you know what happened to Friend. More farmers departed. The offspring of those who remained left when they grew up. Their labor wasn't needed (machinery had taken care of that), and brighter callings beckoned in the cities.

Friend lived into the age of the zip code and became 97025. As this book was going to press the fourth-class post office was open two hours a day in a gloomy corner of The Friendly Store, which had gone out of business about a decade before.

Some day, of course, the post office will be closed and the store will be dismantled. The name of Friend will remain on the state map for years afterward, as always happens, which will bewilder visitors, as such things do now. And there will come a time, after the name is finally deleted from the map, when some wandering romanticists will see the name of Friend in a book and set out to find it.

I wonder if they will succeed.

Directions to Friend: From Dufur (U.S. 197), 5 miles south to Friend Jct. Turn right, or west. 5 miles, Friend.

A Varied Song in Sherman County

I'm thinking now of a beautiful land,
Oregon, Oregon.
With rivers and valleys and mountains grand,
Oregon, sweet Oregon.

Sweet Oregon, composed by Henry S. DeMoss

Three miles north of Moro, the withering seat of Sherman County, we passed DeMoss Memorial Park, once the settlement of DeMoss Springs, a village founded by the most celebrated family of entertainers in the annals of Oregon.

At Moro we met and spoke at length with John M. DeMoss, the last surviving male member of the illustrious artists. He was seventy-six years old then, hadn't sung in public for more than sixty years, and was less interested in telling about his family than in talking about his own hard but fruitful life as a man who had chased the dollar, through good and bad times, with honest hand. He had been a farmer, worker, storekeeper, salesman, and a lot of other things, and to him they were as important as any singing career. But he did discourse about the DeMoss show-business history, and not without some pride.

Actually there were two families of DeMoss entertainers. Only one person participated in both — the father, James DeMoss. He and his first wife and their five children, one of whom died young, established themselves as the DeMoss Family. The second entertainers consisted of James, his second wife, and their two children, Ruth and John — our man at Moro.

After the death of his first wife and fifth-born child, James and the four remaining members of his family (two girls and two boys) crossed the Atlantic and were heralded in Europe as "America's World-Famous Concert Family." When the father left to remarry, the four children, now grown, continued on their own, winning more laurels as the DeMoss Lyric Bards and the DeMoss Quartette.

"My father said," John DeMoss related, "that the first DeMoss Family performed not only in every state of the Union but in almost every county of every state." They also gave concerts in Canada, Great Britain, Germany, Switzerland, Belgium, and France.

The second DeMoss entertainers quickly disbanded after the father died. The first family continued on until the third decade of the twentieth century.

"The family actually did more than sixty years of work," said John DeMoss, a rugged man with a face well plowed by time and a gruff briskness in his voice that crackled across the room like a spring wind snapping through the willows on the creeks of Sherman County. "From 1872 to 1932 they went by wagon, overland stagecoach, train, ocean liner and automobile. A stagecoach they traveled in for years is now at Oregon State University. They entertained everybody from miners and cowboys to royalty and presidents.

"They weren't exactly an amateur group," the man at Moro grinned. "All the older children — my half-brothers and half-sisters — they had excellent musical training in this country and in Europe. Altogether they played more than forty instruments. And they played and sang everything for their times: you name it — religious, classical and popular. And they made up a lot of their own songs.

"They were always making up songs," John DeMoss said, shaking his head a bit in wonderment. At the World's Columbian Exposition in Chicago in 1893 the DeMoss Lyric Bards wrote a song for each of the states.

"Yes, they did!" John DeMoss exclaimed. "And the songs were sung at the different state celebrations during the fair. They were named the official song writers of the Exposition."

DeMoss turned to his wife, Etha, who had been in a wheelchair for three years, victimized by arthritis. "Are you all right, honey?" he asked.

There was a story about her, too, his Etha.

In 1916, when he was twenty years old and had been working the ranch he had been renting from his half-brothers for two years, he decided he needed help. "I couldn't find a couple but in Grass Valley I found a man and his daughter to come down. Well, the first time I ever saw her was on the 19th of September and on the 29th we got married. I proposed the day we got married. It was love at first sight all right. She was a good-looker. And I tell you, she could cook! We've been married all these years and closer than ever — and we've always been close."

It was exactly a century back in time from the year we spoke to John DeMoss in Oregon's smallest county seat that the DeMoss Family took to the road on a career of entertainment. But the story goes even further back — to an ordained minister of the United Brethren Church and his wife. The minister, who was also a gospel singer, had volunteered for missionary work in the West.

With three yoke of cattle and a covered wagon, James M. and Elizabeth Bonebrake DeMoss started overland from Iowa in 1862. "Crossing a wilderness of mighty plains and rugged mountains, through alkaline dust and sagebrush desert, they were glad when a day's drive was accomplished and they were ten or fifteen miles nearer their goal." The descriptive prose is taken from a booklet, *The DeMoss Entertainers*, written in 1927 by John's half-brother, George.

Only when other emigrants were met was the monotony on the long ordeal broken. Then church services were sometimes held, and occasionally a funeral or marriage ceremony would be performed.

Like many other pioneers of the cloth, James DeMoss did more than preach. He had a hand in establishing post offices at Weiser, Idaho and at

DeMoss Cemetery

North Powder, and at Cove, where the couple settled. Being a civil engineer too, he helped survey and build bridges across the Grande Ronde River. And he located the first sawmill in eastern Oregon. "He worked all day in the mill and would conduct revival meetings or singing schools week nights besides maintaining two regular church services on Sunday," wrote George.

By now the singing preacher was in demand from Boise to Walla Walla. He and Elizabeth lifted their voices in song everywhere they paused. Someone, with the instincts of a business agent, suggested: "Why give all that music away free? Why not charge money?" James and Elizabeth laughed and went on — but the words were to ring in their ears.

The turning point came in 1872, after their fame had spread throughout the mining territory and James and Elizabeth were now the parents of five children, all of whom were early incorporated into the family singing.

Reverend Harvey K. Hines, a Methodist minister who had crossed the plains to Oregon in 1853, knew talent and God's will when he saw it. The Reverend Mr. Hines was no backwoods hick; he had been around and done a thing or two. Before his death he was to gain distinction as a clergyman, educator, territorial legislator, editor and author. He was then presiding elder for the La Grande district.

One day in the spring of 1872, Reverend Hines told DeMoss: "I'd like your musical family to give concerts. I have an organ for you."

Family discussion ended in acceptance. For weeks everyone, from parents to youngest child, was busy arranging a program. It consisted of madrigals, vocal duets by James and Elizabeth, a solo by each of the children, and a lecture on the science of music by the father.

By midsummer the family was ready to start its tour. DeMoss said: "I have the spring wagon all fixed up, a good team, a camping outfit, a rack behind for the organ, and seats for all."

En route to their first pay concert, the family camped on Summit Meadow of the Blue Mountains. "We placed our little organ under a big evergreen tree," remembered George, "and Father said, 'This first evening we will build a bonfire and will go through the entire program just as we shall in our regular concert.' There was a large Indian camp across the meadow and when we started the music the Indians came sauntering over with blankets wrapped about them and squatted in a circle around us. Thus our first public rehearsal was given to the wild men of the mountains. The grunt of the Indians as we finished the program pleased Father greatly, and he said, 'If we can please the preachers at Walla Walla, and with the same program please the wild men of the mountains, we surely ought to please the multitudes of the world.' "

The first effort was a roaring success and the family moved forward in jubilation. "We were booked at all the settlements and towns in the valley and over at the Boise mines," wrote George fifty-five years later. "The miners were especially fond of Mother's singing and they would toss money on the platform when she was singing her beautiful solos."

Beyond the mining camps lay the isolated land — but it was the way east, and that was where the DeMoss Family was bound, though they had been warned of danger ahead.

"From Fort Boise," wrote George, "we launched out into the great Shoshone desert. In that arid country only one gray sagebrush plain meets the vision, until the horizon merges into the blue desert sky. For days we drove along without meeting any save the rambling old stage coach with its tired looking occupants.

"After crossing the dreary old Snake River and had passed through the same undulating sage-brush waste and over a divide, we came to the head of Raft River and camped in a little mountain meadow with a willow-bordered streamlet coursing through it. Twilight deepened and the Autumn moon cast into the stream its weird reflections. Father stepped out on a knoll, pointing, and said, 'Do you see those fires? Those are Indian signal fires, we are to be attacked early in the morning.' Everything was soon placed in the wagon and the team hitched up and started. 'Now Henry, you stay and build a big fire until we are out of hearing, then follow as fast as you can and we will make a drive for our lives.' Little Henry did as he was told and we drove hastily down Raft River and arrived at City of Rocks at daybreak. There we met the U.S. Cavalry, who told us the Indians were on the war path, had massacred hostlers, driven off stage stock, and there was a general outbreak."

In their anecdotage the children would recall such hair-raising episodes in the Wild West as easily as the thunderous applause which resounded for them through the great concert halls of Europe.

At Ogden, Utah the family sold its team, wagon and organ and purchased tickets on the Union Pacific, which only three years before had commenced transcontinental travel. It was a primitive train, and fifty years later the children still shuddered when talking about it. The seats were hard as iron and the only night light came from wheezing candles in

John M. DeMoss

brass candlesticks attached to the sides of the coaches. There could be no near-misses; the train had no airbrakes.

The plains and prairie states were hospitable to the singers and when the DeMoss Family ended its first annual tour at Des Moines, it knew where its future lay.

For the next ten years the entertainers traveled widely, from the Mexican to the Canadian borders and from the Mississippi River to the Colorado and Montana mining camps.

Business boomed at roundup time. Cowboys charged into town, whooping it up and shooting off their guns as they spurred their horses to the singing site. They were quiet during the vocalizing — whether it be sacred, classical or patriotic music — but as soon as a song ended they expressed their enthusiasm by shooting out of the open windows or hammering on the floor with their gun butts.

Nor was there any trouble at even the most reckless of the mining camps. DeMoss smilingly, firmly, turned down every offer, no matter how large the sum guaranteed, to have the family play for a dance. And the miners understood. He raised a polite but strong hand to ward off every drink extended, and the miners did not press the matter. They came from all over the hills, walking or riding mules or horses many a mile through heat and cold to hear the music. At the close of the concert they cheered fervently, then quietly left, except for some with close-home memories who shyly muttered or piously whispered to Elizabeth DeMoss, "God bless you, ma'am. You have the voice of an angel. God bless your dear family."

The family had grand plans of a triumphant Eastern tour but Elizabeth's health was bad and she seemed to do better in the West. In 1883, passing through central Oregon, the weary woman expressed a strong interest in making a future home amidst the poplars of their campground. Quickly her husband and sons sought out the owner, one Pierre Couture, and from him purchased a large tract of unplowed land. That fall they selected a townsite and the family became part-time farmers, growing wheat.

Elizabeth Bonebrake DeMoss saw only the promise of DeMoss Springs. She was still alive when her husband platted part of the tract, with the streets running east and west named for famous musicians and those running north and south honoring renowned poets. The town plat was not filed until after she was dead and the second DeMoss family begun. She was still singing when C. W. Dickenson came to DeMoss Springs in 1885 and opened a store after he had agreed not to sell liquor. Others had approached James DeMoss in seeking land on which to build a store, but until Dickenson all had retreated when they were told of the ban on liquor. Elizabeth passed away before a seminary, which had a few years of successful existence, was established. That she truly would have liked: She was fond of teaching.

The year 1886 was not a happy one for the troubadors. While touring in northern California in September, the family was "stricken with typhoid malaria fever," and at the Siskiyou Mountains village of Henley, now Hornbrook, ten miles south of the Oregon border, the youngest girl, May, perished, and was buried.

Three months later, at Roseburg, Oregon, a fast-failing Elizabeth breathed her last. Her passing was poignantly told by George DeMoss in his brief history of the first family:

"As the glorious sun rose over the mountains, reflecting its bright rays on the sparkling diamond drops of dew on the trees, we were called to her bedside. Henry stepped forward and clasped her hand. She exhorted and closed by saying, 'And never forget to pray.' George knelt by the bed and she placed her hand on his head. 'Be a good man and never forget to pray.' Lizzie and Minnie took turns at the bedside. 'Trust in Jesus and never forget to pray, I know that my Redeemer liveth.' Then she requested us to sing for her. Father stood on one side of the bed, the doctor on the other, and we four children at the foot. Mother called for the different selections which we sang and during the singing her face was brilliant with a triumphant smile. At the close of the last stanza of 'The Sweet Bye and Bye' she closed her eyes and Mother was gone."

James M. DeMoss met Julia Emily Shatto in Des Moines in 1890 and they were married in 1891. A wedding picture shows the groom, then sixty years old and at least twice the age of his new mate, as a high-domed, full-bearded, virile-looking, self-confident man and the bride as slender, strong of eye, and handsome in the romantic sense. He is the portrait of the dominating church elder, she of the country schoolteacher who dreams of far-away places.

James took Emma, as she was called, back to DeMoss Springs and he alternated between the farm and the concert hall. He was in Europe, where the family entertained for kings and queens and Kaiser Wilhelm before continuing their tour into Switzerland, when John DeMoss was born.

Two years later John's sister, Ruth, was born, also at the DeMoss Springs home. John and Ruth were close only as children John told us. "My sister and her husband — and she married early — drifted around and got down to California and I never seen her after 1919, not from 1919 until the 8th of August 1971 when we had the DeMoss picnic down here at the park. Somebody pointed her out to me; that's how I knew it was her. We had a lot to talk about but she was only here one day and there was over a hundred there."

The man at Moro remembered with relish and nostalgia the family picnics of the past. "Around 1915, 1916, 1917, the DeMoss reunions on July Fourth brought hundreds of people from all parts of the country. They came with wagons from miles around. I had the hay ricks fixed up, and they were good places for sleeping."

By 1972 the family picnic was down to John and Etha, their three sons and the wives of the sons, six grandchildren, ten great-grandchildren, and friends. "I've got a nephew, in Salem I think, but I haven't seen him in a long time." The children and grandchildren of the two boys and two girls of the first family were strung across the continent and if there was communication within that clan, it did not reach Moro.

After the birth of Ruth, James stayed home awhile. "The older children formed their own group," said John, "and went on to even greater success. They wrote a lot of songs. I guess the best one is 'Sweet Oregon.' It was sung at the Chicago Fair in 1893 and throughout America and Europe. It was supposed to be the state song, but it never went over. It's difficult; hard for children to sing."

The story of how "Sweet Oregon" came to be written was told in *The DeMoss Entertainers* by George in 1927:

" 'Twas a cold foggy morning many years ago in one of the larger cities of America that Mother heard music in the hotel parlor. Quietly entering the parlor she found Henry seated at the piano, his fingers rambling o'er the keyboard. 'Henry, what is that beautiful piece you are playing?' He said, 'Mother, I'm homesick,' and commenced singing the song he had just composed, 'Sweet Oregon.' "

John DeMoss took up the story of the second family. "As soon as we were big enough my father formed a musical group of the parents and us two kids. We played from 1900 to 1911.

"Music was taught to me by my father and mother mostly off that chart you see up there," said John, pointing to the wall at the side of his desk in the tiny office of his rambling house that stood only a stone's throw from the state highway that is the main street of Moro. "My mother was musical and, of course, so was my father. But they spanked it into me. I like to hear music but I don't like to make it. I had to practice an hour every day on the organ or the violin. No, I don't play any of 'em now. All

I do is play the radio. I got to play all right. I used to play in the Moro band, the cornet. I love music but I don't like to make it. I don't know why."

Between tours the family returned to their ranch. The town grew steadily. In 1896 it lost the county seat to Moro by only six votes. By then, recalled John, DeMoss Springs had two stores, a blacksmith shop, a school, warehouses and a church. "There was more church there than we have here in Moro. And we had a nice park started, which is still there. In 1929 they gave it to the county as a memorial park and there's people stopping there all the time now to stay at the park.

"Why did DeMoss Springs fade away?" the man at Moro said, repeating the question. He chuckled. "Why, everybody there worked for Tom, Dick and Harry and, like the story goes, pretty soon Harry had everything."

He glanced solicitously at his wife, asked her if she was comfortable, and when she said she was and wheeled away, to do the dishes, he returned to his childhood.

"We traveled by wagon and team all over the Pacific Northwest here, giving concerts and moving picture shows. The picture show was four foot pictures, the biggest we could get, with a carbide light, and it was amusing to see what we looked at — people come from miles them days — and we also had an Edison round-cylinder phonograph and that caused more excitement than anything, to hear people's voices, and we would record pretty near every night. People would get around and we would record and play it back to 'em. We done that in many places. And we traveled mostly through the summers and then we'd come to DeMoss Springs usually for the winters. My first school was in Willamina, Oregon, in nineteen-six, if I remember right. Five or six, I can't remember which year. My schooling was mostly on the road. I rode a bicycle and took it on the wagon and when we got into a town we scattered handbills around and had a show that night or the next night. The folks were acquainted all over and we done that for years.

"We toured the Willamette Valley in 1911 and we got home Thanksgiving eve. We come up on the *Dalles City* from Portland and we got into The Dalles and it seems like when the horses got there they knew we were headin' home. And we drove all night."

His voice broke then and he started to cry. All the memories of that last journey home had swiftly engulfed him. Perhaps he had not thought about them for a long time. It was the end of his boyhood he was weeping for, the robbery of his youth. Soon thereafter the family broke up and he was thrust swiftly into manhood.

"Just a minute," he muttered, wiping away his tears and blowing his nose. He paused until he felt his voice firm again.

"So it was some experience coming over the old free bridge at the Deschutes River. And that was in 1911. Well, we stayed in Portland before that, we stayed in Portland two weeks, going to Gypsy Smith's evangelist meeting. That's where my father throwed out hundreds of dollars of gold pieces, them days. It made me sick to see the money going out, because I just couldn't see it. [He laughed then at the absurdity of the scene.]

"And then we got home in November, as I said, and then in January, the twelfth of January, why, he had a stroke and on the seventeenth, why, he died on the seventeenth. And it was a cold, snowy day. And believe it or not, we had less than ten dollars of cash on hand. So, little John, he went out and went to work. I wasn't sixteen yet.

"I went to work in February for twelve dollars a month and I worked all spring for a man over at Monkland. I carried mail from Monkland to Nish, down on the railroad, and I worked in the field, and at harvest time I did get up to a dollar and something for a day, for harvest time. And then I went to farming in the winter of thirteen-fourteen, started in there on the DeMoss ranch — my mother got married again and took off in 1914 and left me to ranch — I had eighty acres, that I rented from my half-brothers, and I went to farming and batchin' out there for two years."

And then he went looking for a couple to help him, met Etha, and ten days later they were man and wife.

There was a time when the name of DeMoss was associated with one of the most famous singing groups in the nation. That was all in the past. John DeMoss had paid his own dues through life. He and Etha had toiled their way out of the pit of poverty and made it by a shoestring. But it was avarice which first did them in and lost them their family home. Like others of the unwary multitude they were suckered by a con artist. No rube who bought the Brooklyn Bridge or invested in Florida real estate that turned out to be ten feet under water was as ready for guile.

"In 1927," said John, grinning about it now, "a fast-talking mining expert came along and convinced us we'd get rich quick if we'd help him finance his quicksilver mine near Tiller, Oregon. Well, we got taken. We lost everything, including a ranch we had leased near Wasco."

They lost their shirts just as the big hard times arrived to snatch at their underwear. John and Etha both went to work at whatever they could find. "Right on top of our private depression came the national depression," John said, matter-of-factly. "We had four children to support." One of the boys died later from a beesting. He was only ten, and John still wept when telling of his death.

In 1936 they got their home back. "We heard that part of the old place was foreclosed on for taxes and was for sale. So we come to The Dalles from Bonneville Dam, where I was working, and darned if we didn't make a deal to buy part of the old place with a twenty-five dollar post-dated check. That's how much money we had."

He pounded his right fist into his left palm. That was luck, he was exclaiming, but it was a break he and Etha deserved for all the lean years and the scrounging to keep body and soul together.

Twelve years later the couple rented the place to a son, Curly. So the original DeMoss home, built by James, was still in the family.

At the north end of Memorial Park a gravel road leads east into a canyon. A mile down, in a field of stubble backgrounded by canyon wall, is the DeMoss Cemetery. Here lies the patriarch, close to the wheatlands he loved and under a vast umbrella of sky that was the only roof the family had for so many of their early concerts.

John DeMoss looked upon the cemetery as the burial ground into which he and Etha would eventually be laid. It had no more historical significance than that. And every time he passed the park that had been DeMoss Springs he did not stop to tell himself that once the village was, in parts of America and Europe, better known than Portland. For him it was just the place where he was born, where his family had fallen to pieces, and from which he had been pushed into the world of breadwinners.

"It was a great little town," said John, interlacing his fingers, "but it's gone and you can't bring it back.

"The same with the family," he added. "They were very celebrated. But they're history now. A nice part of Oregon history that maybe more people ought to know about — but you can't live in the past. When the sun goes up in the morning, that's the day I look to."

Come Along to Hay Creek

Between Madras and Ashwood the sky swells over the rolling land. This is Western country, the sere grass rustling in the drought, squawberries scrambling along the sparse shoulder of the sleepy dirt road, lean wild flowers filling the gullies.

A buffalo-bodied red barn with a sheepskin nailed to its door humps on a knoll peering down a pond that flings glinted arrows back at the rays of the encroaching sun, a yellow-piled haywagon hauled to rest on a tuft of meadow squints under the bony branches of a wind-scoured cottonwood, and a deer squirms out of the brush to stare at the intruders churning up pebbly dust and to shiver at the thunder of rocks slingshotted against hubcaps, oil pans and fenders.

If at the junction you turn for Grizzly instead of continuing straight for Ashwood, the Hay Creek Ranch is a mile down the pitted pike.

It seems out of place here, in the silence and space of nature, until you remember that it is a ranch, a cattle ranch, and if it did not belong here, where would it be at home?

It belongs all right. It has belonged for a long time, for longer than a century.

After homesteaders had stood in awe at the natural forage that prospered in the valley, and bestowed upon the life-giving streams the appropriate name of Hay Creek, sheepmen moved in. Most of them were from the Willamette Valley but the one to leave his mark was a New Englander. He was Dr. David W. Baldwin, a Vermont physician and farmer and a breeder of Spanish Merino sheep. In 1873 he found the place he had looked for everywhere and established the Hay Creek Ranch. From Vermont he shipped his woolies as far by rail as he could and then had them driven to the green swale oasis that became the center of his empire.

Out in Oregon, Baldwin was more than a sheep rancher. He planted the first alfalfa in the eastern part of the state and he gained a reputation for humanitarianism as a doctor, riding as far as a hundred miles to minister to the sick.

After Baldwin there were a host of owners: individuals, partners, corporations. In the early 1900s the big stockholder was Henry Louis Pittock, founder of the paper-making industry of Oregon, a state printer, and best known as publisher of *The Oregonian*.

At its peak the ranch grazed thousands of sheep, some of which were shipped to the young Soviet Union. (There was a joke at the ranch that the offspring, nibbling on the foothills of the Caucasus, had a Jefferson

Courtesy Oregon Historical Society

Hay Creek Ranch in its prime

County twang to their Russian "speech.") But the depression of the 1930s forced the great spread to its knees. It hasn't been the same since, and where it was once all sheep, it is now mostly cattle.

In 1875 the Hay Creek post office was opened, primarily to serve the homesteaders. It operated almost continuously for forty-five years, finally shutting down in June 1920, when the small farmers had departed, unable to compete with such giants as the Baldwin Sheep and Land Company, which had its headquarters at Hay Creek. Those who remained lie buried on a crusted hill half a mile west of the ranch.

The old post office was a recreation room at Hay Creek Ranch, the last time we were there. There wasn't any town; whatever there had been of Hay Creek had long belonged to the ranch. Some of the handsome managerial dwellings on the horseshoe-shaped road burned down or were torn down, but not too much had been added in the last few decades. You could shoot a Western film at the ranch without having to clutter the place with false-front structures.

We were most impressed by the round barn, one of the few such left in the state. Some people from Western Oregon travel way out to Diamond Valley, south and east of Burns, to view the round barn built by the legendary Pete French. They could see as much at the Hay Creek Ranch, now owned by a Portlander.

The foreman, puzzled by the flurry of visitors, advanced cautiously, to get the feel of the newcomers. He was a middle-aged, leathery faced, clear-eyed man who looked all workingstiff. "Shoot away," he said, when I wondered if we could take pictures.

He told us the ranch ran about 2,000 cattle over 190,000 acres, most of which was leased from the government. "It's a pretty good-sized spread," he remarked evenly. "I've seen bigger, I've seen smaller."

As we were ready to leave I asked him if Hay Creek Ranch didn't remind him of settings from *Bonanza* or *Gunsmoke*. "Never thought about that," he replied laconically, probably saying to himself that he didn't need television to find his own corner of the Old West.

Directions: In Madras (U.S. 97), take B St. east. 10.5 miles, Jct. 1.1 miles, Hay Creek Ranch.

Round Barn at Hay Creek Ranch *Ralph Friedman*

The Wonderful Baldwin Hotel

Back in the Hard Times of the Thirties, when I was a young migratory worker, I didn't have enough money to put up at the Baldwin Hotel whenever I passed through Klamath Falls. But I knew the hotel because of a very basic need. Headed west out of town, to hitch a ride across the Cascades, I paused at the Baldwin to ask if I could use the rest room.

There was nothing about the Baldwin in those days that struck me as special. For one thing, it seemed fairly modern — only about thirty-five years old then, as I learned later. I had stayed in many hotels much older. For another, I had seen a passel of hotels, from South Dakota to California, that had a lot more Western flavor than the Baldwin.

Time passes. Practically all the colorful horse-era hostelries I knew in the Depression years have been torn down. And the Baldwin is now a national historic site. That's how young and transient and profligate with history our country is.

Still, the Baldwin deserves full credit for what it has been stamped. It is a moving portrait of an earlier Oregon period.

Long after western Oregon had acquired some touches of sophistication, south-central Oregon was still frontier range country and far removed from the heartland of the state. Klamath Falls had had its current name changed from Linkville less than ten years when construction started on the Baldwin. Materials for the hotel had to be carried over the Topsy Grade Road on the Lower Klamath River. Ten-mule jerk lines hauled three wagons to bring furniture to the Baldwin. It required three days to haul one I-beam. From Ashland, you had to go down to California at least as far as Montague and come up the Lower Klamath to get to K Falls.

The four-and-a-half story hotel was built into blue bedrock, so that all of it sits on solid rock. The hotel was literally tiered into a hill of rock, which had to be blasted out to make the stairway from the lobby to the mezzanine.

We learned the above from Vera Moore Jones, who with her husband, Mart, ran the Baldwin. The silver-haired, loquacious proprietor, as energetic in body as in tongue, plied us with details that seemingly left no stone unturned. But, she insisted, "It would take me at least three days, maybe more, to tell you all about the Baldwin. There's enough here to write a book about. Why don't you come back and stay a few months and

Baldwin Hotel, Klamath Falls

write a book about the Baldwin? There isn't another hotel like it in Oregon. There's pioneer spirit here."

Unfortunately, we had to leave for an appointment in Ashland. Sadder, too, we never found the time to return. (We will, of course; we always say we will and pray to whatever gods that be that we are good prophets.) But there was no denying, even in the few hours we were there, that Vera Moore Jones knew a great deal about the hotel, considered it a close part of her life, and had the credentials of native heritage.

She was born in Bonanza, about thirty miles east of Klamath Falls, the daughter of a Missouri-born couple who opened a general store in Bonanza in 1910.

"When Mother was eight years old her folks took part in the Cimarron Drive, that opened Oklahoma Territory to white settlement," Mrs. Jones declared proudly.

She was as high on her father. "I have a story for you," she said, in between telling us about the construction of the hotel and orally cataloging the items of interest. "My father drove out his competitors in Bonanza because he sold corsets to Indians. That's right. He had a freight-car load of colored corsets from St. Louis. The Indians would come in and buy the colored corsets and walk out wearing the corsets on the outside."

In 1920 the Moores closed shop and went to Oklahoma, to be with her mother's family, but three years later they were back in Oregon and purchased the Baldwin Hotel. "I have lived here most of my lifetime," asserted Mrs. Jones with a gleaming smile. "The most I was ever away was a little over three years. My husband and I have been running the place since 1951. That's quite a while, isn't it?

"I love the hotel now as much as I did when I was a kid," she went on. "It gets kind of tiring sometimes but we can't get away; there's so much pilfering. A lot of people who come to Klamath Falls stay overnight. Bob Straub and his wife always stay here. He likes the big beds. He wrote in our guest book: 'It's the best hotel in Oregon.' "

This was before Straub was elected governor and became warier in his remarks.

Mrs. Jones bade us be seated on overstuffed nineteenth century chairs in the lobby — and the lobby was something else; it looked like a cow-country inn waiting for the cattlemen to come trooping in through the old doors — and told more about the building:

"The wood up to the third floor is thirty inches thick and from then on it is fourteen inches thick. Every board in the hotel is original; not one has been changed. There's not a knot in the wood in all the building. It's clear, selected native wood. The pillars are single pieces of wood slapped around I-beams used in building bridges. All the work was hand done. They didn't have machinery to do it with. The building has nineteen chimneys on top and fifty-one flues inside. It took five years to build the hotel. And the engineers say this is the strongest building in the Northwest because it's built on rock and can't settle."

It was a dizzying rendition of facts and I brief-handed beyond my normal speed to keep up with her. But before I could catch a deep breath she was unloading more information upon us:

"The hotel was built by Sen. George Baldwin, after whom it is named. It has entertained Presidents Theodore Roosevelt, William Howard Taft and Woodrow Wilson. Zane Grey visited here and there is a photo here — I will show you soon — of his horse in front of the hotel.

"Now, let me tell you a bit more before I take you on a tour. The hotel has thirty-two hollow Western brass beds; thirty-six wood-burning stoves; original oval flush boxes in six rooms, each with footrail; Quaker spinning wheel; a one hundred-fifty-year-old mahogany sleigh bed; a seventeenth century cast-iron bed; an Aladdin lamp more than a hundred years old; and cheval dressers. One bed is so old it was floated down the Mississippi River on a barge. Most of the furniture and fixtures are originals. And one other thing: The hotel has registration sheets going back to at least 1907."

"Somewhere I heard, or read," I mused, "about the hiding of secret money in the hollow brass bed frames."

Mrs. Jones laughed. "That may be true. A lot of strange people roomed here and a lot of strange things went on. I haven't found any of that money but it's a good story, and this old hotel is full of such. Come down here for a few months and I'll give you enough material to fill a book."

Of the sixty rooms in the hotel, she added a moment later, forty-

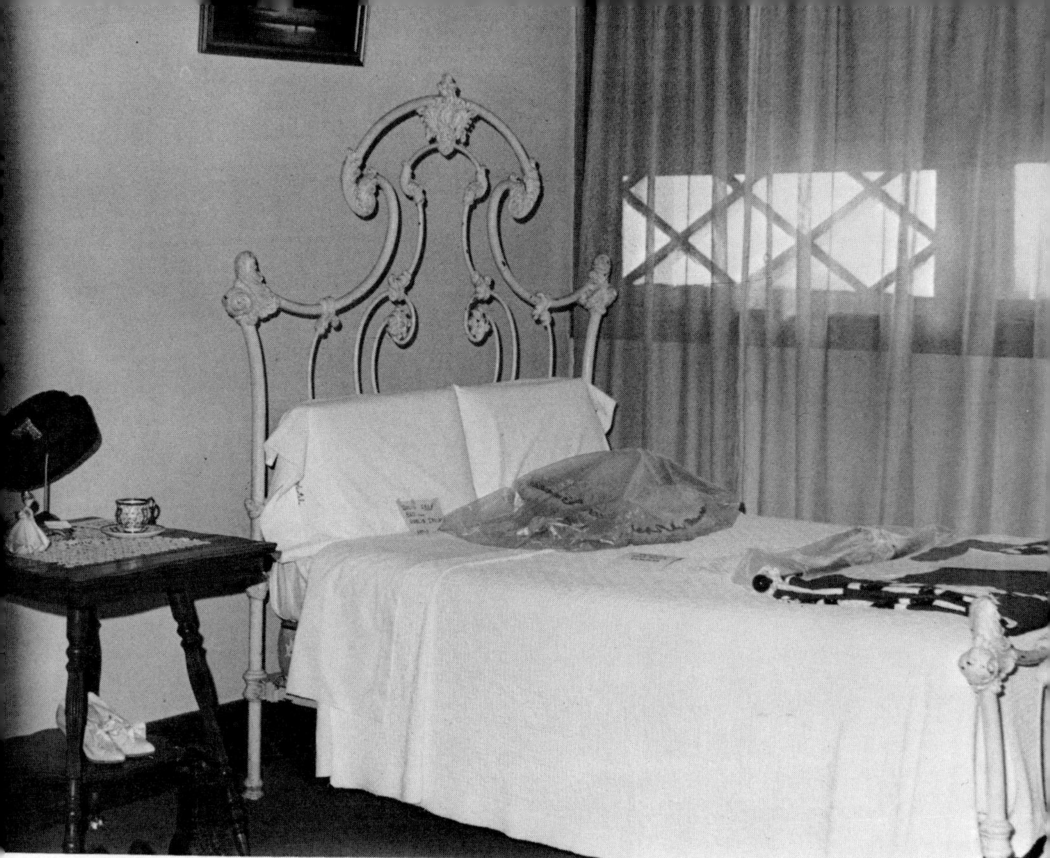
A room at the Baldwin

seven were for rent. The others were used for storage or display. The display rooms had all the appearance of tasteful, expertly arranged museum sets. One of those display rooms alone would probably cost an antique-buyer a fortune, I guessed aloud. Mrs. Jones winked at my materialistic impulse. "That's right," she agreed, with all the security of a poker player who starts off with four aces, "but they're not for sale."

Who patronized the hotel now, long after the glamour and wealth had gone? "Mostly working people and retired folks, who want quiet," Mrs. Jones replied. A small hand-printed sign on the second floor read: "NOTICE! Please Keep Unnecessary Noise Quiet After 10 P.M. People Are Sleeping Near By And The Floor Under."

Minimum rent then, when I made these notes in 1972, was $12 a week, without bath. That probably was about the tariff for a single night's stay at one of the plush motels just a few blocks west.

I tried the mattresses. They were firm. The rooms were clean. The carpets weren't frayed. I said to my wife: "I don't care about Theodore Roosevelt, William Howard Taft, Woodrow Wilson, Zane Grey, and Bob Straub. I don't want to sleep in their glory. I like this place for what it is now. The next time we come to Klamath Falls, let's stay here."

Friend wife nodded amiably. "Be my guest."

"Mine," chimed in Mrs. Jones. "You'll love it here. I do. And when you come, plan to stay a while. I haven't begun to tell you the first thing about this wonderful Baldwin Hotel."

Two Apart: Winema and Captain Jack

I feel bad for my people in the lava beds. I would cry if I didn't see my people at Yainax. I don't know the new country, and they wouldn't know where they were. I know no country but Shasta and Pitt River. But I say yes, and consent to everything and go away. I don't want to live here any more, because I can't live here any more in peace. I wish to go to southern country and live in peace.

Captain Jack, March 6, 1873

If you ask in Beatty where Winema is buried you may find yourself running into blank faces. That may seem strange, because Beatty is regarded as an "Indian town," and in Oregon history Winema is looked upon as one of the greatest of the state's Indians.

Better you should ask for the location of the Chief Schonchin Cemetery. You are on more neutral ground there.

We inquired about Winema of a few young Indians we met on the main street (which is state highway 140) of Beatty. "Who is she?" one of them asked, looking puzzled. His companion said, "I think I heard of her from somewhere." The others seemed bored or irritated by the question.

The only people in Beatty who really knew something about Winema were whites, and maybe that fixes her place more meaningfully in today's scene than the inscription on her tombstone in the Chief Schonchin Cemetery:

"Modoc Heroine — Interpreter For Peace Commission— Pensioned by Congress For Courageous and Loyal Service, Modoc Indian War, 1872-73."

She was, in short, though perhaps unwittingly, an agent for the Yankee conquistadores.

The plaque was placed by a chapter of the Daughters of the American Revolution on May 30, 1932.

I know of no plaques placed by the DAR on the graves of Indians who fought and died for the rights of their people.

Winema was born about 1846, near Link River, also in Klamath County, the daughter of a Modoc chief. She was sixteen when wed to Frank Riddle, a white Indian trader, who is also buried in the cemetery. Many Riddles lie here. Winema and her husband had four children, three of whom died in infancy; the survivor, Jefferson Riddle, is best known as the author of *Indian History of the Modoc War*.

It was during the so-called Modoc War that Winema gained her fame. By then she was ten years married, had adopted the ways of her husband's culture, bore the name of Toby Riddle, and was a round-faced, beaming young woman of awesome drive and energy.

On February 28, 1873, Winema, her husband, and three other white men rode into the Lava Beds, just south of the Oregon border, to talk to Captain Jack, the leader of a Modoc band seeking refuge from white power. Only because Winema was his cousin and he trusted her did Jack consent to talk to the other three whites, who constituted a Peace Commission sent out by Washington, D.C. to remove the Modocs to a warm place in the south.

Born Kintpuash, Captain Jack had been given that name by merchants in Yreka City, California, where the Modocs of the Lost River Valley often traded. Until the war he was forced into, he believed he could live in peaceful coexistence with whites. "I have always told white men when they came to my country," he said, "that if they wanted a home to live there they could have it; and I never asked them for any pay for living there as my people lived."

As always, the greed for land determined federal policy, and the Modocs were moved to the Klamath Reservation. It was a stupid and wicked decision. The Klamaths, who for centuries had occupied the land that was now a reservation, strongly outnumbered the Modocs and made life miserable for them. Captain Jack pleaded for protection, but the Indian agent was deaf to their cries. The Klamaths were fed and clothed; the Modocs were not. The powers in Washington, D.C. had even neglected to vote money to purchase supplies for the Modocs. Every effort on the part of the Modocs to develop a life of self-sufficiency was frustrated by the Klamaths. Finally the Modocs could take no more and departed.

Captain Jack had arrived at the Klamath Reservation with less than fifty people; he left with 371. But dissension within the Modocs quickly broke out. One group settled near Lower Klamath Lake, away from both the reservation and Captain Jack. Another, led by Old Schonchin, returned to the reservation, more fearful of the white man's wrath than of Jack's authority.

The plaque on Schonchin's grave in Chief Schonchin Cemetery reads: "Head Chief of the Modocs — His Courageous Loyalty to His Treaty Obligations Kept the Bulk of his Tribe From the Warpath and Saved the Klamath Settlement 1872-73."

That, of course, is why a butte in Lava Beds National Monument, where the Modoc War took place, was named after the chief.

Those who stayed with Captain Jack in the Lost River Valley, to which they had returned, resumed their old ways. Captain Jack urged the Great White Chiefs to create a Modoc Reservation on Lost River, rather than return them to the Klamath Reservation, as the Indian Bureau decreed. For a fleeting moment the bureau leaned in Jack's favor but quickly regained their adamant stance after vigorous protests by white ranchers, who did not want one acre of their rich grazing lands taken

Courtesy Shasta-Cascade Wonderland Association

Captain Jack's band used caves such as this one, in the Lava Beds, to fight the white soldiers.

from them. So, of course, the army was dispatched to bring the Modocs back by force to the Klamath Reservation.

Captain Jack was willing to return rather than spill blood. "I will take all my people with me, but I do not place any confidence in anything you white people tell me," he addressed the commander of the First Cavalry. But the bullying tactics of Major Jackson precipitated a conflict — and the Modocs fled.

They retreated to Tule Lake, an ancestral home, and from there continued south to an ancient sanctuary, the Lava Beds of northern California. Eons ago, volcanic upheavals and rivers of fire had turned a gentle plain into a labyrinth of oddly shaped caves, natural bridges, fumaroles, fissures that could be seen only up close, trenches that sliced through the terrain, and narrow rocky gullies a hundred feet deep. The tortured wasteland was ideal as a fortress and as a base for guerilla operations. Captain Jack exploited it for both. And if the government had approved, he would have consented to live out his life on a Lava Beds Reservation.

It is another one of those ironies, repeating itself as regularly as the coming and going of the seasons, that the protector is betrayed by the protected. The day after he established a stronghold for himself and his family at the Lava Beds, Jack was visited by a old companion, Hooker Jim, who arrived in a froth with thirteen other Modocs. They told a story that Jack first found incredible. Then, as the truth sank in, the tale broke his heart and left him with the anguish of despair.

Hooker Jim's group had been outside the camp when the firing between Major Jackson's troops and Captain Jack's men started. They had fled, explaining that white settlers had started shooting at their location at the time Captain Jack's people had been facing the First Cavalry.

"I ran off and did not want to fight," Hooker Jim said later, when the smoke of all the battles had drifted off into history. "They shot some of my women, and they shot my men. . . . I had very few people and did not want to fight."

But Hooker Jim's group did kill. In a madness of revenge they rode to the Lava Beds, pausing only at isolated ranches to gun down anyone they found. They had slain twelve settlers before they reached Captain Jack.

Not all whites were hostile to the Indian. Some of the murdered settlers had befriended Jack; he could trust them to keep their word. "What did you kill these people for?" he cried. "I never wanted you to kill my friends. You should have done it on your own responsibility."

Courtesy Oregon Historical Society

Captain Jack

Perhaps Jack should have tried to turn Hooker Jim and his men away. As he faced execution he probably realized that he should at least have tried. But it was different that day, long before the bitter lesson was learned. He knew that, as leader of the Modoc band, he would be blamed for the slayings. To turn Hooker Jim's group away might save the rest of Captain Jack's people. Or it might not. But Hooker Jim had come to Jack for protection, one Modoc brother appealing to the other, and Jack could not say no.

There was yet one way out; surrender himself and assume equal guilt with Hooker Jim's men, whom the soldiers now wanted most of all. But by a 37-to-15 vote of the warriors his proposal was turned down.

Then, after the Modocs had repulsed a charge by the soldiers, Winema, her husband, and the three commissioners came riding into camp. Frank Riddle, whom whites called a squaw man, acted as interpreter, and a peace council was agreed upon. One of the terms to be guaranteed, the commissioners promised after Captain Jack pressed the issue, was that all Modocs at the Lava Beds, including Hooker Jim's cohorts,

Courtesy Oregon Historical Society

Winema

would be removed to a reservation — in Indian Territory or Arizona — far from the hated Klamaths. Surrender as prisoners of war would place the Indians outside the jurisdiction of Oregon law, the commissioners declared.

Swiftly as they learned the word, Hooker Jim and his partisans rode hard to the headquarters of Gen. E. R. S. Canby, who had veto power over the commissioners, and turned themselves in as prisoners of war. The astonished Canby jubilantly wired his superior, General Sherman, in Washington, that the Modoc War was over and asked for instructions on what to do with the vanquished.

Had Canby put Hooker Jim and the eight who came with him under guard, as was regulation in such circumstance, the violence and the tragedy that followed would probably — or at least might — have been averted. It was one of those mental lapses that change the course of small streams of history. In his exhilaration Canby let his discipline slip. The nine wandered around the armed camp and, in one of those fortuitous events that sometimes alter the destinies of individuals and groups, met an Oregonian who denounced them as murderers and added with grim relish that the governor of Oregon would have them arrested and hanged.

Back to the Lava Beds fled Hooker Jim and his followers. Even before they dismounted they were exhorting Captain Jack not to go to the peace council. It is a trap, they warned. The soldiers will give you to Oregon to be strung up, they admonished. And they argued and shouted and tongue-lashed and proclaimed.

Winema and Frank Riddle returned bearing messages. It was not true, Canby said, that all of Captain Jack's band would be handed over to Oregon. That would apply only to Hooker Jim's group.

Jack pondered and returned to the question that was now a thorn in his being. Could he desert Hooker Jim? Was he a chief if he did not protect all his people? There had been wrong on both sides, he concluded. Let the white men understand this and there will be peace.

With some assistance from his sister, Mary, he wrote a letter to the commissioners. It is interesting to note that he did not ask his cousin, Winema, or Frank Riddle, the husband of his cousin, to help him. Nor did he give the letter to the Riddles to deliver. It was Mary who brought it to the commissioners.

"Let everything be wiped out, washed out, and let there be no more blood," Jack wrote. He asked the commissioners if they would "give up their people who murdered my people while they were asleep?" He added, "I never asked for the people who murdered my people." He could not, he said in summary, give up his men to be hanged.

General Sherman, who had broken the back of the Confederacy in his everything-to-the-torch march from Atlanta to the sea and then bluntly asserted that "War is hell," advised Canby to give the Modocs a reservation in the Lava Beds, but first turn it into a cemetery, so that they would stay there forever. But Canby wanted one more try for peace. Back to the saddle went Winema and Frank Riddle.

The general and Captain Jack spoke briefly. Canby promised the moon and brought more soldiers. Jack accused Canby of hypocrisy and pleaded, as he had done so often before, that all the Indians wanted was to be let alone.

There were more meetings. Each time Canby was more audacious. Now he talked tough about the fate of Hooker Jim's men. Jack replied he could not give them up. Canby sent Winema to Jack with a proposal: Any Modoc who wanted to surrender could ride back with her.

Hooker Jim was outraged. He and his men, who had slain the settlers, swore they would kill any of the band who surrendered. Vehemently they accused Canby of trying to seduce Jack into capitulation and Jack of listening to Canby's persuasion. The hour of doom was at hand.

Canby had ordered a tent to be erected on the sageland halfway between where the soldiers stood and the first defenses in the Lava Beds. There the final council would be held. Armed with the formidable power of their artillery, whose gunsights held the canvas tent in full view, Canby and the commissioners came without guards or weapons, except for two derringers. But the Indians arrived with concealed pistols.

Winema had urged the commissioners to stay away. One of Jack's band, also related to Winema, had cautioned her not to come to the stronghold again and begged her to convince the whites for whom she worked to keep their distance. But the commissioners waved off as unreal the entreaty she delivered, and she and Frank Riddle accompanied them to the council.

For three days Captain Jack had tried to resist the pressures put on him by Hooker Jim and his followers that Jack kill Canby. One after another of Jack's friends turned against him. The Modocs were desperate. Every day they faced new soldiers and more field pieces. Steel and shot were hemming in. Death in the Lava Beds was imminent, so why wait?

Hooker Jim taunted Jack, sneered at him, reviled him as a coward, a betrayer, a fish-hearted woman, and named the terms: Kill Canby or be killed by your own men.

Jack fought back. He spoke eloquently of life; he spoke calmly of death. His words were received by stone. Three-fourths of the warriors voted that he kill Canby.

There was one last hope, the last of the last. If Jack could extract from Canby a promise that the general would meet the terms of the Modocs, Jack would not kill.

One white man quickly sensed the situation in the council tent. He was Alfred Meacham, a former Superintendent of Indian Affairs in Oregon, appointed by President Grant in 1870. He had come to know Captain Jack and the Modocs well and had proposed a Lost River Reservation. That was too much for the War Department, which feared conflict between the Indians and the settlers, and at the insistence of the brass, Meacham had been fired.

Meacham could feel the tension that crackled through the Modocs. Danger stalked grimly inside the tent. For the first time in his dealings with Indians, Meacham was shaken. When Captain Jack implored Canby to remove the troops and guarantee the Indians a home — anywhere, anywhere but with the Klamaths — Meacham almost screamed at Canby to promise Jack anything. But before Canby, probably momentarily confused by the commotion, could speak, Jack shot him dead.

Riddle and a peace commissioner fled in the confusion. Another peace commissioner was killed. Meacham owed his life to Winema, who rescued him after he had been badly wounded and his clothes ripped away. Then she nursed him back to health.

The Modocs retreated deep into the Lava Beds, and the war began in earnest. Despite the heroism and brilliant tactics of the Indians, their end was only a matter of time. But some who had boasted that they were ready to die for freedom abandoned Captain Jack when the mortar fire came close. Gone soon were Hooker Jim's group, who quickly made a deal with the army. They joined forces against Jack and were granted amnesty.

There was something of high Shakespearean drama in the confrontation between Hooker Jim and Captain Jack when the turncoat found the leader he had betrayed. If Jack had read Othello he might have thought of Iago as Jim cajoled, "Return with me and the soldiers will be just to you; the soldiers are your friends; they will give you all the food you need, all the clothes you need, you will never be in need again."

Jack was fierce in his denunciation. He mocked Jim and his men for gaining their freedom at the expense of his, for having become lackeys of the soldiers, for having renounced all their grand words. And he angrily gestured them away, threatening to shoot them if their shadows again came within the range of his rifle.

The finish came soon enough. Only three of his band were with him when Captain Jack surrendered.

A trial — with the verdict never in doubt — was held at Fort Klamath in July. The star witnesses against Jack and his three codefendents were, as you can readily guess, Hooker Jim and his men. It was the ultimate act of betrayal. The protector had been delivered to the hangman by those he had protected. It was another one of those ironies of history that are as regular as the coming and going of the seasons, and out of which few of us learn.

Captain Jack used his chance to speak in court to denounce his Judas. In a speech translated by Winema's husband, Frank Riddle, Jack summed up the essence of the struggle in the Lava Beds: "You white people conquered me not; my own men did."

He died on the gallows October 3, 1873. The 153 Modocs still remaining — Hooker Jim's group among them — were shipped off to Indian Territory. There the Okmulgee Council, which had shown its solidarity with a message of "sympathy and brotherly feelings," held a ceremonial reception for the delegates of the exiled. In 1909, when the Modocs were allowed to return to Oregon, and again placed on the Klamath Reservation, fifty-one were alive. A few chose to remain in the southwest; in 1970, according to historian Angie Debo, about forty of the descendants still lived in Oklahoma.

Seventeen years after the killings at the council tent, the government granted Winema a pension of $25 a month. She spent it on impoverished Indians of the Klamath Reservation. For a while she was a celebrity, touring the East, telling audiences of the redskins in the far off West, and

Grave of Winema

lionized by the press. Everywhere she went she was hailed as a truly good Indian, the sweetest laurels a white society would present to her.

The last years of her life were spent at Yainax, on the Klamath Reservation. She died in 1920 at the age of seventy-four, the same age as Frank Riddle when he passed away. She was born and died fourteen years later than he. In death she fared better than her husband, the whites giving the name of Winema to a post office (no longer existent) about twenty-five miles north of Chiloquin; to the basalt spires (Winema Pinnacles) about half a mile east of Multnomah Falls; and to a national forest in southern Oregon.

Enclosed on three sides by pines and on the fourth by a pasture, the cemetery in which Winema sleeps is ablaze with wild flowers, their blooms gorgeous in spring and stalk-dry in summer. As though to add to the color, many plastic flowers have been placed on the graves, some of which are nameless mounds, the inscriptions on their board markers having been erased by wind and rain and sun and snow.

Captain Jack, too, lies in a nameless grave, but not here. You cannot find his grave; there is no certainty where it really is. Before the cock could crow to the world the news of his execution, his body had been dug up and wagoned to Yreka City, where it was embalmed. Then it was shipped across the country and exhibited at carnivals. And there is a story that his head was severed and sent to a museum in Washington. How fortunate we are to be civilized!

Suppose, suppose now in your imagination, that at the second confrontation at Wounded Knee — if one can call the first time, a massacre, a confrontation — Winema and Captain Jack had arisen from the dead. Each had had time to survey the past — for Captain Jack, more than a century; for Winema, almost six decades. What would they have done?

Captain Jack would at least have sent greetings, and warned of those who speak too boldly and thirst for blood. But Winema, would she have learned? Or would she have found it more comfortable still to be esteemed by whites than to join with the rebels of her first and last people?

Directions: Take Oregon 140 east from Klamath Falls. 36 miles from downtown Klamath Falls, Sprague River Jct. (Beatty is 5 miles further.) Turn north at Sprague River Jct. 1.2 miles, turn right on gravel road. 0.7 mile, Chief Schonchin Cemetery.

Phantom Legend on the Crooked River

I guess you have heard of Meek's cut off. Well, it came pretty nigh cuttin' off the ones who tried it.

Susannah Johnson Peterson, member of the Meek Party

About five miles west of Paulina we paused at the South Fork of the Crooked River, brought here by my fascination for Oregon history and folklore.

It is an interactive process with me: The books compel me to the places and the places turn me to the books.

I walked along the banks, wondering what the river looked like in 1845. Undoubtedly it was wider and deeper then, irrigation having drained so much of it in recent decades. And the land greener — much greener — thick with bunchgrass. The homesteaders broke the earth and the land had never been as green since. Now there are areas where green grass is seldom seen.

So there it was, a piddling stream no bigger than a minor creek now, and lost in the dust of history.

Let me try to remind you. You have heard the legend of the Blue Bucket Mine. It was born in the wake of the grim trek of Meek's Cutoff Party of 1845.

Stephen Meek, at thirty-eight, three years older than his illustrious brother, Joe, sold several hundred emigrants on a short cut from Fort Boise, Idaho to the Willamette Valley. (Those who continued along the Old Oregon Trail arrived in the Willamette Valley six weeks earlier, and in much better shape.)

It did not take the members of the caravan, which came to be known in some quarters as the Lost Wagon Train of 1845, too many days to realize that old Steve didn't really know the country — but by then they were hopelessly disoriented. Frequent threats were made on Meek's life and at one point some intensely frustrated men — who hated Meek with boiling blood for having suckered them into a hellish wasteland — might have shot him if he hadn't gotten wind of the plot in time to ride away fast with his bride. She was the former Elizabeth Schoonover, a seventeen-year-old lass he married a week after the wagon train he'd hired on to guide westward took off from Independence, Missouri.

(Theirs was a courtship of only seven days but they stayed close until her death twenty years later.)

At Wagontire Mountain, after drifting confusedly as far south as Harney Lake, the party turned north and bumped along in clouds of acrid dust and blazes of curses until it reached the present site of the G. I. Ranch, a few miles below the headwaters of the South Fork of the Crooked River.

There the train divided, for reasons no one could later recall. One section headed west and eventually reached what is now Bend. The other followed the South Fork north to the place where this photo was taken. Then that group turned west, as the South Fork does here, and adhered to the stream, which in twenty miles joins with the North Fork to become the Crooked River, all the way to present Prineville. Somehow both sections of the train came together — some miles above Madras.

It was the South Fork section which supposedly discovered the Blue Bucket Mine — if, indeed, any gold was found.

Out of the hills the emigrants stumbled — weak, bitter, disheartened, death almost a daily notation in soggy ledgers, and illness a part of every wagon. They had no idea where they were; they only knew that somewhere in the westering arc of the sun was the Deschutes. The Deschutes would take them to the Columbia and the Columbia to the Willamette Valley. But where was the Deschutes?

South Fork of the Crooked River

Courtesy Oregon Historical Society
Peter Britt photo

Stephen Meek, colorful to the end

At last they found the river and suffered the ordeal of crossing it. "The means finally resorted to for the transportation of the families and wagons were novel in the extreme," wrote Joel Palmer in his much-quoted *Journal of Travels Over the Rocky Mountains*. A careful reporter, he had taken pains to learn what had transpired. "A large rope was swung across the stream and attached to the rocks on either side; a light wagon bed was suspended from this rope with pulleys, to which ropes were attached; this bed served to convey the families and loading in safety across; the wagons were then drawn over the bed of the river by ropes. The passage of this river occupied some two weeks."

Samuel Parker jotted dolefully in his diary on Oct. 3: "Crossed the deschutes river in a wagon body and tuck the wagons Apart and tuck a wheale at a time by rope this day my 2 small boys tuck sick gideon and george and susan my forth girl 6 of my family sick at one time" On the same day Jesse Harritt wrote tersely: "spent the day in crossing the river had no timber to make boats ware compelled to make boats of our wagon beds to cross our families and goods."

By the time the contrite and frightened Steve Meek and his wife reached The Dalles to summon aid, a rescue expedition was already on the way, alerted by the emigrants who had reached The Dalles by the Old Oregon Trail and who had become alarmed by the absence of their former comrades of the plains.

Leading the Good Samaritans was Black Harris, the old Mountain Man, as able and resourceful as anyone in the Oregon Country. The main body of the Cutoff Party probably could have made it to The Dalles on their own but straggler families, too weak to keep the pace, would likely have perished without the relief column. They were at the end of their rope, their provisions almost depleted and their hopes forsaken.

So I stood here, at this quiet little stream, so low in water that even the shallow rocks were drying out, and strained to turn time back.

A camper stopped and a man with a Bend dealership plate got out and asked if anything was wrong. Everything's fine, I said. "Fishing?" he asked. No, I replied, I'm just looking. "Anything for?" he asked. Well, I said, Meek's Cutoff Party came down this stream. He peered oddly at me. "When do you expect them?" I don't know, I replied, but I'm trying hard.

He had a resonant voice and when he got back into the camper we heard him say, "Let's go, Mary. That guy's been out in the sun too long."

Directions: The point where this photo was taken is fifty miles southeast of Prineville, on a country road, and 5.5 miles west of Paulina.

Fording on the Oregon Trail

Five miles east of Wasco we had a picnic lunch on some hay bales outside the old store building at the ghost town of Klondike, the stiff breeze swirling slivers of straw into the glint of the central Oregon sun.

Most abandoned buildings get torn down within a few years, but half a century after the Potter mercantile store closed the weathered structure still stood.

Having finished lunch and cleaned the area, I asked my Oregon for the Curious class, "Who would like to look with me for a place where the covered wagons on the Oregon Trail forded the John Day River?"

"Me!" cried everyone in unison, so off we took down a gravel road covered by stillness. We paused briefly, three-tenths of a mile from the store, at the shell of a brick schoolhouse that hadn't served a pupil for many decades, and then continued 4.7 miles, through open wheat country, where we slanted right. I had never been to the fording but I had in my mind a sketch of a map drawn orally for me by an elderly lady I had palavered with a year back, at The Dalles.

Now, on a narrow, twisty, droppping trace, we bumped five miles, passing the mouth of a canyon that is a deep trough in the tall grass, and halting at an Oregon Trail marker. At this point the wagon trains had crossed what was now our road, going from right to left.

We had not passed or seen another car since leaving Klondike. Here there was not a house or barn or animal in sight. This is the way the choppy contours of the land must have looked to the comers. But travel was far more trying for them. In all the diaries I have read there is not a kind word about the terrain.

"The hill on leaving John Day River," wrote John S. Zeiber, an emigrant of 1851, "is one of the worst we have met with; about one and a fourth miles long, not very steep in any part of it, but about one-third of it is very rocky and contains many short turns which makes it impossible for more than a yoke or two of cattle to draw at the same time."

The "very stony, rocky and sandy hill" was to Cecilia Emily McMillen Adams, who crossed the plains in 1852, "as bad as any we have had, all things considered."

Three miles ahead on the boulder-strewn, erratically indented pike we came to a small granite monument bearing a plaque that tells of the wagon train fording at the John Day River. A minute later we were at the storied waterway, which Mrs. Adams described as "a very rapid stream."

Most emigrants were concerned with what was — or wasn't — on the west bank. "The valley of the river is narrow and without timber," wrote John Zeiber. "A few small willows afforded a scanty supply of fuel and we shall have to travel 36 miles before we get to wood." But there was a bright note: "Fish appear to be plenty in the river."

Like many other emigrants, E. W. Conyers, a pioneer of 1852, found that earlier caravans had devoured the natural feed. "There has been very good grass in this valley," he jotted in his journal, "but the ground is now barren, the grass having been eaten off." He found a solution, though: "We drove our cattle to the table lands back of our camp, where we found good bunch grass."

The wagons came down to the river following Rock Creek, a shallow bite in the low but sharply angled hills. The creek was sometimes too low to water stock, but in 1847 Ralph Carey Geer observed: "At Rock creek, we had several head of cattle drowned in a short time after we stopped and we called that creek Drowning Creek."

Between Willow Creek to the east and the John Day River, a wagon-wheel distance of almost twenty-eight miles, John Zeiber found "no water for the cattle." From the tablelands east of the John Day, the emigrants, wrote Conyers, "descended a very steep hill." Other emigrants described

Ralph Friedman

John Day River at point where covered wagons crossed stream

Ralph Friedman

Old Oregon Trail plaque near John Day River.

the descent as "dusty" and "rough" and almost all called the entire terrain "barren" and "desolate."

In 1858 Thomas Scott established a ferry on the east bank. The wonder is that no one had done it before. Evidently the comers were more anxious to reach the end of the rainbow than to profit from their fellow travelers.

Near the ferry the town of Scotts was started in 1867. In 1878 the name was changed to Rockville and moved a couple of miles up Rock Creek. In 1889 the post office was closed. A post office called Rock Creek had had a shorter life; it had lasted only from 1872 to 1874. The first waves of homesteaders were washed out by isolation, hard times and poor crops. At what was the hamlet of Rock Creek there is only a school, and past the rise on which it stands rolled hundreds of prairie schooners.

Daniel Leonard had a better way to cross the river than by ferry. In 1866 he built a bridge. Like Scott, he accumulated a small fortune from the emigrants. There is now no trace of the wooden span.

A plaque near the river says that settlers came this way until 1884, when the railroad to Portland was completed. The fact is that wagons continued on the trail into the twentieth century.

Legend has it that near the river crossing on the west bank of the John Day a saloon was established for thirsty emigrants. It was so profitable, legend continues, that about a dozen more saloons arose within five or six miles to the south. If legend is true, they all disappeared long ago.

Bill McDonald arrived in 1904 and started up a ferry service, Leonard's bridge no longer usable. That same year a post office was established to serve the new generation of homesteaders, so McDonald's Ferry became McDonald. The post office lasted until 1922, about the time most of the homesteaders left. Search up and down the riverbank and as far back as you want and you won't find anything of McDonald except an ugly rock wall which Bill McDonald supposedly built to "fence in" his place at its western boundary.

We were met at the crossing by Evan Burnett, a bright, muscular young man who breezed barefoot out of the ranch house he shared with his wife and three dogs. There were nineteen of us, and Evan hadn't seen that many people so close together since the last time he had been to The Dalles. Unless there's a planned meeting of some kind you don't see nineteen people in one place at Wasco.

Evan and his father owned a spread that had once been occupied by a passel of homesteaders and they ran about 100 cattle on this far-flung land. I asked him if he ever used the cable handcart to get across the river. "Sometimes," he replied. So I talked him into coming with me on the trip and together with Pat Kimoto, a veteran of our group, we crossed high above the John Day, Evan pulling on the cable. Downstream, one of his dogs swam the river diagonally, wisely keeping to the current. Returning, the four of us traveled by an outboard motor skiff that had been beached on the east bank.

Standing at the now all-but-forgotten fording, so important in the great years of the westering march, I told Evan that I had been looking for Oregon Trail ruts wherever the wagons had rolled and had seen very few.

"I can imagine," he replied. "I've been all over these hills, covered every square foot of them. I know where the wagon trains crossed the river, I know which course they took, I can take you just about where they traveled from here to Wasco, but I've never seen a single wagon-train rut. Men, machinery and time have wiped them out."

And so, I thought, all that remains constant is the John Day. But a moment later I asked myself, "With all that has happened since the land was settled, especially irrigation, is the river really the same?" I didn't know, but I was sure that I would see the drama of the wagon trains fording the stream not on a plaque but in my mind. So I lifted my eyes to the hills and between the sheets of dust I spied the schooners looping down a cut in the ridge to the stream, and seeing that brave procession, I hiked up and down the bank, looking sharp into the water, so that I could call across the best place to come out on the western side of the John Day River.

Directions: From Wasco, take Airport Road to Klondike. Turn left. 5 miles, slant right. 5.1 miles on right, Old Oregon Trail sign. 3 miles, on left, Oregon Trail marker. 0.2 mile, John Day River, where wagons forded the stream.

Ghostly Sequel to the John Day Fording

Perhaps I should have included the following story of cached loot at the site of McDonald in the preceding sketch. But I did not think it wove well with the rest of the telling. It stands out too strongly alone.

There is a local legend, said Evan Burnett, about a McDonald farmer who robbed a bank in a nearby town and made off with $20,000. He was then murdered by his two partners, a man and a woman. The money was supposedly buried, but before it could be unearthed the couple got into an argument and shot each other to death. The cache, added Evan, had never been found.

A year later I was told a different version of the buried boodle tale by Jim White, a native of these parts then living at Lincoln City, on the Oregon coast. I had written to White because his name was suggested to me by a Sherman County woman who said White had once related to her a fascinating story of gold secreted at McDonald. White replied to my inquiry with one of the eeriest yarns I have heard in my tracking down of Oregon. It is as much a ghost story as a tale of buried treasure and with White's permission I give you herewith his full reply:

"I know nothing of the story of a bank robbery. The story, as I know it and as was told to me by my Grandfather, W. H. Yancey; my Mother's Aunt, Maude Bargenolt; and my Mother, Adria White, is as follows:

"A man named Leonard and his wife ran the stage station at McDonald, which was on the main route to and from The Dalles to the gold strikes near Canyon City and Baker. Over several years time they are supposed to have murdered some of the travelers for their gold and money. Eventually a family tiff developed, and Mrs. Leonard killed her husband. She was brought to trial and convicted. Before she left to serve her sentence she asked that her saddle be brought to her. She tore the saddle open and retrieved some gold and money from it.

"A number of years later, probably about 1907, while my Great-Grandfather, Grandfather, and three of my Grandfather's brothers were each homesteading land near the breaks of the John Day River in Gilliam County, Mrs. Leonard was released, and came to my Grandfather's homestead, and asked for his help in finding and digging up the treasure that she and her husband had buried. According to Mrs. Leonard, a light was to appear at midnight to show where it was buried. Apparently her prison stay, as well as the recollections of her deeds, had taken their toll on her mind. My Grandfather accompanied her at least once, if not more times, but no light appeared, and Mrs. Leonard gave up her search and was never seen by my family again.

"Even though my Mother was a small girl then, she still remembers seeing Mrs. Leonard when she came to the homestead. She had long white hair and a wild appearance. My Mother remembers how very afraid she was of the old woman.

"Several people who subsequently lived in the old stage station tell of seeing apparitions of an old woman, with long white hair and wearing a long white flowing dress, roaming the old house, of her going through walls and closed doors, and of her then disappearing when spoken to. The old house was torn down 20 or more years ago, and a new house was built in its place, so no one will ever know what it was that was reported seen, except those who saw, and they *know* what it was.

"I do believe that the buried treasure does exist."

That should have been enough for me — but I had to spoil the story with additional research. Anxious to know how long Mary Leonard served in prison, I wrote to the clerk of the Circuit Court of Wasco County, at The Dalles. Back came word suggesting I correspond with Fred W. Decker of Corvallis, and the state archivist in Salem.

Decker, the great-nephew of Mary Leonard didn't think Jim White's story held much water. His own exhaustive research, summed up in a lively article in the New Hampshire *Sunday News* of Manchester, on December 18, 1975, disclosed that Mary Gysin had married Daniel G. Leonard in 1875, after Leonard had separated from his common-law wife, Sarah. Two years later the Leonards sued each other for divorce. "Sometime during the night of Jan. 4, 1878, Leonard suffered a small-bore wound in the head, and he finally died on Jan. 18, 1878," Decker wrote.

From the Oregon State Archives I received a sizeable package of materials, most of which pertained to the trial of Mary Leonard for the shooting of Daniel.

If we can backtrack a moment, there is a notation in the handwritten documents that Sarah E. Leonard sued D. G. Leonard in 1874 "for payment for labor and services rendered" and was awarded $1,500 and costs. Small payment for the sixteen years she lived with him, during which she bore four children, only two of whom survived.

It is possible that, if the story of the heinous activities at the river are true — the robbing and murdering of travelers — it was Sarah, not Mary, who was Dan Leonard's partner in crime.

On a further note, Leonard filed for divorce action in "1877-78" but the case was dismissed because "D. G. Leonard deceased since continuance."

The day after Leonard was shot, Mary was arrested and put in jail. On June 26, 1878, together with Nathaniel Lindsay, a telegraph lineman who was the only other regular resident at the John Day River inn operated by D. G. Leonard, Mary was indicted "with the crime of murder in the first degree."

Mary was charged with "unlawfully, feloniously, purposely and of deliberate and premeditated malice" killing Leonard by shooting him in the head with a pistol. Lindsay. who was not present at the shooting, was charged with having incited and counseled Mary to commit the alleged crime.

A question never resolved: Why was Mary, then estranged from D. G., at the river? Had she come to ask for money due her for separate maintenance? If an answer was given at her trial it was not recorded.

Bond was set for Mary Leonard at $2,000 but she could not make it and remained behind bars. On July 23 she complained of her incarceration in a letter to the Circuit Court. "I was arrested about the 5th day of January 1878," she declared, "and I have been in prison ever since that day. I am not guilty of the crime with which I am charged, and I desire a speedy trial to the end that my innocence may be established and I may have my liberty. I have been ready for trial at any time since my arrest and am ready now." She concluded with an attack upon the district attorney for having delayed the trial on the pretext that key witnesses were not available when all that was needed to find and summon them was "the use of diligence."

On November 19, 1878 the case against Mary Leonard came to trial; she and Lindsay had requested separate trials. The following day the jury, "after a short absence," returned a verdict of not quilty. Immediately the district attorney moved to dismiss charges against Lindsay, and he was

In the Circuit Court of the State of Oregon,
For the County of Wasco:

In the name of the State of Oregon:

To any Sheriff or............... *in the State of Oregon:*

An indictment having been found on the 26 day of June .... A. D., 1878..
in the Circuit Court of the State of Oregon for the County of Wasco, charging Mary Leonard .... with the crime of .. of murder in the first degree

You are therefore commanded forthwith to arrest the above named Mary Leonard..... and bring him before this Court

to answer the indictment, or, if the Court have adjourned for the term, that you deliver him into the custody of the jailor of the County of Wasco.

Dated at Dalles City, the 26 day of June .... A. D., 1878

By order of the Court:

Witness my hand and official seal, the day and year above written.

R. F. Gibons

CLERK.

Courtesy Oregon State Archives

Warrant issued for arrest of Mary Leonard. Although warrant was issued June 26, 1878, she had already been in jail since January 5, 1878. Notice that the warrant directs the sheriff to "deliver him" to the Wasco County jail. Even when accused of a crime, a woman was "him," not "her."

discharged. Who shot D. G. Leonard remained — and remains — a mystery.

What happened to Mary Leonard after her ten and a half months of incarceration in the Wasco County jail? According to her grand-nephew, Fred Decker, she went to Seattle to study law and in 1884 was admitted to the bar. Two years later and then living in Portland, he added, she was admitted to practice before the Oregon Supreme Court.

There are indications that in her old age her mind began to wander. She seems to have suffered hallucinations. So perhaps she did return to the John Day River, and if you mix up all the facts you can see how a story is born.

Maybe there isn't any buried gold and money at the Oregon Trail fording. Years of chasing many a will-o'-the-wisp have taught me that legend is hardier than history and that, indeed, it becomes history. But if there isn't any cached loot on the banks of the John Day there is a precious bit of folklore there, and for those of us who seek to plumb the soul of the state the legend itself is a treasure.

The Sage of Pilot Rock

A former student of mine said that if I ever got to Pilot Rock I'd be a fool to leave town without meeting Jim Hoskin.

So here we were in downtown Pilot Rock and just as I started toward a cafe to ask where Jim lived I spied this medium-size, stocky fellow in faded and patched overalls come smiling out of a store and head for an old sedan, his step having the spring of a gentle bantam that was all get-up-and-go.

"Mr. Hoskin?" I called. Don't ask me why, but that's what I did.

He turned quickly and with a crinkly smile replied, "No mister. Just Hoskin. Who are you?"

"Ralph Friedman," I said.

"Well, Ralph," declared Jim, his cheerful face a map of rugged cordiality, "I know you, don't I? But I ain't seen you in a long time, have I?"

"Don't reckon we ever met," I said, "but somehow it seems right off like I've known you for about forty years."

He grinned infectuously, instantly recalling for me Will Rogers and Reub Long, fast charmers both of them. "I think I know you, too," he declared, his blue eyes twinkling as he rubbed a couple of fingers over a side of sandy hair.

"I heard tell you're ninety years old," I said. "I don't believe half of it!"

Jim slapped his blue work shirt and chuckled. "Lots of people guess me down to sixty-five and seventy."

"Can we talk to you?" I asked.

"Sure," said Jim heartily. So we followed him home, where he told us many a good story.

Here, measured against the living, was a true pioneer, a genuine son of the soil, a man who was thirty years old when the first automobile came into eastern Oregon. And he was an authentic local. For more than eighty-eight years he had lived within a fifty mile radius of Pilot Rock.

None of his tales were of great moment, but pieced together they gave a vivid folk picture of late nineteenth and early twentieth century homestead and ranch life. His language was so beautiful — so rich with the idiom of his time and place — that I would not have changed a word for love or money. We taped Jim Hoskin, and in transcribing I went over some words as often as ten times, just to get the shading right. If sometimes he says "for" and sometimes "fer" and if he shifts from "and" to "an'," that's the way he spoke. He was not a body to stay glued to a single track of utterance.

In 1883, when Jim was fifteen months old, his family left Asotin, Washington, where he had been born, to see the parents of Jim's father, who lived on Rock Creek, southeast of Pilot Rock.

This is the way Jim told of that trip, hearing it only from his father years later, for his mother died when he was a small boy:

"First we stopped overnight at what they called Pine City. And Dad had been in the sheep business up at Asotin. Old Man Nieves owned that place then at Pine City, and the sheep was comin' in and Dad, they kinda excited him, an' he called for Mother to come out an' look at the sheep. An' he says, 'My, I'd like to have an outfit like this,' an' Nieves says, 'I'll sell it to you.' An' Dad had sold his sheep up at Asotin, so he bought it, right there that night, both sheep an' the ranch."

Jim flopped one leg over another and went on with the story of the trip.

"Then we started over to Rock Creek to see Grandpa an' Grandma an' we stopped to noon on Willow Creek, an' John an' Mary, that was my

Jim Hoskin

brother an' sister, they come down an' washed their hands in the creek and I stepped into a hole and would have drownded if Dad hadn't pulled me out."

That set Jim off to telling about a later near-miss at a different stream in Umatilla County.

"Another time, my brother and I, after we'd come down to Butter Creek, a colt jumped through the fence and kinda excited us. I was between two and three years old then, and we went over to tell Dad about it, an' he just cut some brush and throwed it into the creek an' he'd just jump on this brush and then jump across the creek but it was up about, oh, that much water, you know," and Jim ran a hand across his knees, "an' so we went over to tell him, 'We got across all right,' but we couldn't find Dad, so we come back to get over to the other side again, and I got across all right but my brother, he fell off. He was younger than I and I've often thought, it must have been the good Lord with us because I ran down about thirty steps below an' the water was a-blowin' him down — there's a deep hole there — and I run out an' as he come to me I grabbed him, and pulled him out, and he was a-crying and he say, 'You didn't want your little brother to drown, did you?' an' I says, 'No,' " and, Jim recalled with a hearty chuckle, "but I've often thought of the judgment I'd taken in running ahead of that stream and waitin' fer him to come rather than to just to follow down, you know, and got into that deep water myself. But it turned out all right." And Jim laughed quietly, pensively.

Just because he was born in Asotin didn't mean his roots were short in Oregon, Jim wanted us to know. His father had gone to Dayton, Washington in 1864, twelve years after the first wave of the Hoskin clan arrived in Oregon.

"Now my folks landed in Oregon in October, 1852, at Scio, a town out from Salem," Jim told in his soft sagebrush drawl. "And Grandpa Llewellyn put out an orchard there and filed on a homestead. But when Grandpa left the east — he was goin' with three brothers — his Grandpa Dillon, he split apples and saved the seeds until he got a quarter of a can full of seeds. An' he gave them to Grandpa. 'Now,' he says, 'you plant those seeds where you think they will grow all the way out because someday there will be fruit and people will need it.' And Grandpa did, but they had quite a little seed when they got out here. Jesse, his cousin, went on down to Roseburg, an' he filed on a homestead there and he planted an orchard with these apples. Well, they just growed wonderful, you know, an' he says to his wife one day, 'I'm gonna give Dad the honor of havin' these apples,' he says. 'We're gonna call 'em Jonathans.' And that's where we got our Jonathan apple. Yeah, with Jesse Hoskin comin' out in 1852 with Grandpa Hoskin and named them after his father, Jonathan."

You could easily perceive by listening to him that Jim Hoskin was largely a self-educated man who had used his nimble mind and good memory to make up for what he lacked in formal schooling.

"I didn't have any education, other than just a little part-time," he said, a bit wistfully, starting a story of school-day memories out in the homesteader country.

"The school was three months in the spring and three months in the fall. It was just a little grade school, with a teacher and seventeen or eighteen of us kids. The first teacher I ever went to school to was my cousin, Herman F. L. Hoskin; that was in eighty-nine; he taught there at Pine City. And in those days there was people went to school growin' whiskers in the face, back in the grades. And an old man — well, I can't remember his name, he stayed at our place too — he was forty-eight years old, an' he was goin' to school when I was, in eighty-nine. Then there was Bob Beard and Bernie Prestly and George Pearson, and all of 'em was well up in their twenties, close to thirty; they was goin' to school there too.

"That was my first experience at school. The next teacher, if I remember right, was a woman by the name of Thomas, and she taught one or two terms.

"They taught good thought, but I had to herd sheep, you know, so I didn't get in much. I had to quit in the spring to help with the sheep. I just got ten weeks of school from the time I was ten years old until I was sixteen."

He grew old fast and piously. "Never went to a dance in my life. Never took a drink of whiskey in my life. When I was young those things were wrong and I wouldn't do 'em, that's all."

He laughed heartily, perhaps wondering what he might have missed, and at this stage in life just curious, though knowing he would have acted the same again, because all his life he had been a God-fearing Christian: United Brethren, Methodist and Presbyterian, taking turns at each denomination.

Then Jim launched into an account of his early days with sheep. His eyes glowed and his lips took on the damp of nostalgia as he seemed to relive experiences more than three-quarters of a century back.

"I started in the sheep business as quick as I was able to talk with the sheep at all; I was seven years old. I didn't have much to entertain myself. When I was twelve I was a-herdin' two thousand sheep out in the mountains and doin' my own cookin' and nobody around. My brother come up four times in the whole summer, pretty near five months, so the next year I vowed I wouldn't herd until they hired a camp tender, and they did, and I got along all right but, boy, I tell you, this here one time, it got late, it was in November, it snowed about eight inches deep, and nobody there, so I cooked me a kettle of mutton, and wrapped it up in a sack and took a quilt and I started home.

"Well, I went that day and I lost a bunch of sheep and then I had to go back and I found 'em back to the band about dark an' I slept in under a tree and o' course I had all the food I'd taken ate up, so I started out and I got out to a sawmill out here on the head of Butter Creek and I went down to the sawmill there, and the fella there, his name was Hart, he says, 'Have you had dinner?' and I says, 'No, didn't have no dinner,' and he turned around to his wife and says, 'Can you set him a lunch?' and the sheep was out on the road, and they was tired, and been in the snow all the time, and they was bunched up, and she says, 'Yes,' so she did. Well, I went up to a meadow, about two miles over, to a fellow named Hurst, Jim Hurst, and he had a garden, fenced in with boards, so I put the sheep in the garden, the snow was quite deep, and I stood all night with him.

"Early the next morning my feet was swollen so I couldn't get my shoes on. Well, I wore a number four shoe and Jim, he wore a number eight, but he loaned me a pair of his shoes. I put 'em on an' started on home. His missus fixed me a lunch. An' after I got down about two miles, three miles, out of the snow, to where there was no snow, and the sheep was so bad I went into Nels Jones's place there an' there was big, nice grass an' I turned the sheep loose to eat, you know, to feed, and here come a fella — I know just by the way he was comin' — to give me the dickens. And when he got up there and he saw me, just a little spoon-faced kid, and I guess he felt sorry fer me, and he talked awful nice. He says, 'Mr. Jones is been a savin' this for our poor sheep. This was his favorite spot. Would you take your sheep back and put 'em in the corral there an' come down to the house and stay all night?' I thanked him, told him I would, and I went back, and there was some sacks in the old cabin there, a bunk, with just hay on it, and being kid-like I didn't want to go down so I just fixed four or five sacks together and crawled in those sacks and stayed all night.

"Well, the next morning I started on down, Jones was separatin' sheep down about a mile from there, he come right to the road, says, 'Young man, how you makin' it?' And I says, 'Oh, makin' it pretty good, Mr. Jones.' He says, 'You been to breakfast?' And I says, 'No.' 'Did you have any supper?' 'No.' 'Did you have anything to eat yesterday?' 'Oh yes,' I says, 'I had me a lunch fixed up for me.' So we talked a while. I says, 'Mr. Jones, how much does my father owe you for me goin' into your pasture up there?' He says, 'You don't owe me nothing but you tell him he owes me fifty dollars.' "

Jim broke off his story in a gale of laughter. By golly! That was something he would never forget. When the laughter had ebbed away, he continued:

"I says, 'Well, if he owes you anything I'd like to have him pay you.' 'No, son,' he says, 'you go down to the house and tell that old man to give you your breakfast and to give you a big lunch to go on.' So I did, and the old man, he set out a breakfast fer me an' I told him about the lunch, so he says, 'you'll have to wait, you've ate up everything I've got cooked.' " And Jim threw his head back and laughed again. "I says, 'It can't wait, the sheep's goin' now.' I knowed they'd be scattered. So I went on.

"Well, I went on all that day an' about night, eleven o'clock, I was on Little Butter Creek, an' I was leanin' up against a tree, my back was; I'd left my quilt, however, everything. I heard some horses comin' down the road an' when the driver got opposite of me, he knew the sheep was there, you see, an' he hollered at me, an' I answered him. He says, 'Can you tell me where I can find a place down here to feed my horses?' He says, 'I got a wagon up here but I was afraid to come down this steep hill.' Yes, I directed him, told him where to go, toward old man Vincent's down there. So, he woke up old man Vincent when he got there and while he was feedin' the horses he told Vincent, he says, 'I ran into a fella up here with a band of sheep, and he told me he didn't have no bed, nothing to eat,' and brother and Dad was sleepin' up in the hay mow an' they'd been a-lookin' fer me that day and John, he woke Dad up, Dad was hard o' hearin', and told him, he says, 'James,' and he told where I was, so they got up, hitched up the team, an' come up to get me, two o'clock. So I got somethin' to eat."

That was a time to remember! Jim shook his head from side to side and laughed and chuckled out, "I guess that was pretty rough goin' for a kid."

He worked constantly with sheep until he was twenty-three, he thought, and he left that life for two or three years. It was then he married.

"Met my wife at the academy down here at Pendleton. She was born at Pilot Rock. Her name was Porter. How I fell for her . . . I went to school three months and then I was out two years, I thought I'd go back to school — that was when I had quit the sheep business — and the older kids had all graduated and the young kids, they didn't remember me, so I was pretty badly disappointed and I figured, well, I'll just try it another day and if I don't feel any better I'll quit. And the girl come down the street drivin' a gray cayuse on a one-horse buggy and I looked up at the girl, and she knew me, and she spoke kindly, and that was the girl I married.

"She was nineteen, I think, and she come back there to school to take a review for her teaching and I got better acquainted with her. I knew her the first time I went to school there but I had forgotten all about it. But of course I knew her face an' when she seen me goin' up the street she just spoke to me as she passed. But when she come back to school the next day to take her review, well, we got acquainted, we went together, oh, six months, I guess, and we were married. Then we lived together fifty-seven years. Pretty good life to live, you know. Raised three girls, all good Christian women. Got sixteen great-grandchildren. Countin' in-law, got forty in the family. Well, fifty-seven years, and then she died. She was an awful good woman. I lived single six years. I got lonesome livin' alone, so I just made up my mind I'd get married, so I married Mary here about the twenty-fifth of June two years ago." He was past eighty-seven when he entered matrimony for the second time.

After marriage, young Jim Hoskin returned to the sheep business — "and when the war was over, the first World War, why, I went out and contracted a lot of sheep, a lot of lambs, and I paid thirteen and a half cents a pound fer 'em. By golly, when the treaty was signed, well, I had a trainload to Chicago, and I only got thirteen cents a pound for 'em. I lost seventeen thousand dollars on that one shipment. That was quite a loss, you know."

Jim Hoskin kept going, though, until he was done in by the depression and a cruel act of conniving. "I was well-to-do until the Hoover administration. I got in debt about thirty-five thousand dollars and the bank down here was in bad shape, and a fellow by the name of Johnson had sold out to his partner, Pearson, and he took a full mortgage on everything that Pearson had. Well, then the bank was trying to, had to, finance Pearson, he owed them a lot of money, but they couldn't get no security, no mortgage. Now Mr. Rice, the president of the bank, didn't do this; they had to vote him out before they could do it because he thought so much of me and he told me, he says, 'You worked like a slave all your life,' and he says, 'You oughtn't to be throwed out this way,' but they throwed him out, so he didn't have anything. He took my liabilities and assets; he called 'em in; he says, 'Now, here it is,' he says, 'He has his assets of a hundred and thirty-seven thousand and his liabilities of thirty-five thousand,' but you couldn't go and borrow thirty-five thousand at the time. So they, Johnson, took my stuff all over.

"Oh yes, we lost our ranch then. We moved out of a ten thousand dollar home (it was about eight inches of snow) and into a tent.

"Well, then Frank Sloan and I went into buying; we made quite a little money out of that, and I've often thought, the other day I was lying there in bed, thinkin' about the past, and thinkin' what the Bible says, 'What does it profit a man if he gains the whole world and loses his own soul?' and you know, Dave Johnson didn't live over a year after he took my outfit over. Yes, I thought about that the other day."

Jim Hoskin had done a lot of pondering in the last half century, and his mind returned often to what he is certain is a miracle.

"In 1917 I got sick, I started a sickness, and for ten years I kept failing and failing and failing. So I went to almost every specialist between Seattle and San Francisco that other doctors would tell me to go and see and I kept gettin' down, gettin' down. One trip up in 1927 I went up to Spokane and comin' back I stopped in to see a doctor in Walla Walla. He told my wife, 'If you don't have him operated on he'll be gone in sixty days.' I was yellow and it was hard for me to get around and, 'Well,' I said, 'I'll be gone then.' My wife come up and talk to me, because, I says, 'I'm not gonna be operated on.' I had one operation, for 'pendicitis, an' that was enough.

"Well, I come home and I believed in prayer, an' I went in prayer, an' in my prayer I says, 'Lord, if it's Thy will, take me, and if it isn't, let me get well.' An' you know, it come to me as plain as I'm settin' here. I went in an' told my wife, 'Momma, I'm gonna get well.' She says, 'What makes you think so?' 'Well,' I says, 'ain't no think about it, I'm goin' to. But,' I says, 'there's gonna be a doctor just come along; we don't know who it'll be, but I'm gonna see him an he's gonna cure me.'

"Well, she couldn't believe it, you know, so next week I went up to Pendleton to get an electric treatment — I always felt better when I got an electric treatment — an' I got up there a little early to see the doctor, so I went over and thought I'd talk to Jim Sturgis, he was a-workin' in a grain office, an' Jim was gone. Some of the boys was in there, several in the office, an' I seen a fella come out through the back door, an' I says to the fella close to me, 'Isn't that Chris?' That was Jim's brother. An' he says, 'Yes,' and I hollered at him an' Chris come out an' shook hands with me. I'd went to school with him, him and Jim both, and he talked to me a little while and he says, 'Why, Jim, what's the matter of you?' I'd forgotten about Chris bein' a doctor. And he didn't expect ever to see me, he didn't know me to be sick or anything, you know, and I told him, 'I'm pretty well knocked out, Chris.' And he says, 'Let's see your arms.' And I rolled up my sleeves and showed them to him. He called in Doctor Brennan, and he says, 'Do you know what the matter is with this fellow?' Brennan says, 'No, I doctored him a little; I give him up.' An' Chris says, 'Oh doctor, this is myxedema.' Well, they talked back and forth and Brennan says, 'My goodness, would I let him died and never recognize it?' Now, he and Chris studied this in the college at the same time; they was going to school together; but Chris did know it, and Brennan didn't. I says, 'Well, Chris, can you do me any good?' 'Oh,' he says, 'cure you sound and well in two weeks.' And he says, 'If you'd let 'em operate on you' — they all wanted to operate on my liver — and he says, 'You never would have been well.' I said, 'What's about this cirrhosis?' — they all said I had cirrhosis of the liver. 'Well,' he says, 'myxedema hardens the liver.' And he says, 'But quick as you get some thyroid back in your system the liver will be all right.'

"Well, that was the whole thing, and how I come to run into Chris, that was another kind of miracle. Jim Sturgis wasn't a Christian but he would tell anybody that it was a miracle. I heard him tell a big crowd there one day. He says, 'Chris and I got in the car to go out to the reservation. Chris didn't know anything about James being sick or anything; he just come out to see mother.'

"The way Jim Sturgis told it," Hoskin went on, "Chris asked, 'Where is the bottle?' And Jim says, 'We haven't got any.' And Chris says, 'Well, we've got to have a bottle to go out there.' And Jim said, 'You'll have to stay here if you do because you being a stranger I couldn't get it, bootleggin' what it is.' Chris got out of the car and while he was there, Jim told the crowd, Chris met me. 'If Chris didn't want a bottle,' Jim said, 'we would have gone on and Chris never would have seen James.' "

Jim Hoskin laughed again, laughed until he was out of breath, and he sighed triumphantly, "And I was cured."

After the sheep business, Hoskin tried another line of work. "I trucked for nine years, out of Stanfield, and I did very well in the truck; when I quit I had twenty-five thousand dollars. Then I sold the little ranch I had got and come up here, in forty-one. I was supposed to retire but I built these duplexes over here, for rental, and then this little house. Then I owned that building down there where I was when you come to me, that old hospital building."

Ever since he was a youngster Jim was a pilgrim in search of progress. As long as it came within the boundaries of his approval, he was for something new. In 1913 he paid $600 for the first Ford to come into Umatilla County. He couldn't get electricity fast enough. There wasn't a gadget around he didn't want to try. And when it came to church business he was a leader in dividing the jurisdiction of two congregations, so that the churches wouldn't cannibalize each other's membership. But he outdid himself while living at Stanfield, so that when he moved to Pilot Rock he had to become a Presbyterian. That wasn't too bad, Jim's wife being that, but the way Jim had planned it, the church at Stanfield would be Methodist. It was, which made Jim happy — until the Hoskins relocated from Stanfield to Pilot Rock and Jim found himself a parishioner of his own manipulation.

We asked Jim, as relaxed as when we had met, if he could remember any of the songs he had sung in his youth. There was one in particular he liked, "There's a Dear Spot in Ireland I'd Love For to See."

"I learned it from an Irishman," he said. "We'd get together of a night in the mountains, you know, an' sometimes we'd sing songs, 'til midnight. I was about twelve, thirteen then."

Sing it, we pleaded. "I've got such a cold, and my voice ain't no good," Jim protested mildly, but we persuaded him anyway, and, cold or no cold, he sang better than I could, and I was more than a third of a century younger. And he knew every word.

The best time of his life, he thought, "was right along in those days when I was a kid. I've often wondered why older people would always stop and talk and ask me questions. Uncle Tom Scott, I used to go up there, he run the post office there at what they call Calloway, it was named after my grandfather, and old Uncle Tom, he'd always invite me in and visit like I was an old man. I don't know, but the old folks always liked to hear me talk."

Jim Hoskin gazed at us, his eyes untroubled and his soul at peace. He sat completely at ease, merged with every leaf of grass and stalk of stubble, a child of nature, a rumpled Buddha of the plain spinning out his wisdom of four score and ten. But for the next half hour, as he talked on, there was an intertwining of his boyhood and old age, as though perhaps he was never young, or as though now he felt young again, or, I thought, as though his boyhood and his ninety years were coming together, so that in the last pages of his life there were sentences and paragraphs from the first chapter.

Once he paused for a moment, sighed heavily, and said, "Oh, I've done a lot of work in my lifetime; I don't know, I kinda wonder sometime why I did so much but my stepmother, she says to my father there one day, she says, 'Why did you send James out to the mountains when he's such a little kid?' When I was fourteen I weighed eighty-seven pounds. 'Well,' Dad says, 'I didn't realize he's being little, he's always done anything he wanted to,' and he says, 'I knew he's competent in doing it and that's all there was to it. I didn't realize he was just a little kid that way.' "

He looked at my wife, then me, then ahead, and, with the glow in his eyes softening, said in humor that came out as wistful, "Oh, those years go so fast, looking back it don't seem . . . When I was a kid I thought a hundred years was so long it would never pass, but looking back now it don't seem any time since I was a kid."

He could get away from a lot of memories — but never from sheep. They would probably haunt him, I thought, until the end of his time. They were the strongest part of his boyhood and somehow, though he had been away from sheep for decades, he could not see any part of his life absent from them, and even if he could, they would not let go of him.

Jim Hoskin, ninety years old, ran still-strong fingers across his sandy hair, as though trying to find where the trouble was, pressed his lips together, as though that might squeeze out an answer, and said simply and wonderingly:

"I never dream about sheep, and I dream of 'em so often, without having a nightmare about 'em. They're either drownin' or fallin' off a cliff or starvin' to death. I like sheep. Been in sheep most all my life. But I have those nightmares."

A Long Way from Old Long Creek

It isn't often you meet someone like Theron Keeney, whose ties with Long Creek, a Grant County town of some 200 people and about forty miles north of John Day, went back to even before there was a settlement.

Traveling around, we try to find folks whose years and whose ancestors are interwoven with the land and the villages, and when we reached Long Creek we asked if there was a genuine old-timer around. That's how we came to be directed to Theron Keeney, who had been born here in 1901, less than twenty years after the first white family arrived to stay.

There is a lot of folklore you can learn from natives such as Theron Keeney, and some history, and sometimes the two, the folklore and the history, get mixed up, but you can hear things you had not been told before and hadn't read anywhere.

There are whole areas of Oregon history that haven't been covered, and others only scratchily. For instance, no one has delved deeply into the contribution made to the development of the state by the Chinese. I had known, of course, because it is common knowledge, that the Chinese were all through Eastern Oregon as gold miners but not until Theron Keeney talked to me was I aware that Chinese were also sheepherders. It is these bits of information, often randomly and casually given, as though of no importance, that I find more valuable than dates and descriptions of great events.

Actually, Theron Keeney didn't feel he had anything of significance to say and wondered why we wanted to bother with him. He had been a simple wage earner most of his life, hadn't made the headlines, and had scarcely been outside the state. But, since he hadn't anything else to do that afternoon, he reckoned he could give us a few grains of time.

"My grandfather, Joseph Watson, came here in the 1880s and homesteaded where Long Creek is now," Keeney began. "He laid out the town and donated everything west of the highway. They called it the Keeney Addition, this side of the highway. Actually, I'm living on my grandfather's ranch."

What was left of his grandfather's ranch for Keeney was a very modest frame house he shared with his wife. It was all there was to show for the family history.

"Father did a lot of things," said Keeney, going up the genealogical ladder. "Them days, every man who had a family to make a living for had to freight or herd sheep or punch cattle. I worked on ranches and stock until 1928 and then I moved west of the mountains, to Grants Pass. Then in 1929 — you know what happened — I didn't have a job for ten years. I was never on relief but I was on WPA. In 1942 I went to work in the shipyards in Vancouver until the war ended. Didn't do much for a while and moved back to Long Creek in 1947. I farmed four years, down here to Hamilton, had some stock and such, and then I worked in the lumber mill for ten years, right here in Long Creek. In 1961 I had a severe heart attack and I haven't had a hard day of labor since. I've been the municipal judge, city recorder and watermaster for fifteen years and they call me the fire chief too.

"We've got a fire truck and a city hall and one of the best water systems in the state," Keeney went on, explaining his town in a low key of pride, "and we've got a city police here, one man, appointed by the city. We haven't had anyone in jail for more than a year. We'd put a man in jail for disturbing the peace but we don't have much of that. I mean, it's got to get pretty rough before a man is jailed."

Then his mind returned to the past. "We used to have a big dance hall here and a racetrack too. Every three hundred and twenty acres had a family. They sold out. The land barons gobbled them up. I've seen two hundred, three hundred people at a dance and I didn't know a stranger in the crowd. There'd be a violin and a piano and sometimes a banjo. The

Theron Keeney of Long Creek

dance would start at nine o'clock and end at two in the morning. In Dad's time they'd dance all night and have breakfast and then go home.

"There was a big Chinatown over on this side of town when I was a kid. Lots of mines. That's how come they were in this part of the country. Then they became sheepherders but when the sheep thinned out the Chinese starved out. There was a Chinese doctor and a Chinese shoemaker. I remember the Chinese New Year — shooting firecrackers and raising hell."

Theron Keeney still had affection for the town. "Well, I was born here," he philosophized. "We got good air and good water and not too many hippies." But he liked the Long Creek of his boyhood more than the Long Creek of the present.

"There was a lot more natural resources. The streams were crowded with fish and the hills with birds and animals. Nobody had much money, but a dollar was as big as a wagon wheel. There was a lot of things for a boy to do. And there were no roads coming in here, so we had the place to ourselves. Now the natural resources are almost gone — about ninety percent, in my book. And if it weren't for the tourists, the town would still exist, but barely. That's how far things have gone since I was a kid."

Mattie's Monument

There was a time not too many years ago when the only accommodations in the forty-eight miles between Spray and Long Creek were at Mattie Stubblefield's rooming house in Monument.

And that time had passed when last we came through Mattie's town.

The only people who visited Monument regularly when Mattie had her rooming house were — as is just about true today — the farm families, who came in to shop at the general store for everything from butter to saddle blankets, and to socialize.

Hunters drove past in season, as they continue to do; some delivery drivers also wheeled in, as they still do; and the few others who saw the town were wayfarers who took to the quiet roads just because they were there.

That's how I discovered Monument and Mattie Stubblefield.

Actually, the county road from Kimberly, thirteen miles below Spray, is so rewarding that even if Monument blew away I'd still take this pike, as I frequently do when I come to this part of Oregon. There are long vistas of strikingly contoured ranges, deep expanses of pastel grazing lands, islands of verdure that flash in the sun, and Sunken Mountain, a great hill that dropped straight down and left red cliffs on all sides. And then there is Hamilton — spelled out on the official state map, though it hadn't but three houses the last time I was there and not one of these a store, cafe or school.

Monument is an old homestead town on the North Fork of the John Day River. It seems that just about every kid in town has a horse and if you wait long enough you can get a photo of a youngster watering his or her horse in the middle of the stream. It makes a pretty picture.

The first time I saw Monument it had close to 100 people. A hundred years after it was founded, in 1874, it had a population of 150 and boasted a high school, in a beautiful rock building, of about fifty students.

I don't recall ever putting up at Mattie Stubblefield's rooming house, which was built before the twentieth century showed up, and still looks like a stagecoach hostelry, but I remember hearing some about Mattie on every trip. She was quite a girl.

Born in 1885, Mattie homesteaded a 320-acre claim in her twenties, a single woman on the frontier. She hammered together a pine log cabin and then added a little storeroom and dug a cellar at the back. Most of her fare was beans and potatoes; money was tight and what there was had to go for improving the cabin.

One night at a horse-and-buggy dance Mattie met Murd Stubblefield. They kept proper company until she was thirty-one. Then she was sure he was the man who would make a good hitching-mate. It turned out he was. In 1966, before he passed away, the couple celebrated their golden wedding anniversary.

In 1945 Mattie and Murd purchased the house in Monument and moved to town. The upstairs bedrooms were opened to take in roomers, by day, week, or month, and, before she grew too weary of it, Mattie also served meals.

The first time I saw Mattie she was sharp-eyed and could hear a cat purr from the other end of town. By 1970, though, her eyes were fading a bit. She wore a hearing aid and kept asking me if I had come to adjust it. Otherwise, she was as straight and brisk and long-striding as ever. And her house was fringed with flowers, which Mattie tended, and the inside of her home was spotless.

Looking back at her after we had said our goodbyes I thought of her as a poplar deeply rooted that would stand tall in all seasons. But not too long after that Mattie stopped taking in roomers. By then Long Creek,

Cora Stubblefield

Mattie Stubblefield and two great-granddaughters

twenty-one miles east, was reaching out its hand to tourists and the motel at Spray, twenty-seven miles west, had such a high rate of occupancy in its two units that it was planning to expand.

The last I heard of Mattie, in the summer of 1976, she was past ninety, still living in the same house, and pretty well taking care of herself, though her hearing continued to diminish and her eyes were growing dimmer.

So that's Mattie Stubblefield, a saga in her own right. As for Mattie's house, it typifies all of Monument, with its still cowtown appearance. And it belongs in that land, where the fractured face of Sunken Mountain looks out to a weathered rail fence bending toward the call of a hidden creek.

Wings in an Odd Fortress

We were sitting in a John Day cafe when a man we had met the day before asked: "Have you heard the story about the stone fort that was built just to protect a single horse?

"The place is still standing," he continued, "and it's only about six miles from here. Why don't you go and take a look at it?"

We did, but before we set out we listened to one of the most remarkable yarns we had heard in all Grant County. Later, after the photography was done, we returned to John Day for verification of what we had heard, and in the process gathered enough new information to fill out the tale.

The story begins in 1863 with the coming into the John Day Valley of David Jenkins, his wife, and their year-old daughter. In 1864 Jenkins took up a homestead and built a house about fifty yards to the east of where the strange barn stands. It is a bit ironic that the horse dwelling has far outlasted the Jenkins home. But, then, the horse outlived Jenkins by some years.

About 1876 a dusty traveler stopped at the Jenkins house to offer the weary sorrel mare he was riding in exchange for a fresh horse.

"This horse," confided the traveler, with the oozy assurance of a snake-oil drummer, "has been bred to the best, the very best, trotting stallion in the whole bluegrass state of Kentucky. Her colt will be a champion, mark you. The only reason I'm willing to make this swap is because the mare is tired some and I've got to get to where I'm going."

So the story goes.

Sight unseen, you could say, David Jenkins took a chance and came up a winner. The mare's chestnut-sorrel colt, which Jenkins named Mount Vernon in honor of the village where he traded, was born to run. It came into the world with a stiff breeze at its back, ballet slippers on its hoofs, and invisible wings on its flanks. Watching the horse bound across the meadows in enormous strides that seemed more gliding than running, a local rancher who knew a bit of Greek mythology thought the sorrel should have been named Pegasus.

When Mount Vernon was three years old Jenkins heard rumors that some Indians planned to steal his horse, so he hired two Scottish stonemasons to build a stronghold. With stone from a hillside back of the ranch the masons constructed a shelter whose walls were more than a foot thick. For the roof, the only part of the barn which had been altered when we saw it, the Scotsmen used clay dirt supported by poles. The attic, reached

The stone barn "fortress" of Mount Vernon

from an entrance above the window at the north end of the structure, was held up by hewn beams. Heavy doors guarded the openings. Each wall had two gun slots but no shot was ever fired from within the barn or at it.

As Mount Vernon's fame as a trotting horse grew, Jenkins accepted challenges to trotting races around the state. Horses were brought from all parts of the Northwest to vie against the 1,100-pound champion. Only once was the handsome chestnut sorrel beaten, and that was at the old racetrack where the Dennis Lemons ranch is now located, west of Mount Vernon town.

A man from Washington came with his pride, Black Hawk, and shrewdly waited until David Jenkins had raced Mount Vernon three times, each time winning. Without giving his horse a rest Jenkins entered the fourth race and Mount Vernon, gallant but spent, was beaten by the spurt of the fresh Black Hawk in the back stretch.

In 1893, when he was about seventeen years old, Mount Vernon was sold by Jenkins to a Portland man, who bought the famed trotter for breeding purposes. By then Mount Vernon had sired numerous colts. As late as 1918 some stallions from his lineage were seen on farms in the John Day Valley. Genetically, the strains of Mount Vernon may still be alive — but no one knows where.

After he was sold to the Portland breeder there is a long gap in the history of Mount Vernon. He was probably sold at least several times more, each time a step downward in prowess and prestige until, many years later, a rancher from Izee, Bill Alsop, spotted Mount Vernon in Athena. The great chestnut sorrel, now battered, old and half-blind, was the lead in a eight-horse team.

As a young man Bill Alsop had watched Mount Vernon race and had been thrilled by the graceful and powerful trotter. There was no mistaking Mount Vernon. The J brand was plain on the horse's left shoulder but even without that mark, and even with Mount Vernon a pale and exhausted shell of his former beauty and strength, Alsop knew immediately.

The man from Izee had no practical use for Mount Vernon but sentimentality has its own reward. Mount Vernon was taken to Alsop's ranch and turned loose on the lush bunchgrass above the South Fork of the John Day River.

His end came peacefully in 1917, when he was forty-one, and forgotten or unknown by most of Grant County. His only testimonial today is the stone barn, probably the only fortress in Oregon ever built to house an animal.

Directions: Stone barn is on north side of U.S. 26-U.S. 395, 2.1 miles east of Mount Vernon city center and 6.3 miles west of John Day city center.

Sawdust at Seneca

Bill Pearce looked up from filling a beer order at the Bear Valley Tavern in the Hines Lumber Company town of Seneca, twenty-five miles south of John Day.

"You say you're a writer, huh? Well, you've come to the right spot for a story. Who told you about us?"

"No one," I replied. "We just came in for some ginger ale. What's special about this place?"

Bill Pearce rolled a cigar around his mouth — we were told later that he was never seen without a cigar in his mouth — and pretended to be mortally wounded.

"What's special about it?" he cried in mock umbrage. (His friends said later he always kept his cool.) "Why, this is the only tavern in Oregon that has got sawdust on the floor!"

"That's right," echoed a lanky fellow at the other end of the thirty-five-foot-long bar. "I've been in taverns all over the state. This is the only one with sawdust on the floor."

Sawdust on floor in Bear Valley tavern, Seneca

"He should know," nodded the going-on-sixty Pearce, a chunky, round-faced, pleasant, droll man. I couldn't tell whether he had passed a compliment or issued an indictment.

"He's been around," added Bill's wife, Freda, a doe-eyed, gentle-looking woman who helped him run the tavern. The expression in her eyes carried the message.

Bill slid a schooner of beer down the bar and asked if we were interested in history. "This tavern was built in 1930, but the back bar was made in 1857. That makes it way over a hundred years old. Ever since the tavern opened, there's been sawdust on the floor. We get it from the planer mill in Seneca."

Why sawdust? "To keep the calk boots from cutting up the floor. The sawdust gives the floor a cushion. It also keeps a nice smell. It's sanitary. It keeps the dust down and absorbs the mud."

"Helps in fights, too," volunteered the lanky fellow down the bar, as he called for another beer.

Bill Pearce affirmed with a tilt of his cigar. "When the loggers get into a brawl the sawdust absorbs the hard shock."

He studied my skepticism and continued. "Do they really have fights here? Are you kidding? Hang around a while and find out. Nothing serious, just a friendly argument. Did you ever see loggers who don't argue? It's a way for them to express themselves and get the point over and to exercise their muscles."

"And what do you do with the sawdust?"

Pearce rolled the cigar from one corner of his mouth to the other, as though it were a log in a pond, and answered deadpan, "I screen it and pick up the diamonds and all the extra change."

"Good luck," I remarked wryly.

Bill grinned in conciliation. "I put sawdust on the floor at least once a week, depending on the condition. I like fresh sawdust. It takes out the musty beer odor."

The tavern seemed to have a lot of spittoons, I noted.

"That's right," Pearce agreed. "this being a logging town, the boys like their snoose."

"And spittoons are better than sawdust for snoose juice," Freda added. "You can empty the spittoons every day."

There was something else about the Bear Valley Tavern that was different. When the lanky logger had finished his third glass of beer he slapped an octagonal coin on the counter. Bill tossed it in his cash register and handed back coins I had never before seen.

"This is the only tavern in the Pacific Northwest, far as I know," said Pearce, answering my bemused expression, "that has its own money. These coins have been used here for many years. That octagonal one is worth five dollars. Other coins are worth a buck, fifty cents, and two bits."

He went on to explain that the loggers signed scrip chits, with the amount deducted from their checks, and the change given in company coins.

"They're also good in the grocery store next door," said Freda. "Company town, company money."

The tavern and the grocery just about made up the business district in this windswept town of four hundred. The tavern was one of three social centers in the town, the others being the V.F.W. and Union halls. "But most of the social activity is right here," Bill said. "And a lot of town and union business is discussed here."

"And a lot of B.S.," put in a burly fellow who had wandered in a few minutes before.

"Yeah," said Pearce, his eyes frowning. "The people of Seneca work together and stand together against outsiders but they fight amongst themselves."

He put down some glasses he had been washing and sighed, "You've got to have the patience of Job to run this place."

"So it isn't all starlight?" I said.

"Absolutely not!" exclaimed Freda. "But it's an awful lot of sawdust." And she and Bill and everybody else at the bar roared until the floor shook.

The Gray Ghost of Hines

One of the strangest manmade sights in Oregon is the cavernous hulk of a three-story concrete apparition that faces a glimmering greensward in the center of Hines, two miles south of Burns.

For almost fifty years it has stood empty, defenseless against wind, snow, time and vandals. Actually, it never had a tenant, and therein lies the weirdness of its sad history, which I dredged up in Hines and Burns.

The gray ghost was born at the wrong time and in the wrong place. A Burns lumberman, Charles Silbaugh, started construction in the fall of 1929 on what was to be the elegant Ponderosa Hotel, with an up-to-date emporium on the ground floor. Well, you know what happened in the fall of 1929 — which is why, after construction was halted a year later, the aborted Ponderosa became know as "Hoover's Hotel."

Hines was just being founded when Silbaugh's dream was taking form in stone and steel. The Edward Hines Lumber Company mill, around which the town revolves, was going up. Streets were being laid out, houses built, the talk of greatness was in the air before the first bucket of cement was poured. Silbaugh was certain that Hines would supplant Burns as the prime city of Harney County. But Hines never became more than an industrial outpost of Burns.

Nobody knows how much money Silbaugh put into the Ponderosa before he ran out of credit. The best guess is $60,000. The building then was two-thirds finished, with all the electric wiring completed, the subfloors laid, windows and window casings in place, and a sawdust-burning furnace installed in the basement.

Silbaugh hired a guard to protect his beauty when he halted construction but after a year he gave up on the future and the phantom of the sagebrush country was left to the mercy of human scavengers. They took the lumber and the wiring and a lot more. A bit of folklore about the hotel has it that the window glass in half the homes in Hines came from the Ponderosa.

I stood in front of the eerie hulk, scanning the graffiti which covers much of the building. The scrawlings ranged from a peace symbol to a swastika to the best-known of the four-letter words. And there were the usual adolescent proclamations: I LOVE TONY, TILLY IS A BITCH, LANETTE AND BOB.

A husky young fellow in a T-shirt drove up in an old sedan and asked: "You the fella that's going to buy that?"

"No," I replied, "Do you live here?"

He grinned. "I'm the town policeman."

"When are you going to erase all that stuff on the walls?" I asked.

"Aw gosh," he stammered, "it would cost too much."

I smiled. "Don't do it on my account. It doesn't bother me."

He tilted his head to suggest indifference. Then he called, in a boyish voice, "Want to climb up to the roof?"

"No," I said wryly, "I went to the second floor and there are too many boards torn out. I'm too old to play Batman."

He laughed. "I had to go to the roof once to get a guy down. Crazy galoot!"

"What would you like done with it?" I asked.

"The city would like to tear it down," he said. "If a kid falls off the second floor he could sue hell out of the city."

"And if I fall off?"

"You could sue too."

"I think I'll stay on the ground," I remarked.

"See you," he grinned, and drove off.

If the gray ghost weren't so dangerous to mess around in, I'd say, keep it. There's nothing like it in the state and I've seen a lot worse-looking tombstones.

The Gray Ghost of Hines

A Stately Meeting at Wagontire

I never come to Wagontire without thinking of the time Oswald West, then thirty-nine, and Bill Brown, eighteen years older, had their simple and colorful meeting here. That was an encounter of strong individualists, and the fact that both men handled it casually not only shows of what stuff they were made but reflects the unvarnished democratic spirit of the frontier — and less than seventy years ago.

There is more to Wagontire now. Today it has a cafe, a couple of gas pumps, a few motel units, and a paved road runs by it. But no matter how large Wagontire has grown, the meeting between West and Brown is larger in my mind. What Western writer would not have deemed it fortunate to have been witness to that inelegant and impressive scene!

Oswald West, the state's greatest governor, and Bill Brown, the legendary stockman, were surely two of the most picturesque and vivid characters in Oregon history. Though one was a glad-to-see-you officeholder and the other a crusty denizen of the range who didn't have much use for oiled tongues of politicians, both had much in common: They were mavericks, completely without pretension, close to earth, and unawed by station and fame.

West is cherished for his pioneer conservation policies, his unequivocal support of woman's suffrage, and his far-sighted leadership of social legislation. But his contemporaries spoke most eloquently of his openess, salty wit, refreshing mind and flexibility.

At the height of his fortunes Brown had holdings in Eastern Oregon of some 30,000 acres and, apart from his thick flocks of sheep, was known as the "Horse King of the West;" at least 5,000 horses carried his brand. He is best remembered, though, for his "eccentricities," some of which are detailed in my book, *A Touch of Oregon*. Compared to the gregarious Bill Hanley, the renowned rancher of Harney County, Brown was a hermit. Set against the swashbuckling Pete French, whose derring-do now seems enshrined in mythology, Bill was John the Baptist in the wilderness.

In the early summer of 1912, West set out from Salem on a black standard-bred saddle mare to attend a Western Governors' Conference in Boise. That was Os West for you: Why take the train when he could save the taxpayers a few dollars by riding a horse? And why go straight to Boise when he could poke along and palaver with his constituents en route?

At Prineville, West turned north and followed a longer and less

Wagontire: present and past

Courtesy Oregon Historical Society

Oswald West

traveled way so that he could go through Wagontire and see Bill Brown, of whom the governor, like everyone else, had heard so much.

Thirty-seven years later West recalled the encounter:

"It was toward evening when I reached Wagontire, where Brown's home, ranch buildings, and general merchandise store were located. Asking the housekeeper and cook if I might find food and shelter for the night, she referred me to Brown, whom she said was cutting hay in a nearby meadow. Upon my approach Bill halted the mowing outfit and acknowledged my introduction. The fact that he was about to entertain the governor of the state made little or no impression upon the old stockman. However, he agreed to my spending the night at Wagontire.

"The ranch house was large and roomy, but Bill's bedroom, of which I was to become a joint occupant was quite small, and hardly afforded room for its double bed and a desk which occupied one corner. The desk was littered with, and surrounded by check stubs, which appeared to be Bill's only method of bookkeeping.

"When it came time to retire I found that Bill, my sleepmate, had been wearing red woolen underwear — it was a hot July — while hay making and had perspired quite freely.

"Bill's charge was 50 cents for my supper, 50 cents for bed, 50 cents for breakfast and 50 cents for my saddle animal. After breakfast, I mounted and headed for Idaho and the Western governors' conference."

Great Basin Blues

This Oregon of ours is so varied. There is not a single mile that is dull, if you know what is there. Behind the prosaic tone of the high desert is a teeming life current; go a step beyond and you come to homesteader lore. Wastelands might seem as barren in tale as in flora, but for the geologist the landforms are exciting and the writer sees ancient Indians, scouts searching out cutoffs to the Willamette Valley, cavalry in defile, prospectors scouring every butte and crevice for trace of gold, cattle kings whose sway extended farther than a man could ride in a single day.

Will you not join with the geologist and the writer in finding pleasure through knowledge even in that which repels the eye? Then regard no sight as absent of interest.

Twenty-five miles east of Burns, on U.S. 20, at a point where the pale chlorophyll pasturelands thin out to high desert grazing, there stands a roadside marker which tells about the Great Basin, that enormous oddity of nature in a rancid mood.

The marker is two-tenths of a mile east of Buchanan, a map dot consisting of a single store. Westward the land starts to green and ranch houses and barns pimple the landscape. Eastward, the sneering slopes skulk up to the malodor of Stinkingwater Pass.

So turn to the marker and the legend:

"This site marks the northern limit of the interior lying between the Rocky Mountains and Cascade-Sierra Nevada and divides of Columbia and Snake Rivers and Colorado River. This area has no drainage to the sea."

It is an immense region, thousands of square miles, and devoid of any sizeable stream. And a big chunk of the Great Basin is in Harney County, the largest of Oregon's thirty-six counties.

In all of Harney County only one river finally reaches the sea. This is the Malheur. The main branch is born in the forests of Grant County, to the north, and in the northeast corner of Harney County the Malheur picks up the sluggish creeks of Pine, Wolf, Stinkingwater, Squaw and Cotton. The South Fork of the Malheur, rising in the Crow Camp Hills north of Crane, swallows Indian Creek before it merges with the main branch at Juntura, in Malheur County.

The Malheur joins the Snake near Ontario and the Snake empties into the Columbia at Pasco, Washington. A long way to go, from Stinkingwater Creek to the Pacific, but somehow the journey is made.

Every other county in the state makes Harney look bone-dry — or maybe it would be more accurate to say dusty — when it comes to rivers. Pick a county at random. Try Wallowa. It has the Minam, the Wallowa, the Grande Ronde and the Imnaha. Take another: Crook. A score of cold creeks pour into the Crooked. Wheeler? The John Day bisects the county. Jefferson? It has the Deschutes, the Crooked and the Metolius. Look at the map and see what I mean.

Harney County is earthwormed with lonesome creeks spawned on snow-glazed hills and dribbled out between fence posts bleached as buffalo bones on the naked plain.

Here is Ramon Creek, slapped into life on the Pueblo Mountains, wiggling down the wild cliffs, skiving the foothill stubble, oozing across the Nevada line, and lapped up on the Charles Sheldon Antelope Refuge.

And here is Skull Creek, splashing down the Steens with drunken exuberance and dying of thirst on the scurfy sage below Catlow Rim.

And here is Jackass Creek, pushing off the rocky slopes of the Jackass Mountains, but not having steam enough to reach the sinkhole called Foster Lake. And Home Creek, which has no home to go to; and Rawhide Creek, about as wet as leather; and Fifteencent Lake, which hasn't a nickle's worth of water. And the Donner und Blitzen River, which whispers its way (lest someone discover and put an end to it) into Malheur Lake, the stewpot of Malheur Slough and the Silvies River.

It's an immense land, and if there's a lesson to be learned it's this: Here in the Great Basin, if you follow water you won't get to the sea.

Yes, and knowing, as the geologist and the writer do, that Edwin Arlington Robinson was right in saying that "hell is more than half of paradise."

Great Basin Marker

Great Register on Crooked Creek

About six miles east of Burns Junction there is an historical marker that tells of Camp Henderson. The camp, established in 1864, and of short duration, was located due south, below the sandstone cliffs which mark the eastern boundary of the shallow valley that lies between sagebrush plains and alkali flats.

I reckon I passed the marker half a dozen times before I got smart enough to do some reading on Camp Henderson and then to knock on the door of Hazel and Julian Zimmerman, whose Crooked Creek Ranch is where the makeshift army facility was located.

Camp Henderson's brief history belongs to the Indian outbreaks of the 1860s. Military units were stationed throughout the state and each built its own garrison. Those that were temporary, as were most, were called camps; those that were meant to stay some years were termed forts. It didn't always work out that way but it was the general rule.

In mid-spring of 1864 a detachment of the First Oregon Volunteer Cavalry established camp on Crooked Creek and named their windswept base after J. H. D. Henderson, a Eugene fruit grower and railroad mogul who served a single term as Oregon's lone representative in the lower house of Congress.

It has been the custom of travelers since time immemorial to leave their names on whatever surface was available, even, as is the case in the American West, on buffalo skulls. All it took was one scrawling to inspire the second. The second set the stage for the third, and from then on there was no stopping so long as space held out.

Right from the start the horse troopers knew they had a natural writing tablet at hand. They started their engraving even before they had set up their tents. Just about every officer, noncom, and private who could stencil his name did so. Word about the inscribed cliffs must have gotten around, for there are many names dated beyond the departure of the First Oregon, including one S. Friedman, who etched his John Henry on March 25, 1866, more that a year after the camp was abandoned.

Hazel Zimmerman had made several trips down to the foot of the cliffs and, like others, hadn't found a thing to indicate that there had been a camp there. "There wasn't much, you know, it was a pretty simple camp, and maybe the Indians or the whites coming through took away or burned up what the soldiers left behind," she explained.

She could have added that nature hadn't been idle either. Sun and rain and wind are no respecters of crudely constructed quarters for people and stock.

Hazel Zimmerman had a romanticist's eye for Western history but a practical view on why people did what they did. "Crooked Creek is the only water in the country and I guess that's why they put the camp there.

"Crooked Creek starts about seven miles south of Burns Junction, out of a spring. It disappears before it gets to us, then it comes out (though some people say it's a different creek) and about five miles from here flows into the Owyhee River."

It was somehow fitting that the Zimmerman Ranch, whose occupants had to drive forty miles to Jordan Valley or ninety-seven miles to Burns for groceries, was on the site of Camp Henderson. The closest drugstore, doctor, hospital, and movie were at Burns. Mail, out of Jordan Valley, came only three times a week. The closest ranch was too far away to see; when winter marched in, the nearest neighbors seemed to be at the other end of the continent.

Maybe that's why the men of the First Oregon Volunteer Cavalry, fellows who came from sociable land, were happy to move on — their

Cliffs above site of Camp Henderson

Courtesy Mrs. Hazel Zimmerman

A name on the cliffs above Camp Henderson

camp was just too far from the kind of life they knew. Anyway, they had left their mark on this far-flung corner of Oregon, and that was enough for one war.

Directions: From Burns Jct. (Oregon 78-U.S. 95), 5 miles west on U.S. 95 to Zimmerman Ranch. 0.8 mile, historical marker.

The (Maybe) Fantastic Walls of Rome

According to the lady who ran the post office at Arock, the real authority on the Walls of Rome was Mrs. Scott, who ran a gas station and grocery store at the east end of Rome.

While we're at it, we may as well place Rome in Oregon; it is between Burns Junction and Jordan Valley, in the southeastern part of the state.

Mrs. Scott, an elderly, cheery woman who sat in her store waiting as much for people to chat with as to sell boxes of cornflakes and jars of pickles, told us to drive to the other end of town and take a dirt road north.

"It's no more than two and a half miles," Mrs. Scott said. "No chance you'll miss it."

"Are you sure it's two and a half miles from the highway to the Walls of Rome?" I asked lightly.

Mrs. Scott beamed assurance. "Absolutely," she said, "give or take half a mile."

Before we left the highway we paused to verify directions and Dave Miller, a tall young fellow with a Pancho Villa mushache, said he had never heard of the Walls of Rome.

"I haven't been here too long," explained Dave, who was running the west end of Rome gas station, tourist cabin and cafe with his wife and his brother and sister-in-law. "We came up from Huntington Beach, in the L.A. area. What interests you in that place?"

"Well," I replied, "I'm a natural-born bum and when I hear about somewhere I can get to I want to go there."

"How'd you hear about it?" asked Dave.

"Just bits and pieces of talk I picked up around Jordan Valley and Burns in the years I've been coming through," I summarized, "and a few sentences in a book that was written more than thirty years ago. Been too busy before, or didn't have a car, or just plain forgot. But now we're here and looking."

"Good luck," he waved, and we started up a dirt road. After plowing along it for a while we met a pickup. I hailed the rancher to a halt and asked him about the Walls of Rome.

"Oh yeah," he drawled wryly, pointing northward with his chin. "It's a little old low chain of hills that some outside folks got excited about."

"A book I read said that the walls are imposing and fantastic formations of fossil-bearing clay," I declared.

Walls of Rome

He peered at me. "Fantastic?"

"Fantastic," I repeated.

"Well," he said, pushing away a frown, "I guess it's all in the eye of the beholder."

"I understand," I continued, "that the formations are about five miles long and about two miles wide and about a hundred feet high."

"Maybe that high," he replied, "But," and he squinted in mental measurement, "I don't know about that long or wide. Don't seem that big."

"Fella in Burns told me," I went on, "that some dark ravines knife into the mounds and buttes."

He nodded. "Good place to lose cattle."

"The book says," I pushed forth, "that some formations are great clay blocks that look like they've been shaped by the chisel of a giant sculptor."

"All kinds of things out there," the rancher shrugged, "but nothing spectacular."

"One final note," I persisted. "Let me tell you what the book says, and I can repeat it from memory: 'At dusk these mesas are weird and sinister in appearance, and moonlight dusts their symmetrical contours with an uncanny splendor.' "

The rancher seemed amused. In the tone of one who asks, "I wonder if the writer was ever here?" or "What night was he here?" or "Is he talking about the place where I graze my cows?" he commented, "Well, I guess he had a lively way with words, wouldn't you say?"

About a mile on we reached a lone ranch house. A woman looked up from hanging wash on a line and was so dumbfounded at seeing total strangers that she just kept staring at us. I asked her about the Walls of Rome and she pointed them out in the distance.

"When you get to a fork in the road," she advised, "take the left road."

Out in that unending sagebrush peneplain, anything that has taken wheels is a road.

"The Walls of Rome are supposed to be a mighty awesome spectacle," I said.

"I wouldn't know about that," the woman replied. "Personally, I think they're overrated. I wouldn't go all the way from the highway to see them."

We found the left fork, which was a narrow brush trail hemmed in by high banks, and bumped down it until I was afraid there would be no place to turn around. I was driving an old Chrysler, not a jeep, and we had already gone three and a half miles from the turnoff. So when I found an indentation in the banks where I might turn around by gaining six inches a maneuver, I stopped and said to friend wife, "There they are. If you want to, we'll walk."

"I can take a picture from here," she said. So I browsed up a ways, keeping out of her line of sight by leaning close to a barbed wire fence on a bank until she had completed her shooting.

"Frankly," I said, when I returned, "they don't really look impressive, and they don't really look like the pictures I've seen of the ruined temples of Rome."

"They look impressive to me," she replied, "and I can see where someone would compare them to the walls of ancient Rome."

"I don't see them that way at all," I insisted.

"Some people just don't see clearly and some people lack imagination," she said, smiling coolly.

"O.K.," I declared flatly. "If that's the way you feel about them we'll go on. There must be someplace to turn around. And let's hope a rock doesn't fracture the oilpan."

"Never mind," she sighed. "I'm getting hungry. Let's go back to Rome and see if we can find lunch."

We had a hamburger with Dave Miller and he asked us if we had located the Walls of Rome.

"You bet," I said. "Pass the mustard."

"How were they?" he wanted to know.

Friend wife and I exchanged glances. "Just the way you see them," I said.

"We'll have to go up there," he promised himself aloud. "We don't want to miss any of the beautiful places in Oregon."

Directions: Rome, on U.S. 95, is 13 miles east of Burns Jct. and 33 miles west of Jordan Valley. Road to Walls of Rome begins from highway just east of service station at west end of village. 2.2 miles, turn left.

The Divided Hill House of Jordan Valley

Two miles east of Jordan Valley town the pavement ends and so does Oregon. There isn't any sign to tell you that you're in Idaho; there is just the gravel, and to the people of Jordan Valley that is identification enough.

Right back of where the pavement ends and the gravel begins there stands a quiet, shaded dwelling. It has been here more than a century and to everyone within fifty miles around it is known as the Stateline Ranch House.

The young woman who opened the door didn't know much about the history of the house; she and her husband had been there only a year or so. But she did know (though it didn't interest her very much, since she was paying rent) that the state line ran right through her home.

Oregon claimed the kitchen and Idaho the living room, or maybe it was the other way around. One bedroom was in Oregon and one in Idaho. If she wished, she could sleep in two states on the same night without leaving the house.

"How does it feel to be walking back and forth across the state line all day?" I asked.

She looked at me oddly. "I never gave it much thought."

"There was a great deal of history made around here; the view from any window must cover a lot of historic ground," I observed.

She pursed her lips. "It's just a place to live in."

"Do you ever feel there's something unusual about this place?" I persisted.

She smiled thinly, her patience running out. "It's just a house, and I don't know very much about it."

I went back to the road and looked hard toward the mountain hovering over Silver City, twenty miles east as the crow flies. Silver City is a ghost town now, as impressive a raw ghost town as any you can see in all the Pacific Northwest, but in its glory days it was a great mining center. Past this house trooped long lines of miners and merchants and pack-trains and ore wagons, the road seldom still, and Jordan Valley town a watering hole on the way to Winnemucca and California.

The house itself was built by one of the most action-packed figures ever to stake out a land claim in all that vast sweep of desert, sage and mountain. He was Marshall Hill, covered-wagon emigrant, sheep grower, cattleman, Indian fighter, cavalry scout, miner, orchardist, churchman, and zealous prohibitionist.

Tennessee-born Hill was sixteen when he came with his family across the plains from Iowa to Brownsville, Oregon in 1852. He was still under twenty when he set out to shoot down Indians. He fought in the so-called Rogue River and Paiute wars and was chief scout for General Crook when that salty Civil War veteran was handed the task of subduing the red men along the Oregon-Nevada border. A devout Christian, Hill was not for denying either heaven or hell to the Indians and the sooner he got them there the nearer he was to God. For their part, the Indians looked upon Hill as a white devil; the fact that he survived can only be attributed to acts of nature and poor marksmanship. Once, while developing mining claims on the Colorado River in Arizona, Hill's party was jumped by Apaches and the palefaces fled for their lives, with the Indians in holy pursuit. In Death Valley a hot, violent sandstorm suddenly rose. Several of the party perished but those who saw another day could thank the simoon for saving their skins. And there was the time when an enraged Indian, who had stalked Hill through a rocky canyon, finally spied him at close range and then discovered, too late, that his last bullet had been fired. Hill heard the click of the bolt and the tables were turned.

In 1868 Hill married Prudence Belinda Thomas and the couple rode off to the plateau west of Silver City, where he tried stock raising. The next year the Hills had a child, Melissa, the first white female born in Jordan Valley. As a silver-haired woman living in Salem in the 1950s she recalled that her only early playmates were Indian youngsters adopted by settlers of the area. Melissa was three before she saw another white child. "It was so strange that at first I thought it must be a little old man."

Hill worked hard on his "big house," Melissa said, so that his next offspring would not be born in a shed, as she was. The dwelling was completed in 1872 and Hill was certain that it was in Oregon. There was no doubt in his mind about it. But he was only half right. Surveyors placed the state line as cutting straight through the house.

Disappointments were no novelty to Hill. He had known some big ones. After fighting the Rogue River Indians he had lost all his cattle, horses and mules in a California flood. Some of his business ventures had gone sour. And down here at the Stateline Ranch he was beset by locusts, cattle rustling, and frosts that decimated his stock. He stayed on a few years, through the Indians shooting at his stock when they weren't blazing away at him, but finally a winter so cold that only the hides of his sheep could be salvaged forced him to leave.

During the Paiute uprising of 1875, Hill hurried his family from Jordan Valley to safety in a log cabin near Fossil, in Wheeler County. There, nine years later, Melissa Hill would start a teaching career that was to span seventy years, in a tiny one-room school with halved logs serving as desks and benches.

After securing the family, Hill returned to Jordan Valley to turn his house into a fortress, prepared to do battle with the Indians to the end. But there was no defense against that last brutal winter, and he departed for good, to rejoin his family. He wound up his days in The Dalles as a wealthy fruit grower. a faithful member of the Baptist Church, and vice president of the local Prohibition League.

In the town of Jordan Valley I found Floyd Acarregui, whose father

Stateline Ranch house, Jordan Valley

came here in 1898 to herd sheep. Later his Basque parents ran a boardinghouse. Floyd was born in it in 1911, a week before the "hotel" burned down. He recalled for me some of the stories the old-timers had told him about the home in two states.

"In the first part of this century," he remembered hearing, "Jordan Valley people would go to Silver City for marriage licenses, because they couldn't get any here. They'd have the civil wedding in the Idaho part of the Stateline Ranch House and then come into town here to have the church wedding at Saint Bernard's. Sometimes they'd go back to the Stateline Ranch House for the celebration.

"A lot of the pioneers around here were married in Idaho," he continued. "Nobody thought anything about it."

But why didn't they get married in Silver City, where they got the license, I asked.

"Because," Floyd said, frowning at my lack of perception, "people around here wanted to get married close to home. I don't care if half of the Stateline Ranch House is in Idaho; the whole house is in Jordan Valley."

Directions: In Jordan Valley, take Yturri Blvd. 2 miles to Stateline Ranch House.

In Search of Monahan

"What be your name?" gruffed the burly Argonaut at the new arrival placering the gravel of Jordan Creek, below the spiraling, mineral-rich Owyhee Mountains in the southwest corner of Idaho Territory.

"Joe Monahan," replied the stranger in a high-pitched voice.

"Kinda small fer a miner, ain'tcha?" remarked the Argonaut who, having been at Ruby City for a week, considered himself an old-timer.

"What's small got to do with it?" challenged the stranger.

"Well," grunted the old-timer, "if you kin do a man's work, you're a man. Shake on that, Little Joe!"

Nobody poked into Little Joe's pedigree. It was never a custom in the West to ask a miner about family or home or what had been done in the past or why the miner had come to this or that place. And no one pried into the backgrounds of the red-light women or dance hall girls. The "civilizing" influences, such as schoolmarms, wives, kitchen help and store clerks, who made much of biography, would come a bit later.

When the color ran thin, Little Joe found work at the quartz mill of the New York Mine in Ruby City, a mile down the new toll road from the great bonanza town of Silver City. It was 1865, silver poured from the mines, the stampede was still on, and Ruby City, with almost a thousand people, was booming day and night.

"Don't see you at the saloon," observed one of the mill hands.

Little Joe shrugged shyly.

"Maybe you're too young," the mill hand teased. "There isn't even any fuzz on your face."

Little Joe laughed, and countered, "Fuzz is for a peach."

The mill hand roared at his joke and slapped Little Joe on the back. "Well, you got a sense of humor. See you tomorrow, mister."

After a while, having saved enough money to go it alone, Little Joe left the New York Mine. Outside a small cabin in Ruby City the now independent farmer raised chickens and hogs and carried slop from Silver City to feed them. Then Joe expanded, adding two cows and selling milk to the miners. For extra money Joe ran a sort of delivery business to the merchants of Silver City. Legend turned the cart peddler into a long-haul freighter.

There was some talk about Little Joe in Silver City but it was passed over quickly. That's why some people came West, to get away from personal questions.

"It takes all kinds," said a grocer, responding to a customer's comment that Little Joe "is mighty peculiar." A hardware merchant was more philosophical: "If you took all the eccentrics out of this mining district, who'd be left but you and me, and I don't know about you." And when a saloon loafer couldn't understand how any man could have such small hands and feet, the bartender retorted: "It takes all kinds."

The 1880s were still very young when Little Joe left the Owyhee mining camps to start a small ranch on the broken hills of Succor Creek, in the still-frontier region of what is now Oregon's Malheur County. From there Joe hired out as a cowboy on the rimrock ranges of eastern Oregon and western Idaho. Size was no measurement of competence: Some youngsters were as proficient as adults. The stock owners agreed that Joe was as good in roundups as the next fellow. "Hell!" spat a foreman when a fresh face wondered about Joe's slight build, "He can handle a lariat, a rifle, and a pistol as good as any other man here!"

Everybody acknowledged that Joe was a loner. Nobody was invited to the Monahan shanty, which was a dugout built into the foot of a hill near what was later the Joe Fenwick ranch. To those who paused to look at it, the shanty seemed almost carelessly put together with whatever materials were at hand or could be scrounged from ranches on Succor Creek.

Almost sixty years after Little Joe passed away the scene was described by Mildretta Adams, who reconstructed a portrait of the shelter from gleanings obtained from Joe's contemporaries:

"The low roof was constructed with willow poles, covered over by packed sage brush and dirt. The door was made of two rough foot-boards nailed together, and was opened by a leather latch string from the outside. Inside, a stout pole served as a bar across the door to keep out intruders when Joe's day's work was done.

"A small stove occupied one corner of the dugout, with a tin lard pail serving as a teakettle setting on its top. A frying pan, baking pan for biscuits, and only such bare essentials as it took to batch with, made up the kitchen corner. A crude bunk bed, filled with hay for a mattress, was built along one wall. The mattress was sometimes used for horse feed when Joe ran short on hay. The bedding consisted of old coats, a canvas, and a shabby blanket."

Little Joe was equally makeshift in dress, padding about in oversize, cast-off shoes stuffed with gunnysack rags to keep them on. Trousers, shirts and jackets were also donations from sympathetic ranchers.

Some people wondered between themselves who was important enough for Joe to live so frugally. It was an open secret: The postmaster at Rockville had told a friend, and that friend had told another, and so it had gone, that Joe regularly sent money to someone in California. But nobody asked the dugout recluse. It just wasn't the thing to do, to poke around in other people's affairs.

Standoffish as Monahan was, there was no shunning civic responsibilities. Little Joe voted in every election that came along and served on juries. "He may not smell so good, but he's got a sharp mind," said a judge.

When the ranchers had odd jobs, they thought right off of Little Joe. And there wasn't a chore Joe turned down, whether it was wrangling sheep in the corrals during shearing time, driving flocks from one range to another, buckarooing — anything. Penny by penny, dollar by dollar, Joe managed to save enough money to build up a small bunch of cattle. The Rockville directory published in 1898 listed "Joseph Monahan, Cattleman," as one of twenty-two citizens on Succor Creek.

Just about Christmastime in 1903, Joe set out for the Boise River, driving the Monahan cattle toward winter pasture. At the Malloy Ranch, Joe took sick. "We'll take 'em on," the Malloy boys said, and did. Mrs. Malloy ordered Joe to bed. "Take the boys' room," she said. "They'll be gone awhile. You've got pneumonia," she diagnosed correctly.

A week or so later Joe felt strong enough to stand up in celebration of the new year. Two days later, resting in a chair in the front room that looked out to snow-covered slopes, Little Joe abruptly broke into a violent cough. There was no stopping it until life itself gave out.

Mrs. Malloy rode swiftly to notify neighbors. Soon the families arrived. The men carried Little Joe's body into the bedroom while their wives waited in the front room. Then the men started to remove Joe's clothing, to prepare the body for burial. Voices were low — and suddenly silence. The men came dazedly out and gasped to their wives, "You'd better go in." They did — and found one of their own sex. Joseph Monahan was a woman.

Her neighbors buried her in the old community cemetery at the Hat H Ranch at Rockville. "A few years ago," wrote Mildretta Adams in 1960, " 'Doc Yak' marked the grave with a sandstone slab."

The day she was buried a local rancher, Bill Schnabel, recalled that he had mailed letters to someone in Buffalo, New York. He could not remember the name or address so he wrote to the chief of police there. By coincidence, an old friend of Monahan's, Anna Walters, was then a Buffalo police matron. Hearing of the letter, she recognized Joe Monahan as Johanna Monahan, who had left Buffalo when still a teenager. Jo had been adopted and raised by Miss Walters' mother after Jo's own mother had died when she was eight and she had fled the custody of her cruel stepfather. At fourteen Jo boldly announced that she was taking off for the West to make her fortune — and that was the last Buffalo saw of her.

However, Jo wrote regularly to the Walters family — without ever telling them that she had taken on the garb and life-style of a man. (Presumably, she asked that letters sent her be addressed to J. Monahan, and evidently her request was honored, though there must have been some wondering in Buffalo.) And what an impression of the lives women in the West were forced to live the Walters must have received from reading Jo's colorful accounts of roughing it in mining camps, on the sheep trails, and in roundups!

When Mrs. Walters persisted in her request for a photo of her adopted daughter, Jo was not caught witless. She traveled to the nearest railroad town, where a photographer's studio was located, and had her picture taken. She explained to Mrs. Walters that the men's clothing she was wearing and her short haircut were only a joke. Upon word of her death a Buffalo newspaper put the photo on its front page, with the caption: "Buffalo woman who masqueraded for years as a cowboy out West."

There were some strange happenings after the news of Jo's passing

Courtesy Mildretta Adams

Jo Monahan dressed as a man

came out. The postmaster of Rockville received a letter from a young man in California seeking the whereabouts of his mother, Josephine Monahan. She had left him in care of others there while he was still a child, he said. On the face of it the letter was a fraud — but to whom in California had Little Joe been sending money? And *The Statesman* of Boise carried a story, datelined Weiser, Idaho, that claimed Jo to be, in reality, none other than the "notorious Kansas murderess," Kate Bender.

"While there is no positive proof that this statement is true," the dispatch continued, " 'Jo Monahan' appeared in Ontario a short time after the escape of Kate Bender." And it added that the parents of Kate presently resided on the Snake River, not far from Ontario.

All the basic data in the above is taken from a sketch in Mildretta Adams' fine booklet, *The Story of the Owyhees*. It was Mrs. Adams who dug up the story, and to her goes all the credit for the factual material. The personal quotations and embellishments are mine — the liberty of a writer who believes that if it didn't happen that way, that is the way it could have happened.

Because I thought this tale one of the most remarkable I had experienced in my many years in Oregon, I decided to pursue it further. Fifteen years after Mrs. Adams' little text was printed, I sought out some old-timers of the area who might personally have seen and talked with Monahan. (Mrs. Adams hadn't; she wrote me: "All that I know about Jo Monahan is in my book.") I wrote to every person suggested to me. It was surprising how many had no firsthand knowledge. Finally, at the end of the long trail, I came upon pay dirt in the persons of Omer Stanford of Jordan Valley and Jess Strode of Vale, both in Oregon.

Mr. Stanford, born in 1893, was recommended by almost everyone as the most authoritative living source on Jo Monahan. Mr. Strode, born in 1898, had strong childhood memories.

One of the things that bothered me about the Monahan story is where, in the one-acre cemetery, which most people agree has about twenty-five graves, Jo was buried. Only about seven graves are marked; there are no traces of the others. Of five fairly large old-style gravestones, three have, or were, toppled.

Mildretta Adams wrote me: "She is buried in the southwest corner, in an unmarked grave. It was one of three marked with a sandstone slab." But Jess Strode (of whom Omer Stanford said, "He is the only one alive that knows just where the grave was in the cemetery.") had a differing opinion.

"There is no marker over her grave," Mr. Strode told me. "There was a wooden marker which weathered many years ago. She lies just about in the center of the cemetery."

The best you can say is that "Little Joe" lies among her neighbors "on the crick," as mysterious in death as in life.

Jess Strode's grandfather, who in 1867 homesteaded below Mahogany Mountain, west of Rockville, knew Jo Monahan. So did Strode's parents, who came to Rockville in the spring of 1903. But Jess does not remember them talking much about her. His own sharpest recollection of her, when he was but five, is brief:

"She came to our house at Rockville, to talk to my uncle, Jack Strode, to take care of her horses as he was going to gather a lot of Strode horses. She was very small and quite wrinkled and had a high pitched voice, and wore men's clothes away too large, and I was just a kid, and she *scared hell out of me*."

And he recounted for me what he had heard from others:

"She would go on livestock roundups, but always had her bed away off by herself and if the men's jokes got a little rough she would just disappear for the time being."

Omer Stanford's letter is more than a remembering of Monahan: It contains some sharply etched touches of the frontier in the last decade of Jo's life. The reminiscing comes from a man who "all my life have been a rancher and a cow man."

"About the year 1884," wrote Mr. Stanford, "my grandfather settled on land at the mouth of Jackson Creek. This would be about five miles from where Jo's dugout was; her cattle ran on the same range as my uncle's. My mother was the oldest daughter, and after she and Dad were married we lived on Reynolds Creek, about fifteen miles north, over the mountains. Several times a year we would go to grandfather for a visit, and most everytime we would see Jo Monahan, as she liked to come here to visit and also to get supplies that she was short of.

"My uncle would tell us boys that she was some kind of witch, so we gave her a lot of room. I remember her as very small, dark-haired and very dirty. She also smoked a pipe. During those years she had a buck herd. She would take these buck sheep from the local sheepmen and herd them during the summer at so much per herd. She had one set of corrals on Jackson Creek and one on Chimney Creek. When she came to the ranch she always had a horse, but I never saw her riding it. She always led it, and she always had a gun.

"At the time of her death she had twenty-seven head of cattle, branded JO, and a few range horses. Sid Knight, a local rancher, was administrator and it took all the stock to settle the estate. The Knights used the JO brand for many years.

"As to the mining and freighting, the old timers said all she done was drive a delivery wagon from the towns to the mines.

"At the time of her death there was a man, Bill Schnabel, a very colorful writer, that wrote a lot of stories about Jo. According to him, she was everything from a circus performer to the infamous Kate Bender. Her parents were to have lived at Weiser, Idaho, but I had kin there and they didn't know. Also, she was supposed to have a son in California that wrote after her death, but no one knows.

"In the early days of Owyhee County there was a lot of young women come to the camps, some as hookers, others as dance hall girls. These dance hall girls were O.K. If you danced with one of them, you paid so much per dance. If you took her, or a friend to the bar, it cost one dollar, and she got a percent of the take. Later in life I knew a number of the women that married local ranchers and they made good wives and mothers.

"I think Jo just took a different route, as she loved the hills and was a loner. To me she was just another old-timer."

There are disturbing indications from the letters of Jess Strode and Omer Stanford that the ranchers knew all along that Monahan was a woman. If true, this would devastate the discovery scene at the Malloy Ranch. But what filters through after seven decades is not always the essence of the original. The litmus test of reality is not in treating hindsight as direct vision but in focusing upon the appearance of the moment. In his letter to the Buffalo chief of police, dated January 6, 1904, Bill Schnabel expressed a judgment that was probably shared by all who knew the scroungie recluse of Succor Creek: "There died near here a little man, known to all frontiersmen, such as miners, cowboys, etc., as Joe Monahan. . . . Now poor Joe is dead, and the long and deep mystery is cleared up. He is a woman."

At another point in his letter, Schnabel wrote:

"He was a small, beardless man with hands, feet, stature, and voice of a woman." These physical features and some of her social characteristics, such as tacitly expressing discomfort at the telling of raw stories, sleeping away from the other cowpokes, and bolting her door, must have given rise to doubts and whispers. But no one sought to embarrass her with a direct question or innuendo. "The cowboys treated him with respect, and he was always welcome to eat and sleep at their camps."

(There is also an Owyhee legend, told by an old-timer of Malheur County, that when Jo's true sex was learned she was so despised that she was buried without the presence of a preacher. It may be correct, but I take it with a grain of salt. If anything, it is further testimony that the female anatomy of Monahan came as a surprise to her neighbors.)

In the summing up, no one could be sure. She was not the only cowboy with small hands and feet and short, frail stature. (Some frontier women, as is true today, were larger than their male contemporaries — and some women of that time could revel in bawdy tales.) A few other buckaroos had high-pitched voices. Loners and puritans were not that rare. And as for the lack of hair on face, it was pointed out that if some women can be bearded, some men can be beardless. "It takes all kinds," said the judgmatic cowboys, who reckoned they had seen everything.

The critical value test was not as much in dress as in work. Women could wear pants and shirt; some on the frontier did. But anyone who lived the rugged, dangerous life of a cowboy had to be a man. (When a prominent writer suggested to cowboy-author Andy Adams that Andy put a woman in a novel about trail-driving, Adams wryly replied that a woman with a trail herd would be as useless as a fifth wheel on a wagon and that he would not insult reality by including her in the cast of characters.)

Despite the doubts, Little Joe therefore had to be a man, and that is why the husbands walked ashen-faced out of the bedroom at the Malloy Ranch.

Directions to Rockville Cemetery on old Hat H Ranch: From Rockville School, 25 miles north of Jordan Valley, take road up McBride Creek (it heads north toward U.S. 95.) 3 miles to Hat H Ranch. O.5 mile past Hat H turnoff, look to right. Cemetery, in neglected condition, is about an acre of fenced-in land.

Leslie Gulch: A Fantasy For Real

More than thirty years after a Malheur County cattleman who had a small spread on Succor Creek showed me Leslie Gulch, I brought friend wife here.

Phoebe is no stranger to Oregon beauty. She had seen just about every other part of the state before setting eyes on Leslie Gulch. And on the way to the gulch we passed through Succor Creek Canyon, whose walls shoot up to 300 feet and then slope skyward another 700 feet to culminate in a remarkable gallery of pinnacles, towers, mounds, cones, spires, faces, monuments and monoliths, gorgeously dyed with free-wheeling reds, greens and yellows. But at Leslie Gulch she really gasped.

According to the cattleman, the gulch had been named for a stockman, "coot by the name of Leslie," who supposedly had been struck down by lightning, about 1882, while trying to roust some cows out of the brush. (The Department of Interior says Hiram Leslie was a Silver City pioneer.)

What did the stockmen who came riding in from the Mahogany Mountains and the eastern shore of the Owyhee River and the lower clefts of Succor Creek to get their mail at the tiny post office of Watson, at the end of the canyon, think about Leslie Gulch? There is no record of their thoughts and as little history of Watson, which opened in the summer of 1898 and closed before anyone had gotten used to it..

Leslie Gulch Marker

Maybe some saw the gulch as wild country that couldn't be tamed — and for that reason left. And maybe some saw it as too far from market and town — and departed because of that. "A pretty place stops being pretty when the odds start running against you," the Succor Creek rancher had said. A stampede of beauty can become a choke of dust when your back-breaking toil is defeated by the terrain, the elements and the loneliness. That's what probably happened to a lot of the homesteaders.

We found a few people squatted in their trailers and campers on the shore of Lake Owyhee, where the gulch runs out. They hadn't come for the splendid spectacle of Leslie; they had driven here to fish. For some people a fish freshly taken from sparkling water is more majestic than the Taj Mahal. But not for me — and certainly not for friend wife. She left with a deep frustration at not having enough time to photograph as much as she would have liked, and I can explain my feelings by what I jotted down there:

Leslie Gulch is a stunning, breath-taking, daffy world of incredible rock windows, parapets, battlements, stony hogbacks, bunched rocks, free-standing rocks, pillars, columns; rocks in the shape of apes, frogs, comic cartoon characters, armadillos; rocks towering and twisted and

The road through Leslie Gulch

Leslie Gulch formations

tumbled; and all in the most wondrous pure and mixed-up colors: pinks, yellows, blues, browns, purples, reds, greens. Some of the formations appear to be covered by chocolate syrup. One hill seems to have a city of rocks built upon it — and cliffs shoot out in all directions. Desert flora stitch the seams of the Mahogany Mountains, weaving a trail of brilliance through the hills. Truly, truly, this reality is fantasy and this fantasy is real — and if I lie, may lightning strike me as it did Hiram Leslie.

Directions: From Adrian (12.4 miles south of Nyssa, U.S. 20-26) on Oregon 201: south 8.3 miles to Succor Creek State Park Jct. 12.5 miles, entrance to Succor Creek State Park. 15 miles, Leslie Gulch Jct. Turn right. 8 miles, start of Leslie Gulch scenery. 6.8 miles, Lake Owyhee.

From Rob to Riches at Joseph

Did anyone ever tell you about the man who became president of a bank he once robbed?

(Actually, he was only vice-president, but why spoil a good story?)

We heard the tale in Joseph, up in the Wallowa highlands, from several people, including the town banker. And we were shown yellowed clippings about the robbery by Homer Hayes, now deceased, who put in some time helping run the Chief Joseph Museum, closed after his death.

The museum was once the First Bank of Joseph, which was the one robbed, and Hayes pointed to the safe from which the money was taken.

Better yet, Hayes recounted the holdup. He was there, probably the last person alive to have witnessed any of the action. He was only a boy of

Joseph bank

Homer Hayes inside bank that was robbed

nine then, back in that year of 1896, but he was sure he hadn't forgotten a single detail.

"We were at school, recessed," he recalled, "when these three guys came up. We thought they were Negroes, because they were blackened up. We never saw a Negro so we didn't know.

"The school was just across the street from the bank. Next thing you know, we heard shots.

"You see, that was dividend day and a lot of folks come to the bank to collect their money. The word went out that the bank was being robbed and all the businessmen grabbed their guns and rushed out.

"Well, the three guys ran from the bank to their horses. The guy with the money got shot right off his horse and killed. His name was Brown. Another robber, Fitzhugh, jumped down and got the money sack and jumped back on his horse and rode off. I heard they got him later in another state; Joseph didn't want him. I heard that, but I'm not sure about it. I know the money was never recovered.

"The third guy, he put his hands up in surrender but they shot one of his fingers off. His name was Dave Tucker.

"Tucker went to the pen. He got seven years. I think that after three years he got paroled. He come back to Joseph and started in the sheep business as a herder. Finally he became a sheep rancher and owned a lot of country. He bought into the bank and eventually became president. He was pretty well fixed when he did.

"Dave Tucker was just a kid, about sixteen years old when he was in the robbery. I knew him well. He was just a helluva good guy. All the people respected and trusted him. He never put the squeeze on a farmer or held out for blood money."

I wrote a small thing about the Joseph bank and soon I received a letter from Dean Pollock, who had grown up in Wallowa County and was the author and illustrator of a fine text, *Joseph, Chief of the Nez Perce*. I felt flattered all-out to get personal word from Pollock and especially tickled to have him add this footnote to the bank story:

"My father, at the time of the episode, was owner, editor, compositor, pressman, reporter, advertising and circulation manager of the Joseph *Herald*. His shop was in the back room of the bank. His 'printer's devil' was a very pretty eighteen-year-old girl who became my mother.

"The pressman (et al) was busy printing the weekly blat on the Washington hand press when interrupted by the turmoil. Immediately after the excitement the reporter-compositor composed his story before the type case with a stick in one hand while his flying fingers sought to keep up with his racing thoughts. On the stone, now as makeup man, he set up a diagram with brass rules, with X, Y, Z marking the points where blood was shed. The sheet was then run off on the foot-power job press (my father's foot), and inserted in the weekly edition. It was really hot news.

"Fred Wagner lived a block west of the bank. At the height of the fray he rushed out into the street and unlimbered his trusty Winchester and, according to my father's version, shot the money bag out of Brown's hand. Finding that this did not stop him, Fred drew a bead in deadly earnest. I believe it was Fred's bullet that killed Brown.

"Fitzhugh was the ringleader, a dastardly stranger in town who corrupted the local boys. He escaped with one other man. It was found that they had fresh horses awaiting them on upper Prairie Creek, from whence they disappeared into the depths of Hells Canyon. The loss was $3,000."

Except for a few years at college, Homer Hayes had lived all his eighty-three years in Joseph, when we saw him, and nothing had been as exciting as that wild morning in 1896.

"That's quite a story about Tucker, isn't it," said Hayes, grinning. "If they put it on television no one would believe it. But it happened, yes it did, and that makes it kind of odd, doesn't it?"

The Wrong Kind of Monument

I hope that no more groans of wounded men and women will ever go to the ear of the Great Spirit Chief above, and that all people may be one people.

Young Chief Joseph

A mile south of Joseph, facing Wallowa Lake in the ancient Nez Perce Valley-of-the-Winding-Waters, there has stood for more than half a century a monument to Old Joseph, a gallant chief in his own right but better known as the father of Young Joseph, or Chief Joseph.

Most Oregonians know of only one Joseph, the son, and though the lettering on the monument clearly states: "To The Memory of Chief Old Joseph," it is astounding how many times I have been told by natives of this state, returning from the lake, that the Joseph of legend, the Joseph of whom so many books have been written, is buried beneath the stone shaft.

It is unfortunate that in white eyes the son has so eclipsed his father, for the father was as wise a leader and as devout a patriot as his son. And he was as compassionate and as much a poet. Riding through the village at morning in the summer camp on the shores of Wallowa Lake, his voice could be heard ringing over water and meadow as he cried:

"I wonder if everyone is up! It is morning. We are alive, so thanks be! Rise up! Look about! Go see the horses, lest a wolf have killed one! Thanks be that the children are alive! — and you, older men! — and you, older women! — also that your friends are perhaps alive in other camps. But elsewhere there are probably those who are ill this morning and therefore the children are sad, and therefore their friends are sad."

He was Tu-eka-kas to his people, the Wal-lam-wat-kin, a band of the Numipu. His father had told him of the coming of Lewis and Clark, the first whites the Nez Perce ever saw, and he often imparted the tale to his son. Many years later, and not without a touch of bitterness, Young Joseph said:

"All the Nez Perces made friends with Lewis and Clark, and agreed to let them pass through the country, and never to make war on white men. This promise the Nez Perces have never broken. No white man can accuse them of bad faith, and speak with a straight tongue."

From their summer camp the Wal-lam-wat-kin looked up to the snow-burnished peaks of the moon-shaped Wallowa Mountains and saw,

Grave of Chief Old Joseph

from a shore of the lake, a ten-thousand-foot-high spire we know as Sacajawea, named for the Shoshone girl-mother who traveled with Lewis and Clark from Fort Mandan to the western sea and back. Suppose the mountain were Sacajawea and she could speak: Would she apologize in the name of Lewis and Clark for the Indians having been driven from their homeland? Father and son must have wondered what Lewis and Clark would have thought. Had not the "Long Knives" told the father of Old Joseph that his people were the friendliest and most helpful Indians Lewis and Clark had met?

It was because of the elkskin captains, who came not with sword and deceit but with friendship and gifts, that the Nez Perce welcomed the whites who came to stay. Tu-eka-kas went a step further; in 1839 he embraced the "spirit law" of the white preachers, being one of the first two converts of the Reverend Henry Harmon Spalding at the Lapwai Mission, in Idaho. Spalding Christianized him "Joseph," and so white history has recorded him, though later he renounced the white man's religion and book. They did not practice what they preached, he said, and their gospel was not to liberate but to enslave the Indian.

Tu-eka-kas had two sons. The oldest was named Hin-mut-too-yah-

Courtesy Oregon Historical Society

Young Chief Joseph

lat-kekht, Thunder-rolling-in-the-mountains. He was to be better known as Chief Joseph. But if not for a war forced upon his people he would not have become the legend he has been for more than a hundred years. It is tragic, but true, that we have been taught (with rare exception, such as Sacajawea, who is associated with whites) only the names of warriors. It must have been a grim jest to this man who loved peace to be pointed out as "War Chief Joseph."

The story of how the Nez Perce land was taken from them has been told too often to repeat. It was a classic example of force, intimidation, skullduggery and bribery. Old Joseph refused to put his name to the government treaty which some chiefs, duped and corrupted (and without real authority), had signed. As he lay in his lodge, sightless and life ebbing out of him, in 1872, he summoned his erect, handsome son, then thirty-two summers old.

The scene was described some years later by Young Joseph:

". . . I took his hand in mine. He said: 'My son, my body is returning to my mother earth, and my spirit is going very soon to see the Great Spirit Chief. When I am gone, think of your country. You are the chief of these people. They look to you to guide them. Always remember that your father never sold his country. You must stop your ears whenever you are asked to sign a treaty selling your home. A few more years, and white men will be all around you. They have their eyes on this land. My son, never forget my dying words. This country holds your father's body. Never sell the bones of your father and your mother.' I pressed my father's hand and told him I would protect his grave with my life. My father smiled and passed away to the spirit-land.

"I buried him in that beautiful valley of winding waters. I love that land more than all the rest of the world. A man who would not love his father's grave is worse than a wild animal."

Five years later Joseph and his people were driven from their ancestral home. There followed what is imprudently called the "Nez Perce War." You've read of it: the 2,000 mile retreat that lasted four terrible months; the brilliant strategy of Joseph and his colleagues, who outmaneuvered the best brains of the American army; the great courage of the Nez Perce, who were, at times, outnumbered better than thirty to one; and the surrender at the Bear Paw Mountains in Montana, only a hard day's ride from Canada and freedom.

Surrender terms guaranteed that the Nez Perce would be taken to Lapwai. Instead they were herded to Indian Territory (Oklahoma), an alien land. Not until 1885 were they returned, 118 to the Lapwai Reservation in northern Idaho and 150, including Joseph, to the arid, desolate Colville Reservation in north-central Washington. Only once was Joseph permitted to see the Wallowa Valley and his father's grave again, in 1900. By then a town was called Joseph and a newspaper the *Chieftain*, but the settlers did not want him back. So fierce was the resistance to Joseph's plea for a small part of the Wallowa Valley to be a homeland again that the government decreed never to permit the Nez Perce to return to Oregon.

The long summer of 1904 was coming to an end and autumn was filtering in. The wind whipped through the tawny hills of the Colville Reservation. Joseph knew his dream of completing the circle of his life in the green valley of his first thirty-seven years was done. He sat heavy and impassive before his fire. One day he was heard to murmur, "Halo manitah"; he would not see another winter. A few days later he collapsed, pitching forward, and all of him sprawled on the floor of his lodge. The agency doctor said, "Joseph died of a broken heart."

Old Joseph, whom his son called the greatest chief he had ever known, had died at the forks of the Wallowa and Lostine Rivers and that night was buried on the ridge. The next day his body was unearthed, carried down the ridge, and buried again on the south slope of the forks. More than half a century later several white men dug up his remains and placed them under a monument at the foot of Wallowa Lake. On September 26, 1926, the monument was dedicated. Hundreds, perhaps thousands, came, including some who had fought tooth and nail to keep the Nez Perce from returning to the Wallowa Valley.

The legendary Chief Joseph lies three hundred miles away, at Nespelem, on the Colville Resevation. Not far from his grave, as distance is spanned these days, a great dam bears his name. But the only monument both father and son ever wanted, they said, was that all people should live as brothers and sisters.

The message is more important than the stone or who lies where — but when will it be heard?

That Troublesome Oregon Trail

Many writers, including myself, have sometimes used the phrases "Oregon Trail" and "Old Oregon Trail" as though both were the same.

Actually, there is a difference between the two. The former denotes an overland passage to Oregon and the latter a route which led into the northern part of the state.

That also can be confusing because for much of the distance to Oregon the same general passage was taken. Thus, in the interchange of language and in the plethora of confusion, most people think that the "Oregon Trail" and the "Old Oregon Trail" are identical.

In reality, there was no "specific" trail to Oregon, if we think of the trail as we do a road. You know exactly where any county, state or national road goes in Oregon. A town may be on it — such as Newberg

Oregon State Highway Division

Marker along Oregon 19

Nebraska Game Commission

Scotts Bluff, in western Nebraska, was well-known landmark on Oregon Trail.

being on Oregon 99W — but between towns the road stands on its own, and a farmhouse half a mile from the road may be near it, but it is not on it.

You cannot say the same about the Old Oregon Trail, or any wagon road to Oregon. In some stretches the trail was forty miles wide. To mark the trail as engineers lay out a road would be an exercise not only in futility but in absurdity.

It comes as a great surprise to some people to be told that there was no such animal as an exact Oregon Trail. Their minds are rooted in the automobile age and they cannot see backward. But you, of course, are brighter. You know that the fuel needed to propel your car down the paved road can be obtained from a service station at the edge of the road. Occupying a relatively small space, the station supplies all the fuel your car needs. But oxen and horses and mules require grass, and if you were driving, say, a team of oxen, and the road were not pavement but grass, you would find that the long march of oxen which had gone before you had eaten all the grass, and therefore you would have to go to either side of the beaten path. If the traces made by others seeking fresh grass had also been denuded, you would go farther afield. You would certainly not drive your stock three miles to graze and then drive them back three miles to the beaten path. Those six miles would constitute half-a-day's travel.

There were other reasons for the wagoners to make their own trails. A scarcity of water would force an outreaching. So would a search for wood. And pilots moved their caravans to different locations to avoid being choked by the dust spumed up by the trains before them.

Ever since the wagons stopped rolling, there has been an illusion that an exact Oregon Trail existed. In 1925, when there were still some Oregon Trail emigrants alive, and when scholars were much closer to the scene than they are now, and when the West was pristine and unblemished compared to today, the Congress of the United States set out to define the Oregon Trail.

Three resolutions, two in the House and one in the Senate, were introduced. After a series of hearings before the House Committee on Roads, the resolutions were laid to rest. The Senate, dazed by the maze of conflicting testimony in the House hearings, did not pursue the matter further.

It was soon apparent in the House hearings that marking the Oregon Trail was no non-partisan matter. Any suggestion of historicity was quickly stampeded by passionate and well-oiled arguments advanced by vested interests. Each chamber of commerce in the broad area demanded that the trail be run through its town.

None of the three resolutions agreed completely with either of the other two in mapping the Oregon Trail. Taken as a concensus, the resolutions had the Oregon Trail pass through places most of which were not in existence when the trail was bearing its greatest traffic. Worse yet, the main flow was away from many of these sites.

One of the resolutions declared that a branch of the Oregon Trail ran from Ontario, Oregon to Weiser, Idaho and thence through Huntington, Oregon. That would be two needless crossings of a river, for it would mean three trips across the Snake in an area where only one fording was made.

Vale, Oregon was not mentioned in any resolution — dozens of towns were — yet hundreds of wagons stopped at Vale, where the emigrants found a much-used hot springs in the Malheur River. Neither was Oregon City, traditionally recognized as the end of the Old Oregon Trail. Hood River was listed, but the Old Oregon Trail did not go through that area; from The Dalles the emigrants either went by boat downstream or crossed the Cascades over the Barlow Toll Road, south of The Dalles. (After some years a shorter route was found, bypassing The Dalles; east of Wasco the pioneers turned southeast after leaving the west bank of the John Day fording and cut across the grasslands to Tygh Valley, where they joined the main Barlow Road by way of what are now Moro and Grass Valley.)

All three resolutions stated that the Oregon Trail ran through "Astoria and Seaside in the State of Oregon, thence through Vancouver and on to Olympia, in the State of Washington."

Oregon State Highway Division

Old Oregon Trail rut in Umatilla County. This photo probably taken in 1950s and by now it is likely that the rut is no longer visible.

The only members of the committee from west of the Mississippi River were from Missouri, Texas and Oklahoma — but surely someone could have looked at the map. (And what of the many Oregon chambers of commerce that heartily endosed the resolution; didn't they know better?) Through Seaside to Vancouver! Ugh!

A witness quoted Hiram M. Chittenden (one of the truly great authorities on the early West, despite the ignorance of him by committee members) to stress the point that it was fatuous to designate any road as the Oregon Trail.

"As travel increased with the inflow of emigrants short-cuts were introduced here and there, while in some places the road became so worn that new locations were necessary, and thus from one cause to another there came to be several parallel lines over many portions of the route," Chittenden was quoted. "Sometimes they were but a few hundred feet from each other; and again they were separated by many miles of distance and occasionally by rivers and mountains. . . .

"It would indeed be a difficult matter to lay down the old line with minute precision. The changes wrought by the settlement of the country have been too great. The land surveys with their rectangular divisions have forced the highways out of their natural course and in many places the old road has long since been plowed up and turned into cultivated ground. The advent of railroads wrought an immense change in the location of names. Although many of the Trail names survive, the towns which they denote are rarely located where the names used to apply. They have probably gone to the nearest railway station which may be several miles away."

(Two comments need to be made on Chittenden's statement. He concerned himself only with the early years, before considerable alterations in the "Trail" were spun out. And he made his assessment about 1900. Consider how much more change has transpired since then!)

The "main" road to Oregon lay not only over the "original" route of 1843, the years of the Great Migration, but through several cutoffs in Wyoming, through parts of Utah, over several trails in Idaho, through a slice of Washington, and through various parts of northern and central Oregon. (The "Southern" or Applegate Trail crossed a tip of Utah, northern Nevada, and a short stretch of northeastern California.)

There was sharp bickering at the committee hearings as to which side of the Platte River constituted the Oregon Trail. At stake was not only prestige but the benefit of tourist dollars.

The Wyoming legislature, for reasons of its own, requested that the Oregon Trail be shifted from the Fort Bridger route — originally used and included by diehards in the "traditional" Trail — to the Lander Cutoff as "the most direct and practical route."

After reporting the sentiment of the legislature of his state, Wyoming Rep. Charles E. Winter added philosophically: "There is no doubt that in time tradition becomes dim; and disputes will continue to arise and become more marked as to what was the trail."

In great measure, his words have proven prophetic. A congressional hearing today would shed even more heat than light.

It is little wonder romanticists speak of the "Old Oregon Trail," meaning the most approximate locations, the most popular route, and that most closely identified with the very first few years of wagon train movement.

To see the road to Oregon for what it was, as a network of trails, would remove all charm and coherence from the storehouse of the romanticists, which is one reason why the House Committee on Roads adjourned the hearings in despair. They were never continued — and no new resolution on the subject was ever again introduced.

Still, I did find a bit of shining gold in the transcript of the committee hearings — a poem, which I did not know existed, that was written by Mrs. John Stack, who is identified only as "a pioneer lady of Baker County, Oregon, who came in 1859."

It was the one solid contribution the committee made on the subject of the Oregon Trail.

Hickory yoke and oxen red,
And here and there a little towhead
Peeping out from the canvas gray
Of the Oregon Overland on its way,
    In Fifty-Nine.

No sound save the creak of the axletree,
And now and then a whoa, haw, gee,
From the driver whose face with dust is gray
Of the Oregon Overland on its way,
    In Fifty-Nine.

Creeping along the mountain side,
Fording rivers, deep and wide,
From the earliest dawn 'til the close of day,
Rolls the Oregon Overland on its way
    In Fifty-Nine.

At ease in a home in some cosy nook,
Near by the sound of a running brook,
Or perhaps asleep beneath the sod,
Forgetting forever the road they trod,
Are the little towheads that peeped that day
From the Oregon Overland on its way
    In Fifty-Nine.

Oregon Names

Land of the ocean shores! land of sierras and peaks!
Land of boatmen and sailors! fishermen's land!
Inextricable lands! the clutch'd together! the passionate ones!

Walt Whitman, *Starting from Paumanok*

In his joyful, poignant and nostalgic reminiscences, *Feelin' Fine*!, Bill Hanley, the legendary stockman of Harney County complained: "They'll be changing our old names that tell people the whole history of the country: Squaw Flats, Yainax, Bake Oven, Rawhide, Stinking Water . . . so many others, given by the boys, often for things that happened there. All mean something. Every one a story."

A lot of old names were changed or obliterated before Hanley's book was published in 1930, and a lot more since. A high butte down in Klamath County is still called Yainax, but the hamlet of Yainax on the Klamath Reservation isn't around any more. Neither is the settlement Hanley called Bake Oven, which is just farmland now, eight miles northwest of Shaniko, on the Bakeoven Road to Maupin. Rawhide is too far back in time for even the ancients to recall and Squaw Flats is a pale and doubtful memory. Stinkingwater Creek is still around but the first village to the east was better known to the boys as Gouge Eye than the post office name of Drewsey.

What happened to some of the good old Oregon names that had real meaning in their time? Axhandle Spring became Kilts, Civil Bend was changed to Brockway, Tell Tale was turned into Eckley, Skunk Cabbage was sweetened to Marshland, Latchaw's Mill was diluted to Pine, Express Ranch was starched to Weatherby, Cross Keys transformed into a polite Ridgeway, Yankeetown shortened to Yankton, and Hogum, applied to show the greediness of some prospectors up in Baker County, was switched to Augusta and then to Sanger.

They are gone, lost to the wind and long-forgotten yarns. So, too, are Pheasant, Peak, Reuben, Rural, Fair Play, Four Mile, Greenback, Arrow, Gooseberry, Canoe Landing, Mesquite, Owlville, Irma and Isadora.

And so are Trailfork, Basin, Lick Skillet, Mule, Hiddensprings, Gopher, Burnt Ranch, Bourbon, Scanty Grease, Desert, Crowfoot, Lonely, Lonesomehurst, Lowersoda, Luckyboy and Vinemaple.

Azalea is still there, but before Azalea it was Booth and before that the more graphic Starvout. Shaniko has had that name so long few people know that it was once called Cross Hollows, which sounds more fitting, at

Horsetail Falls

least to me. West Linn was Linn City until 1854 and started life in the early 1840s as Robin's Nest.

Trek to Wallowa County and you'll find Paradise and Promise hanging on for dear life, born in the days when farmers got around in winter by hitching horses to their sleighs. But Joy, Utopia, Arcadia, Eureka, Eden and Lovely are completely of an age past.

I have been in love with Oregon names since I first heard them. Crooked Finger Prairie, Cricket Flat, Billy Meadows, Bitter Lick, Row River, Dixie Jett Gulch, Dutch Oven Camp and God's Valley.

Close your eyes and you can see the life and folklore of these names: Fandango Canyon, Tombstone Prairie, French Prairie, Fashion Reef, Friendly Reach, Chickenhouse Gulch, Gumjuwac Saddle and Mixup Spring.

I have been drawn a hundred miles to a name and I have not been disappointed by Johnny Kirk Spring, Lord Flat, OK Gulch, Deadhorse Ridge, The Dungeon and Peepover Saddle.

Oregon is rich in names beyond its towns and hamlets. Consider some of the creeks: Big Noise, Blue Bucket, Boneyard, Buttermilk, Chaparral, Coffeepot, Cracker, Crazyman, Curiosity, Dairy, Dinner,

Goose, Fiddle, Louse, Murder, Skunk, Sleepy, Soap, Splintercat, Threebuck, Tumtum, Twocolor and Twelvemile.

Or look at a few of the ranges, mountains, hills, buttes and monoliths: Battle Rock, Blazed Alder Butte, Broken Top, Cabbage Hill, China Hat, Devils Pulpit, Elephant Head, Hambone Butte, Parsnip Peak. Postage Stamp Butte, Preachers Peak, Sagehen Butte, Sourdough Mountain, Spirit Mountain, Three Sisters and Tomlike Mountain.

There is grassroots expression in the name of Oregon valleys: Arkansas Hollow, Barren, Company Hollow, Dinwiddie, Happy, Horsefly, Mormon Flat and Thief. And there are pictures in the names of falls: Fishhawk, Horsetail, Steamboat and Umbrella. You can put the names of lakes to the music of square-dance fiddling: Billy Chinook, Loon, Lost, Malheur, Owyhee, Strawberry and Ten Mile. And there is covered wagon history in the names of rivers: the Burnt, the Columbia and the Deschutes; the Grande Ronde, the John Day and the Powder; the Sandy, the Snake and the Zigzag.

It is in the Indian names, though — of mountains and falls and lakes and rivers — that I find the truest chant of beauty in the names of Oregon. Hear them as you go back to the beginning of white settlement, when the invaders anglicized the even more lilting original names: Calapooya, Chetco, Clackamas, Clatskanie and Coquille; Alsea and Imnaha; Koosah and Luckiamute; Metolius, Minam and Multnomah; Nehalem, Nestucca and Oneonta; Sacajawea, Santiam, Siletz, Siltcoos and Siuslaw; Tualatin and Tumalo; Umatilla and Umpqua; Wahkeena, Wallowa and Willamette; Yachats and Yamhill; and a hundred more.

When I die let the wind sprinkle my ashes over Arock and Horse Heaven, into Alkali Lake and Big Muddy Creek, on the last stretch of the Barlow Road and the worst of the Meek Cutoff, at Camas Valley and Cascade Head, above Buffalo Well and Hug Point, on the Painted Hills and at Tollgate, somewhere in a corner of Chewaucan Marsh and into Lost River, at Whalehead Beach and on a slope of Hart Mountain. And may the last grain of me fall to earth at Wagontire.

Index

Abbee, Carrie, 141–142
Abernathy, George, 84
Acarregui, Floyd, 268–269
Adams, Andy, 276
Adams, Cecilia Emily McMillen, 225
Adams, Mildretta, 271, 272, 273, 274
Adams, Thomas, 104, 105–106, 109, 110
Adrian, 279
Alaska, 28
Albany, 4, 61, 65, 99, 135
Albany *Democrat*, 61, 65
Alexander, Charles, 135, 137, 140
Allen, Chuck, 150, 151
Almeda Mine, 165
Alsea River, 5, 296
Alsop, Bill, 250
Anthony, Susan, 102
Applegate, Charles, 162
Applegate, Cynthia Ann, 163
Applegate, Jesse, 84, 101, 160–164
Applegate, Roselle, 161
Applegate Trail, 160, 166, 292
Applegate Valley Garden Club, 176
Apples in Oregon, 184–185, 235
Arch Cape, 12
Arock, 264, 296
Ashland, 4, 206, 207
Ashley, Gen. William H., 126, 127
Ashwood, xii, 203
Asotin, Wash., 234, 235
Astor, John Jacob, 126
Astoria, 11, 30, 36, 40, 41. 63, 65, 81, 118
Athena, 250
Auburn, 89
Augusta (see Sanger)
Aurora, 143
Axhandle (see Kilts)
Azalea, 294

Bacona, 43–50
Bake Oven, 294
Baker, 229
Baker County, 292, 294
Balch, Charley, 186, 187, 188
Balch Hotel, 185, 186, 187, 188
Balch, Mrs. Lois, 186
Baldwin, Dr. David W., 203
Baldwin, George, 208
Baldwin Hotel, 206–210
Baldwin Sheep and Land Company, 204
Ball, John, 6, 10
Baltimore Colony, 25
Bancroft, H. H., 25
Bandon, 18
Bargenolt, Maude, 229
Barlow, 143
Barlow Road, 290, 296
Battle of Hungry Hill (also known as Battle of Bloody Springs), 167
Battle Rock State Park, 19, 20, 22
Battleaxe Creek, 152, 153
Baumgarten, Leona (see Dickerson, Leona)
Baumgarten, Nova, 137, 138, 139, 140, 143
Bear Valley Tavern, 251–253
Beatty, 211–220
Beautiful Willamette, 58, 59, 61, 62, 66, 67,. 68, 69–70
Beaver Creek, 113
Bend, 4, 222, 224
Bender, Kate, 273, 275
Benton County, 111, 112, 113, 114, 115
Bent's Fort, 107
Bertrand, Alex, 74, 76
Bertrand, Pamela (Maud) Law, 74, 76
Big Muddy Creek, 296
Biggs, 179
Blair, William, 107, 108
Blind Sough, 30, 33
Bloss, J., 179
Blue Bucket Mine, 2, 221, 222
Blue Mountains, 2, 142, 196
Bobbie, A Great Collie, 135
Bobbie, The Wonder Dog, 135, 144
Bohemia City, 157, 158, 159
Bohemia Mining District, 153–159
Bohemia Mountains, 155, 156, 158
Bohn, Louis D., 74
Bonanza, 207
Bonneville Dam, 201
Booth (see Azalea)

Bowen, Roxy Ann, 173
Boyd, 181, 183
Bradley Wayside, 30, 34
Bradley, William "Bill," 171–172
Bradstreet, Anne, 118
Bradwood, 30–32
Brazier, Elizabeth, 135, 138, 139, 140, 142, 143
Brazier, Frank, 135, 137, 138, 139, 140, 142, 143, 144
Brennan, Dr., 239–240
Bridger, Jim, 51
Brockway, 294
Brooks, William, 104, 105
Brosnan, C. J., 105
Broughton, Lt. William R., 30
Brown, Bill, 256, 258
Brownsmead, 33–34
Brownsville, 268
Bryan, William Jennings, 178
Bryant, William Cullen, 59, 65
Buchanan, 259
Buffalo, N.Y., 272, 275
Buffalo Well, 296
Bullards Beach State Park, 18
Bunyan, Paul, 5
Burnett, Evan, 228, 229
Burnett, Judge John, 59
Burney, W. T., 67
Burns, 254, 259, 262, 264
Burns Junction, 261, 262, 263, 264, 266
Burns, Robert, 59, 63
Burnt River, 1, 296
Buskuhl, Theo. H., 191
Butler, Samuel, 6
Butter Creek, 235, 236
Buxton, 43, 44, 45, 46, 48, 50
Byron, Lord, 60, 62

Calapooya Mountains, 157, 158, 296
California Gold Rush, 20, 86, 108, 129, 155
California Woman Suffrage Convention, 100
Calloway, 241
Camas Valley, 296
Camp Henderson, 261, 262
Canby, 143
Canby, Gen. E. R. S., 216, 217–218
Canemah Cemetary, 82
Cannon Beach, 11, 12
Canyon City, 229
Cape Blanco, 21, 22
Cape Orford, 21
Captain Gray's Company, 95
Captain Jack, xi, 211, 212–220
Carey, Charles Henry, 89
Carpenter, William, 111
Carver, 134
Cascade Head, 296
Cascade Mountains, 4
Catlow Valley, 2, 260
Cattle in Oregon, 9, 272, 274, 275
Celiast (see Smith, Helen)
Centennial History of Oregon, 90
Chamberlain, George E., 101
Champoeg, 4, 9, 52, 104, 108, 109
Chetco River, 5, 24, 296
Chetco River Attack, 24
Chewaucan Marsh, 296
Chief Coboway, 7
Chief Joseph (Old), 283, 284, 285–286, 287
Chief Joseph (Young), 1, 101, 283, 284–287
Chief John, 24
Chief Schlyhoush (Sly Horse), 118, 120
Chief Schonchin, 212
Chief Schonchin Cemetery, 211, 212, 220
Chiloquin, 219
Chimney Creek, 275
Chinese in Oregon, 174, 176, 242, 244
Chinook Jargon, 7, 30
Chittenden, Hiram M., 291–292
Churchill, A. P., 184
Churchill, Winston, 164
Civil Bend (see Brockway)
Clackamas River, 59, 296
Clarke, Samuel Asahel, 89
Clatskanie, 34, 296
Clatsop County, 30, 38, 42
Clatsop Crest, 30, 34
Clatsop Indians, 7, 8
Clatsop Pioneer Cemetery, 6, 10
Clatsop Plains, 9
Clay, Henry, 16
Clifton, 30, 32–33
Clyman, James, 125–130
Coast Range, 5, 6, 9, 11, 13, 14, 37, 44, 78, 158
Columbia River, 3, 5, 9, 30, 32, 33, 34, 105, 106, 118, 121, 122, 134, 142, 152, 222, 259, 296
Columbia River Scenic Highway, 118, 124
Colville Indian Reservation, 286
Conyers, E. W., 226
Cook, Amos, 104, 106, 109, 110
Cook House, 104, 108, 110
Cook, Mary Frances Scott, 109
Cooke, Susan Isabella Walker, 95
Coos Bay, 16
Coos County Gold Rush, 15–16
Coquille Indians, 21, 22, 23, 24
Coquille River, 5, 16, 18, 22, 25, 296
Corning, Howard McKinley, 61
Corvallis, 62, 111, 112, 114, 116, 117, 230
Corvallis *Gazette*, 62
Cottage Grove, 155, 156, 157, 159
Couture, Pierre, 198
Cove, 195
Crane, 259
Crater Lake, 4, 158

Cronyn, George W., 1
Crook County, 260
Crook, Gen. George, 268
Crooked Creek Ranch, 261, 262
Crooked River, 222, 260
Cross Hollows (see Shaniko)
Cross Keys (see Ridgeway)
Crossing the Plains, 97–98, 128, 173, 194, 196, 225, 289–290, 293
Crow Camp Hills, 259
Crowley, Joe, 16
Crown Point, 124
Culp, 159
Cunninghame-Graham, Robert B., 131
Curry County, 19, 23, 24, 25
Curry, George L., 24, 85

Dalles City, 200
Dart, George, 25
Daughters of the American Revolution, 211
Davenport, Florinda Geer, 148, 149
Davenport, Homer, 146–149
Davenport, Timothy, 148
"Day with the Cow Column, A," 160
Deady, Judge Matthew P., 162
Death Valley, 268
Decker, Fred, W., 230, 232
DeMoss Cemetery, 195–201
DeMoss, Curly, 201
DeMoss, Elizabeth Bonebrake, 194, 195, 198, 201
DeMoss Entertainers, The, 194, 199
DeMoss, Etha, 194, 200, 201
DeMoss Family, 193, 194, 195, 196, 197, 198, 199, 200, 202
DeMoss, George, 194, 196, 198, 199
DeMoss, Henry S., 193, 196, 199
DeMoss, James M., 193, 194, 195, 196, 198, 199, 200–201
DeMoss, John M., 193, 194, 197, 199, 200–202
DeMoss, Julia Emily Shatto, 198, 199
DeMoss, Lizzie, 198
DeMoss Lyric Bards (also known as DeMoss Quartette), 193, 194
DeMoss, May, 198
DeMoss Memorial Park, 193, 200, 201
DeMoss, Minnie, 198
DeMoss, Ruth, 193, 199
DeMoss Springs, 193, 198, 199, 200, 202
Denver, Colo., 141–142
Depression of 1930s, 156, 201, 243, 254
Des Moines, Iowa, 141
Deschutes River, 187, 200, 222, 260, 296
Diamond Valley, 204
Dickenson, C. W., 198
Dickerson, Clifton, 136, 137, 145
Dickerson, Leona, 136, 137, 138, 140, 143, 144, 145
Doane, William, C., 135
Dodge City, 71
Dodge, Orvil, 24, 25
Dog Creek Indian Cave, 171
Dog Tooth Rock, 151
Dolph, Joseph, N., 101
Donner und Blitzen River, 260
Dorena Dam, 159
Drain, 155, 160
Drewsey, 2, 294
Drowning Creek (see Rock Creek, Gilliam County)
Dry Creek Store, 171, 172
Dufur, 184–188, 189, 191, 192
Dufur Orchard Co., 184, 186
Dundee, 44, 46, 50
Duniway, Abigail Scott, xi, 27, 65, 95–103, 109, 110
Duniway, Benjamin Charles, 95, 98, 103
Duniway, Clara Belle (see Stearns, Clara Belle)
Duniway House, 96, 110

Eagle Brewery Saloon, 72, 74
Earp, Ellen, 71, 73
Earp, Nellie Jane (also Nellie Law and Nellie Bohn), 71, 73, 74, 75, 76
Earp, Virgil, 71–76
Earp, Wyatt, 71, 72, 74, 75, 76
Eckley, 294
Elk River, 26
Elkhorn, 150
Elkhorn Junction, 154
Elsie, 41
Emerson, Ralph Waldo, 13
Emigrant Crossing, 55, 57
Eola (formerly Cincinnati), 98
Equal Suffrage Amendment, 101, 102
Equal Suffrage Movement, 99, 100–102
Equal Suffrage Society, 100
Esmond Hotel, 66
Evans Creek, 169–170
Evans Creek Covered Bridge, 169–170
Eugene, 61, 62–63, 116, 261
Express Ranch (see Weatherby)

Fairfield (Marion County), 61
Fairfield (Yamhill County), 57
Fairview Peak, 158
Farewell Bend State Park, 1
Farnham, Eliza Woodson Burhams, 106
Farnham, Thomas Jefferson, 106, 107–108, 109
Father Dominic, 67
Feelin' Fine, 294
Fenwick Ranch, 271
Fidler, W. W., 59, 64, 65
Fifteencent Lake, 260
Fifteen Mile Creek, 187
Finnish Settlers in Oregon, 35, 36, 37, 39–42
First Bank of Joseph, 280, 281, 282

First Oregon Volunteer Cavalry, 261, 262
Fitzpatrick, Thomas, 126
Fletcher, Francis, 104, 106, 109
Fletcher House, 104, 108, 110
Ford, Nathaniel, 127
Forest Creek, 173
Forest Grove, 46, 47
Fort Astoria, 126
Fort Atkinson, 126–127
Fort Boise, 196, 221
Fort Bridger, 128, 292
Fort Clatsop, 5, 118
Fort Davy Crockett, 107, 108
Fort Hall, 160
Fort Klamath, 218
Fort Leland, 167
Fort Orford, 23, 24
Fort Point, 22
Fort Rock, 3
Fort Vancouver, 6, 7, 106, 118, 119, 121, 122
Fort Yamhill, 59, 60
Fossil, 268
Foster Lake, 260
Free Press, 85–86
French, Pete, 2, 204, 256
French Prairie, 4, 6, 8, 9
Frenchglen, 2
Friedman, S., 261
Friend, 189, 190–192
Friend, George J., 191
From the West to the West, 98
Fulton Canyon, 179

G. I. Ranch, 222
Galice, 165
Garrison Lake, 28
Gaston, Joseph, 88, 90, 92
Geer House, 147
Geer, Ralph Carey, 148, 226
Geer, Theodore Thurston, 148, 149
Gervais, Joe, 8
Gilliam County, 3, 229
Glencoe, 54
Goff, David, 84
Gold-Gated West, The, 67, 68
Gouge Eye (see Drewsey)
Government Field Notes, Benton County, 112, 114
Grand Ronde Indian Reservation, 59–60
Grande Ronde River, 195, 260, 296
Grant County, 243, 248, 250
Grant, U. S., 60, 217
Grass Valley, 194
Grave Creek, 166–167
Grave Creek Covered Bridge, 166, 167
Great Basin, 259–260
Great Basin Marker 259–260
Great Migration, 160
"Great Reinforcement," 106
Great Southern Railroad, 186
Grey, Zane, 208, 209
Grizzly, 203

Hagstaff, 22
Hailey, John, 92
Haines, Ray, 150, 151, 152–153, 154, 186
Hamilton, 243
Hamilton, Col. William S., 126
Hamlet, 35–42
Hanley, William, 101, 256, 294
Hanna, Lewis, 181–183
Hanna, Mrs. Lewis, 183
Hardscrabble Grade, 156
Hardy, Thomas, 181, 183
Harkness and Twogood Stage House, 167
Harney County, 2, 254, 256, 259, 260, 294
Harney Lake, 222
Harper's New Monthly Magazine, 16–18
Harris, Moses (better known as Black Harris), 127–128, 224
Harritt, Jesse, 223
Hart Mountain, 2, 296
Harte, Bret, 15, 67–68
Hat H Ranch, 272, 274, 276
Hay Creek Post Office, 204
Hay Creek Ranch, 203–205
Hay, John, 67–68
Hayes, Homer, 280–282
Hayes, Rutherford B., 167
Hedden, Cyrus, 21, 22, 23
Hells Canyon, 1, 282
Hendericks, John, 180
Henderson, J. H. D., 261
Henry, Andrew, 126
Herbert, Elizabeth, 112
Hermann, Dr. Henry, 25
Higginbotham, Mrs. John, 175–176
Hill, Albert, 35, 38
Hill, Mrs. Albert, 38, 39, 42
Hill, Andrew, 35, 36, 39
Hill, Mrs. Andrew, 41–42
Hill, Henry, 35, 36, 42
Hill, Hilma, 42
Hill House (see Stateline Ranch House)
Hill, Marshall, 267–268
Hill, Melissa, 268
Hill, Prudence Belinda Thomas, 268
Hill, Verono, 35, 36
Hillsboro, 53
Hines, 254–255
Hines, Elizabeth, 55
Hines Lumber Co., 251, 254
Hines, Rev. Harvey K., 195
Hines, William, 55, 57
Hin-mut-too-yah-lat-kekht (see Chief Joseph, Young)
Hirsch, Solomon, 101
History of the Northwest Coast, 64
History of Oregon, 89
Hoffman, Mr. and Mrs., 46–47, 48, 50
Hogum (see Sanger)

Holladay, Ben, 88, 89–93, 94
Holladay, Joseph, 90
Holladay Overland Mail and Express Company, 91
Holliday, Doc, 71
Holman, Joseph, 105, 106, 109
Home Creek, 260
Homesteaders in Oregon, 2, 56, 98, 174–176, 190–192, 243, 245, 246, 268, 278
Hood River, 290
Hood River Valley, 4
Hooker Jim, 214, 215, 216, 217, 218
Horner, John B., 59, 60
Horner Museum, 112
Horrocks, Pat, 150, 151
Horrocks, Scott, 150, 151, 154
Horse Heaven, 296
Horsetail Falls, 295, 296
Horses in Oregon, 130–134, 248–250, 256
Hoskin, Herman F. L., 236
Hoskin, Jesse, 235
Hoskin, Jim, xi, 233–241
Hoskin, Mrs. Jim, 238, 239, 240
Hoskin, John, 237–238
Hoskin, Jonathan, 235
Hoskin, Mary, 238
House Committee on Roads, 290–292
Hubbard, 143
Hudson's Bay Company, 6, 82, 106, 118, 121
Hug Point, 11–12, 296
Hug Point State Park, 11–12
Humbug Mountain, 23
Huntington, 290
Hurst, Jim, 236–237

Idaho *Statesman* (Boise), 273
Ilwaco *Tribune*, 63
Imnaha River, 260, 296
Indian Creek, 259
Indian History of the Modoc War, 212
Indian Names, 296
Indian Territory (Oklahoma), 218, 286
Indians of Oregon, 7, 8, 9, 16, 21, 22, 23, 24, 118, 119–122, 161, 196, 211–220, 268, 283–286
Ingleside Farm, 131–134
Irish Bend, 115, 116, 117
Irish Bend Covered Bridge, 115, 116, 117
Iron Mountain, 79
Irwin, Louis Kompp, 112
Irwin, Richard, 112, 113
Irwin, Robert, 112, 113, 114
Irwin Butte (see Winkle Butte)
Izee, 250

Jackass Creek (Harney County), 260
Jackass Creek (Jackson County), 173, 174
Jackass Mountains, 260
Jackson County, 173
Jackson County Museum, 175, 176
Jackson Creek, 274, 275
Jackson, Major, 213, 214
Jackson, Mr., 38–39
Jacksonville, 16, 173, 177
Jefferson County, 204, 260
Jennyopolis, 111–114
Jenkins, David, 248, 249
Jensen, Lon, 114
Jensen's Lazy J Ranch, 114
Jeppesen, Arlena, 44–50
Jeppesen Ranch, 44, 50
John Day, 2, 242, 248, 251
John Day Fording, 225, 227–228
John Day River, 3, 225, 226, 227, 228, 229, 230, 232, 260, 296
John Day Valley, 2, 248, 249
Johnson, Dave, 238–239
Johnson, James, 157
Jones, Mart, 206
Jones, Nels, 237
Jones, Vera Moore, 206–210
Jordan Craters, 2
Jordan Creek, 270
Jordan Valley, 262, 264, 266, 267, 268, 269, 276
Joseph, 280–282
Joseph *Herald*, 282
Josephine County, 64
Journal of Travels Over the Rocky Mountains, 223
Juntura, 259

Kah-nee-ta, 3
Keeney, Theron, 242–244
Kendall, George Wilkins, 155
Kilbourne, Ralph, 109
Kilts, 294
Kimberly, 245
Kimoto, Pat, 114, 150, 151, 189, 228
Kinton, 77–78
Kintpuash (see Captain Jack)
Klamath Falls, 4, 206, 207, 208, 209, 220
Klamath Indian Reservation, 212, 213, 218, 219, 294
Klamath Indians, 212, 216, 217
Klamath River, 206
Klaskanine River, 5
Klondike, 225, 228
Knapp Hotel, 27, 28
Knapp, Louie, 27, 28
Knight, Sid, 275
Krause, Henry, 179, 180
Krieger, Marc, 150, 151, 154

La Grande, 195
Ladd and Tilton Bank, 81
Lafayette, 95, 96, 98, 104, 108, 109, 110
Lake Oswego, 79, 80, 81
Lake Owyhee, 2, 278, 296
Land Grant Act, 92

Lander Cutoff, 292
Lapwai Indian Reservation, 286
Lapwai Mission, 284
Latourell, Clara, 123
Latourell Falls, 118, 122, 123, 124
Latourell, Grace, 122, 123, 124
Latourell, Joseph, 122, 123, 124
Latchaw's Mill (see Pine)
Lausanne, 106
Lava Beds (California), 211, 212, 213, 214, 215, 216, 217, 218
Law, Fred M., 176
Law, George, 74–76
Law, Levi, 74, 75
Law, Magdalen Katherine (Kay), 74
Law, Virgelena, 74
Lawson, Judge G. W., 100
Lee, Henry A. G., 85
Lee, Jason, 8, 9, 104, 105, 110
Lee, Jason Cemetery, 110
Leonard, Daniel G., 227, 228, 229, 230, 231, 232
Leonard, Mary Gysin, 229, 230, 231, 232
Leonard, Sarah E., 230
Leslie Gulch, 277–279
Leslie, Hiram, 277, 279
Lewis and Clark, 5, 118, 283, 284
Limmeroth, Ed, 186, 188
Lincoln, Abraham, 128, 160
Lindsay, Nathaniel, 230, 231–232
Link River, 211
Linkville (see Klamath Falls)
Linn City (see West Linn)
Little Butter Creek, 237
Little North Santiam River, 152
Log Town, xi, 173–177
Log Town Cemetery, 173, 177
Log Town Rose, 173, 176–177
Logg, Francis A., 174
Long Creek, 242–244, 245, 246–247
London, Jack, 28
Lone Fir Cemetery, 58, 59, 61, 67
Long Tom River, 115
Lost River, 212, 296
Lost River Valley, 212
Lost Wagon Train of 1845 (see Meek's Cutoff Party)
Lostine River, 286
Lower Klamath Lake, 212
Lucier, Roy, 114
Luckiamute River, 127, 296
Lundberg, Alex, 159
Lundberg Stage House, 157, 159

Madras, 203, 205, 222
Mahogany Mountains, 274, 277, 279
Main Street House, 82
Malheur County, 1, 259, 271, 275, 277
Malheur Lake, 260, 296
Malheur National Wildlife Refuge, 2
Malheur River, 259, 290
Malheur Slough, 260
Malloy Ranch, 272, 275, 276
Marion County, 59, 109
Markham, Edwin, 59, 68, 86–87
Marshland, 30, 294
Marysville (Corvallis), 112
Mason, Ralph, 114
Masters, Edgar Lee, 57
Matson, Mrs., 40
Maupin, 294
Mayer, Jacob, 99, 101
Mayger, 34
Mayger Downing Community Church, 34
McDermitt, 2
McDonald (also known as McDonald's Ferry), 228, 229
McDonald, Bill, 228
McKee, 143
McKee, John, 173, 175
McKee, Maryum, 173, 176
McLoughlin, John, 6, 82, 87, 106, 109, 119, 120, 121, 122
McLoughlin, Marguerite, 121
McNary Dam, 3
Meacham, Alfred, 217–218
Medicine in Oregon, 41, 47, 172, 239–240
Meek, Elizabeth Schoonover, 221, 223
Meek, Joe, 28, 51–54, 76, 86, 108, 127
Meek, Olive, 52
Meek, Stephen, 221, 222, 223
Meek, Virginia, 53, 54
Meek's Cutoff Party, 2, 85, 221, 224
Mehama Junction, 154
Mengler, Mary, 114
Mengler, Richard, 114
Metolius River, 260, 296
Miller, Col, R. A., 67
Miller, Dave, 264, 266
Miller, Joaquin, 25–27, 68
Miller, Minnie Myrtle Dyer, 26–27
Milton, John, 58, 125, 130
Minam River, 260, 296
Mineral, 156
Mining in Oregon, 3, 15–16, 18, 20–21, 23–24, 156, 157–160, 173, 174, 242, 267
Missouri River, 126, 141
Mitchell, John H., 101
Modoc Indians, 211, 212–220
"Modoc War," 211, 212–218
Molalla, 4
Monkland, 201
Monahan J., 270–276
Monroe, 111, 112, 116
Montgomery, Richard, 87
Monument, 245–247
Moore, Robin, 109
Morrow County, 3
Moro, 193, 194, 199, 200
Mount Angel, 143
Mount Angel Abbey, 67
Mount Hood, 4, 51, 125, 130

Mount Vernon (horse), 248–250
Mount Vernon (town), 248, 249, 250
Mountain Men, 51, 54, 107, 125, 127, 129, 171
Mountain View Cemetery, 82
Munson Creek County Park, 13–14
Munson Falls, 13–14
Music in Oregon, 42, 46, 176, 195, 196, 199, 200, 240, 243–244
Musick Mine, 156, 158

Narrative of the Texas Santa Fe Expedition, 155
National Archives and Records Service, 113
Necanicum, 36, 37, 38, 40, 42
Necanicum River, 39
Nehalem, 12
Nehalem River, 5, 296
Nelly, 24
New Era, 88, 93, 94, 143
New Era Spiritualist Camp, 88, 93, 94
New Hampshire *Sunday News*, 230
New Northwest, The, 99, 102
New York *Evening Journal*, 144
Newberg, 44, 288
Newell, Robert, 86
Nez Perce Indians, 109, 283–286
"Nez Perce War," 286
Nicholson, Charlie, 182
Nieves, Mr., 234
North Fork of the John Day River, 245
North Platte River, 141
North Powder, 195
North Santiam River, 152
North Umpqua River, 158
Numipu (see Nez Perce Indians)
Nyssa, 279

O. K. Corral, Battle of the, 72
Oklahoma Territory, 207
Old Oregon Trail (see also Oregon Trail), 3, 82, 160, 221, 224, 227, 268, 288–292
Ollers, Mr. and Mrs., 36, 37, 38
Onion Peak, 11
Ontario, 2, 259, 290
Opal Creek, 151–152, 153
Opal Creek Falls, 150, 151–152, 153, 154
Opal Lake, 151, 152, 154
Oregon Almanac, 77–78, 93
Oregon and California RR Co., 89
Oregon *Argus*, 95
Oregon Central Railroad Company, 88, 89, 92
Oregon City, 82–87, 88, 92, 93, 94, 128, 129, 143, 290
Oregon Coast, 5, 9, 11, 13, 16, 19, 21, 35, 229
"Oregon Dragoons," 106, 107
Oregon Exchange Company, 82
Oregon *Farmer*, 95
Oregon For the Curious, 190
Oregon For the Curious Class (Portland Community College), 150, 155, 225
Oregon Historical Quarterly, 59, 64, 99
Oregon Historical Society, 80, 112
Oregon Humane Society, 135, 136, 140, 145
Oregon Institute, 109
Oregon Iron Company, 79, 81
Oregon Literature, 59, 60
Oregon Lyceum, 84
Oregon Mission, 8
Oregon Printing Association, 84
Oregon *Spectator*, 84, 85, 86, 109
Oregon State Archives, 230
Oregon State Equalization Society, 99
Oregon State *Journal*, 63
Oregon State Library, 112
Oregon State University, 13, 112, 116, 194
Oregon Supreme Court, 232
Oregon Temperance House, 109
Oregon Trail, 1, 98, 126, 160, 168, 225, 228, 288–292
Oregon, Unversity of, 36, 116
Oregonian, The, 58, 67, 74, 89, 100, 113–114, 162, 203
Osgood, Katie, 41
Oswego Lake, 79
Ough, Betsey, 118, 119–122, 124
Ough, Grace (see Latourell, Grace)
Ough, Richard, 119, 120–122, 124
Overland Stage Line, 90
Owyhee Mountains, 270
Owyhee River, 2, 262, 277

Pacific Christian Advocate, 61
Pacific Ocean, 5, 9, 12, 16, 18, 28, 152, 259
Packwood, William H., 24
Painted Hills, 3, 296
Paiute Indian Uprising, 268
Palmer, Joel, 24, 223
Paradise, 295
Parker, Samuel, 223
Parrott Creek, 92, 93, 94
Parrott, Joseph, 92, 93
Path Breaking, 99
Path of the Rainbow, 1
Paulina, 221, 222, 224
Pawnee Indians, 127
Pearce, Bill, 251–253
Pearce, Freda, 252–253
Pearson, Mr. 238
Pendleton, 3, 238, 239
Peoria, Ill., 105, 106, 109
Peoria Party, 104, 106–109, 110
Peters, George Washington, 187, 188
Peterson, Susannah Johnson, 221
Phantom Natural Bridge, 150–151
Pike, 55–57
Pike Cemetery, 55–57
Pilot Rock, xi, 233, 238, 240

Pine, 294
Pine City, 234, 236
Pistol River, 5
Pittock, Henry Louis, 203
Placer, 166
Platte River, 126, 127, 292
Plumb, Ida M., 141
Poe, Edgar Allen, 59, 62
Poetes, A. S., 178
Polk County, 59, 98, 161
Pollock, Dean, 282
Ponderosa Hotel, 254
Poor Man's Creek, 173
Port Orford, 19–29
Porter, John E., 113
Portland, 4, 43, 58, 61, 63, 67, 73, 74, 79, 81, 82, 88, 92, 93, 94, 112, 136, 142, 143, 144, 172, 186, 187, 200, 202, 227, 232
Portland *Telegram*, 186
Pottsmith, Marie, 36–42
Prairie Flower, The, 127
Preston's Sectional and County Map, 111
Prineville, 222, 224, 256
Promise, 295
Provisional Government, 84, 104, 160, 162
Publishers Paper Company, 82, 84, 86, 87
Pueblo Mountains, 260
Puget Island, 30

Quinn, 30

Radio Park Store, 165–166, 167–168
Raft River, 196
Ragsdale, Bill, 187
Ramon Creek, 260
Ramsey, George, 157
Randolph, 15–18
Randolph, John, 16
Rawhide, 294
Rawhide Creek, 260
Red Bridge, 159
Reed, Col. C. A., 100
Reed, John, 80–81
Reo Cafe, 135, 138, 140
Reynolds Creek, 275
Rhine, Dr. J. B., 135–136
Rice, Mr., 238
Riddle, Edna, 114
Riddle, Frank, 211, 215, 216, 217, 218, 219
Riddle, Jefferson, 212
Riddle, Toby (see Winema)
Ridgeway, 294
Riding Whip Tree, 148, 149
Ripley's *Believe It or Not*, 135
River of the West, The, 51
Riverview Cemetery, 71, 76, 102–103
Robertson, William J., 113
Robin's Nest (see West Linn)
Robinson, Edwin Arlington, 260
Rock Creek (Gilliam County), 226–227
Rock Creek Post Office, 227
Rockville (Gilliam County), 227
Rockville (Malheur County), 271, 272, 273, 274, 276
Rogue River, 5, 22, 165
Rogue River, City of, 170
Rogue River Indian Uprising, 167, 268
Rogue River Valley, 4
Rome, 264, 266
Roosevelt, Theodore, 208, 209
Rooster Rock, 122
Rose City Veterinary Hospital, 144
Roseburg, 93, 171, 172, 198, 235
Roseburg *Plaindealer,* 162
Ruby City, Idaho, 270
Rumgay, Monte, 131–134
Running Fawn, 118
Russell, Majors and Waddell, 90

Sacajawea, 5, 284, 296
Sacajawea Peak, 1, 5
St. Charles Hotel, 66, 67
St. Helens, 9, 30
Salem, 4, 36, 40, 61, 100, 109, 110, 137, 150, 186, 235, 256, 268
"Salem Company," 88, 89, 92
Salem *Statesman*, 61
San Francisco, 16, 20, 21, 22, 23, 27, 28, 65, 81, 88, 109
Sand Dunes, 5
Sandy River, 79, 296
Sanger, 294
Santiam River, 152, 296
Schnabel, Bill, 272, 275
Schools:
Brownsmead, 33; Fort Vancouver, 6–7; French Prairie, 8; Hamlet, 39–40; Kinton, 77–78; Monument, 245; Pendleton, 238; Pine City, 235–236; Wheeler County, 268
Scio, 4, 235
Scott, Harvey W., 58, 100
Scott, Mrs., 264
Scott, Thomas, 227
Scott, Tucker, 109–110
Scott, Uncle Tom, 241
Scotts, 227
Scotts Mills, 4
Scottsburg, 22–23
Sea Gull, 19, 21, 23, 28
Seaside, 36, 37, 38, 40, 41, 42, 291
Seeger, Pete, 71
Seneca, 251–253
Seven Devils Road, 18
Seward, William H., 28
Shakespeare, William, 19, 35, 36, 125
Shakespearean Festival, 5
Shaniko, 294
Sharps Creek, 156

Sheep in Oregon, 1, 203–204, 234, 236–238, 241, 256, 268, 271, 275
Sherar, Joseph, 187
Sherman County, 3, 193, 194, 229
Sherman, Gen. W. T., 28, 167, 216
Shortess, Robert, 109
Silbaugh, Charles, 254
Silver City, Idaho, 267, 268, 269, 270
Silverton, 86, 135, 136, 137, 138, 143, 144, 145, 146, 147, 149
Silverton Bobbie, 135–143
Silvies River, 260
Simpson, Benjamin, 59, 61, 62–63
Simpson, Claude, 67
Simpson, Eugene, 67
Simpson, Julia Humphrey, 62
Simpson, Nancy Cooper, 59
Simpson, Sam, 58–70
Siskiyou Mountains, 4
Siuslaw River, 5
Skelton, John, 115
Skipanon Creek, 9
Skull Creek, 260
Sloan, Frank, 239
Skunk Cabbage (see Marshland)
Smith, Helen, 6–10
Smith, Jedediah, 126
Smith, Mary Elizabeth, 142–143
Smith, Sidney, 107–108
Smith, Solomon, 6–10
Snake River, 1, 143, 196, 259, 290, 296
Sons and Daughters of Oregon Pioneers, 58, 59, 67
Sons of Temperance, 110
South Fork of the Crooked River, 221
South Fork of the John Day River, 250
South Fork of the Malheur River, 259
South Pass, 126, 127, 128, 154
Spalding, Rev. Henry Harmon, 284
Spanish-American War, 65
Spiritual Society of the Pacific Northwest, 93
Spoon River Anthology, 57
Sprague River Junction, 220
Spray, 245, 247
Squaw Flats, 294
Stack, Mrs. John, 292–293
Stanfield, 240
Stanford, Omer, 274, 275
Stanton, Elizabeth Cady, 102
Star of Oregon, 109
Starvout (see Azalea)
Stateline Ranch House, 267, 268, 269
Steamboat, 172
Stearns, Clara Belle Duniway, 103
Steens Mountain, 2, 260
Stevenson, Allie, 73, 76
Stevenson, Robert Louis, 146
Stinkingwater, 294
Stinkingwater Creek, 259, 294
Stinkingwater Pass, 259
Stitzel, Mrs. H. V., 64
Stone, Lucy, 102
Story of the Owyhees, The, 273
Strandbo, Professor, 186–187, 188
Straub, Bob, 208, 209
Strode, Jack, 274
Strode, Jess, 274, 275
Stuart, Robert, 126
Stubblefield, Mattie, 245–247
Stubblefield, Murd, 246
Sturgis, Dr. Chris, 239–240
Sturgis, Jim, 239, 240
Sublette, William, 126
Succor Creek, 271, 272, 275, 277, 278
Succor Creek Canyon, 277
Succor Creek State Park, 279
Sugarloaf Mountain, 11
Sunken Mountain, 245, 247
Sunny Valley, 165–168
Sweet Betsey from Pike, 55
Sweet Oregon, 193, 199
Sweetwater Creek, 126
Symons, Roberta, xii

Taft, William Howard, 208, 209
Talbot State Park, 118, 124
Tell Tale (see Eckley)
Tenasillahe Island, 30
The Dalles, 3, 112, 142, 181, 187, 200, 201, 224, 225, 228, 229, 230, 268, 290
The Dalles *Optimist*, 184
Thoreau, Henry, 13
Thorton, J. Quinn, 61, 62, 84
Tibbet, Gideon, 89
Tichenor, Ann, 23, 25
Tichenor, Ellen, 23, 28
Tichenor, Elizabeth B., 20, 23
Tichenor, William, 19–25, 27, 28–29
Tigard, 78
Tillamook, 11, 13
Tiller, 201
Timberline Lodge, 4
Tippecanoe River, 141
Tollgate, 296
Tombstone, Ariz., 71–72, 74
Tonquin, 121
Touch of Oregon, A, 256
Townsend, 143
Travels in the Great Western Prairies, 107, 108
Troutdale, 30, 123
Trullinger, Hannah Boyles, 80
Trullinger, J. C., 79–80, 81
Tualatin Plains, 51, 52
Tualatin Plains Presbyterian Church, 53–54
Tucker, Dave, 283–284
Tu-eka-kas (see Chief Joseph, Old)
Tule Lake, 213
T'Vault, W. G., 22, 23, 85
Tygh Valley, 191

Umatilla County, 235, 240, 291
Umatilla Indian Reservation, 240
Umpqua River, 5, 22, 89, 296
Umpqua River Highway, 171
Umpqua River Settlers, 22
Umpqua Valley, 4, 161
Union Pacific Railroad, 196–197
United States Army in Oregon, 23, 24, 196, 213, 214, 216, 217, 261, 262
U'Ren, William, 101

Vale, 274, 290
Van Gilder, Milton, 178–180
Van Gilder, Raymond, 178
Vancouver, George, 21
Vanderpool, Dr. Larkin, 187
Victor, Frances Fuller, 27, 52, 54, 67, 71, 76
Villard, Henry, 92, 93
Vinton, Iowa, 141

Wabash River, 141
Wagontire, 256, 257, 258, 296
Wagontire Mountain, 222
Wagner, Fred, 282
Wagner's Butte (see Winkle Butte)
Waldo, Daniel, 147
Waldo Hills, 147
Wal-lam-wat-kin (see Nez Perce Indians)
Wallowa County, 260, 265
Wallowa Lake, 283, 286
Wallowa Mountains, 1, 5, 283
Wallowa River, 260, 286
Wallowa Valley, 283, 286
Walls of Rome, 264–266
Walters, Anna, 272
Warm Springs Indian Reservation, 3
Wasco, 178, 179, 180, 201, 225, 228
Wasco County, 182, 184, 189, 230
Washington County, 53, 78
Washington, George, 125, 128
Washougal, Wash., 118, 122
Watson, 277
Watson, Joseph, 243
Weatherby, 294
Weiser, Idaho, 273, 275, 290
Wells, Fargo and Company, 90, 91
Wells, William V., 16–18
West Linn, 109, 295
West, Oswald, 99, 100, 102, 256–258
"West Side" Company, 88, 92
Westfall, 2
Whalehead Beach, 296
What Come of It, 64
Wheeler County, 3, 260, 268
Whiskey Run, 15–16, 18
White, Adria, 229
White Horse Inn, 2
White, Jim, 229, 230
White Wing, (see Ough, Betsey)
Whitman, Marcus, 54
Whitman, Narcissa, 106, 127
Whitman, Walt, xi, 68, 160, 294
Whitman's Mission, 108
"Wild Life in Oregon," 16–18
Willamette River, 30, 61, 68, 79, 88, 93, 115, 152, 157, 222
Willamette University, 61, 62, 109
Willamette Valley, 4, 9, 36, 82, 104, 107, 108, 109, 110, 112, 127, 160, 200, 203, 221, 259
Willamina, 200
Williams Creek, 64–65
Willow Creek, 226
Wilson, Woodrow, 208, 209
Wimer, 169, 170
Winema, 211, 215, 216, 217, 218, 219, 220
Winema Pinnacles, 219
Winkle Butte, 112, 113, 114
Winkle, Wiley, 113
Winter, Rep. Charles E., 292
Wolcott, Ind., 135, 138, 140, 141, 143
Wolf Creek, 166, 168
Women, Role of in Oregon, 27, 40–41, 95, 98, 99, 173, 175, 176, 275, 276
Wood, Charles Erskine Scott, 101
Woodburn, 143
Woods, George Lemuel, 89
Wounded Knee, 220
Wyeth, Nathaniel, 6

Yainax, 211, 219, 294
Yainax Butte, 294
Yamhill, 55, 56, 57
Yamhill County, 55, 104, 122
Yamhill River, 55, 104, 110
Yancey, W. H., 229
Yankton (formerly Yankeetown), 294
Yaquina River, 5
Yoncalla, 160, 161–162, 163, 164
Young, Brigham, 90
Young, Ewing, 108
Young, Mrs. Jennie, 174
Yreka City, Calif., 212, 219

Zeiber, John S., 225, 226
Ziegler, Maud, 175
Zimmerman, Hazel, 261, 262
Zimmerman, Julian, 261